Urban growth and change in Britain:
an introduction

Frank Brown   is a Principal Lecturer in Geography at Sheffield City Polytechnic. He has taught extensively on urban studies at both undergraduate and postgraduate level in the Department of Urban and Regional Studies. His current research interests include housing policy, nineteenth century urban history and urban deprivation.

Paul Lawless   is a Principal Lecturer in Urban Planning at Sheffield City Polytechnic. He has taught extensively on urban studies courses in Sheffield and London and previously worked in several planning offices in London. He has published a number of books on inner city policy and local economic development.

Urban growth and change in Britain: an introduction

Paul Lawless
and
Frank Brown

Harper & Row, Publishers
London

Cambridge
New York
San Francisco
Singapore

Mexico City
Philadelphia
São Paulo
Sydney

First published 1986

Harper & Row Ltd
28 Tavistock Street
London WC2E 7PN

British Library Cataloguing in Publication Data
Lawless, P.
  Urban Growth and Change in Britain
  1. Cities and towns — Great Britain — History
  I. Title   II. Brown, F.
  307'.14'0941   HT133
ISBN 0-6-318336-6

Typeset by Gedset Limited, Cheltenham
Printed and bound by Butler and Tanner Ltd, Frome and
London.

CONTENTS

1   An Introduction

The background

Any attempt to provide a synthesis of urban growth and change covering a period of over 200 years must be seen as ambitious. It adds a further dimension to the perennial problems facing the authors of any introductory text: what to include and what to leave out. A further issue is the ever-broadening base of research and the growing popularity of 'the city' and 'urban studies' among academics. To the more traditional disciplines, which have long seen the city as a focus of study — e.g. history, geography and architecture — must now be added an ever-lengthening list of other disciplines that have developed an 'urban' strand, among them sociology, politics, economics, planning and psychology.

In the last 20 years an ever-growing stream of research and literature has emanated from a variety of perspectives and disciplines, all concerned with one or more aspects of the urban arena. 'The city' has clearly become an increasingly attractive proposition for academics, though this should not surprise us. The city is seen as harbouring grave socio-economic problems; it breeds unrest and points to a workless future. Its battles with central governments and markets, its financial disasters and its innovations, have all become legendary and have inevitably attracted academics. Furthermore, many of the debates and issues surrounding 'the city' cross international frontiers. British urban problems find striking parallels both on the mainland of Europe and in North America and Australia. All seem to point to the city today as a metaphor for national decline. Yet few would have made that observation a hundred years ago when the city seemed to be the pinnacle of human endeavour.

Despite the burgeoning literature in the field of urban studies, this book has been conceived less through inspiration than frustration at the lack of an introductory text examining urban growth and change in Britain from the beginnings of mass urbanization in the late eighteenth century to the present day. Such texts as are available either cover too narrow a time perspective (e.g. the nineteenth century, or the post-1945 period), or examine change from one disciplinary perspective only (e.g. Hall's admirable text, *Urban and Regional Planning*, 1975), or both. We therefore hope to fill a perceived gap in the literature, though we are aware of the many stones left unturned and the comparative narrowness of our own approach.

The aims

In this book we aim to provide students with an insight into the processes and patterns of urban growth in Britain over the last 200 years. The approach is a comparatively narrow one, necessarily reflecting the academic backgrounds and interests of the authors. We have tried to harness the literature and methodologies of three inter-related strands of the urban web: history, geography and planning. Producing a text drawing principally upon this trinity of disciplines seems to make a great deal of sense. An historical context is vital for an appreciation of the dynamic nature of urban change. An understanding of both contemporary and historical urban development needs to be rooted in some analysis of spatial patterning and processes, particularly in view of the discrete nature of the process of urban growth. Finally, the pattern of such urban growth and the changing physical structure and socio-economic fortunes of our cities have been profoundly affected by local and central government intervention from the hesitant 'enabling' forays of the late nineteenth century to the powerful 'mandatory' post-1945 planning system. It can certainly be argued that these three areas of interest are central to urban studies, provide intellectual devices within which to locate urban phenomena and, most important, sit easily alongside one another as a collective whole. Other students of the city would no doubt adopt different approaches and distinct agendas. There are in effect a number of introductory texts which can be written within the catholic field of urban studies. This is but one.

A broadly chronological approach has been adopted throughout the book. This is not merely a result of the historical dimension; it is for the ease of the reader in tracing themes, the emergence of problems, the development of government intervention and so on. The book is also intentionally based on urban growth and change in Britain. This is partly because of space, but mainly so that readers can arrive at a reasonable under-standing of such growth within one country, rather than having to synthesize processes and themes from a wider geographical base. The disciplines of planning, geography and history, as they have developed in Britain, reflect very clearly the empirical tradition of much British academic research in the arts and social sciences. This tradition is inevitably reflected in this book. Where appropriate, theoretical material from cognate disciplines, notably urban politics and urban sociology, has been included, but we are conscious of a considerable omission here. This is necessitated both by the emphasis on the more empirical urban disciplines and the introductory nature of the text. For theoretically robust views of the city, readers should see Saunders (1979, 1981) or Dunleavy (1982a,). The complexity and variety of themes examined or touched upon here, together with the long time-span under consideration, precludes any one overreaching theoretical perspective within which to place this book.

The structure of this book

The book falls logically into three separate parts. Parts One and Two have a fairly con-sistent historical and chronological structure, while Part Three is rather more thematic in approach.

Part One is concerned with urban growth in Britain from the eighteenth century, through the nineteenth, up to 1939. Within this long time-period, in addition to charting the salient features of growth and change, an attempt is made to examine some facets of this process in detail, e.g. the nineteenth-century housing question and the urban transport revolution. Changing Victorian perceptions of, and attitudes towards, the city are also explored as a preamble to an examination of the origins of the town planning movement, which has had such a powerful impact on post-1945 planning philosophy and policies. The internal coherence of Part One comes from charting the slow evolution of government intervention in urban problems, primarily through housing, prior to the recognition of the need for a powerful centralized planning system in the recommendations of the Barlow Commission and the wartime reports.

Part Two is essentially concerned with the post-1945 planning system in Britain. The basic ideology and structure of the planning system is outlined, together with its impact on land use and urban physical structure. The social dimension of planning is also examined through, for example, an evaluation of public participation. In both Parts One and Two we have sought to examine societal change, with emphasis on its interaction with urban growth and the environment. In Part Two the rapidly changing nature of British society during the 1950s and 1960s provides the context for the basic revision of the planning system in the late 1960s.

Part Three provides something of a contrast to the first two Parts. The title, 'The Dynamics of the Contemporary British City: Some Issues', points to its selective nature — we do not claim to have examined all possible themes here. Housing, retailing, employment and transport can reasonably be seen as central components of the urban system, and all have undergone quite radical change in recent years. The chapter on Inner Urban Policy does not sit easily in this thematic approach to Part Three — it is clearly area-based in nature. We would argue, however, that its inclusion is justified on several grounds. First, many of the changes which have occurred in terms of the other themes (e.g. employment) have had dramatic effects on the 'core' areas of our larger cities and conurbations; secondly, since this book is primarily about urban growth and change, it is fitting that the inner city,the focus of growth for so long, should be given separate treatment now that it is clearly in what some would argue is terminal decline. A further chapter on dispersal and the impact of population decentralization would be a logical sequel, but space does not allow for examination of this here (but see Herington, 1984). In the final chapter we attempt to pull together some of the strands examined separately in Part Three. It also raises broader questions relating to the future role of urban studies and the necessity for students interested in the subject area to embrace theoretical constructions which, of necessity, are not examined in this book.

Frank Brown wrote chapters one, two, three, five, twelve and thirteen, Paul Lawless chapters six, seven, eight, nine, ten, eleven, fifteen, sixteen and seventeen, and chapters four and fourteen were joint efforts.

A note on sources

As we have already stated, this book is relatively narrow in approach and introductory in nature and level. Rather than providing over-long reference lists we have attempted to limit these. Equally, at the end of each chapter we have provided some guidance to more specialized, detailed and often more advanced books under the heading 'Further reading'. In some areas the literature is exceptionally rich (e.g. housing), in others sadly lacking (e.g. employment change). Those readers wishing to explore specific themes or periods in more depth should resort to the further references cited, though, as with our references, they are in no sense exhaustive.

References

Dunleavy, P. (1982a) *The scope of urban studies in social science*, Units 3/4, D202, Urban Change and Conflict, Open University Press, Milton Keynes.

Dunleavy, P. (1982b) *Perspectives on urban studies*. In A. Blowers, C. Brook, P. Dunleavy and L. McDowell Urban Change and Conflict, An Interdisciplinary Reader, Harper and Row, London.

Hall, P. (1975) *Urban and Regional Planning*, Penguin Books, Harmondsworth.

Herington, J. V. (1984) *The Outer City*, Harper and Row, London.

Saunders, P. (1979) *Urban Politics: a sociological interpretation*, Penguin Books, Harmondsworth.

Saunders, P. (1981) *Social Theory and the Urban Question*,. Hutchinson, London.

Part One   Urban growth and societal response,
1760 - 1900

2   Urban growth and change, 1760-1900

The aim of this chapter is to provide the context for Part One as a whole and in particular for Chapters 3 and 4, which deal in detail with specific aspects of the results of urban growth in Britain — the housing question as it emerged in Victorian Britain and the changing attitudes of Victorian observers towards this alien and often frightening phenomenon: the large industrial town. The dates chosen for this background discussion are somewhat arbitrary, and inevitably some comments and statistics may fall chronologically outside the 1760-1900 bracket. The year 1760 is taken as a broadly accepted date to herald the onset of the Industrial Revolution; 1900 is even more arbitrary but does mark the advent of mass public transport in our towns and cities which had such profound effects on urban growth, and which is therefore treated separately (see Chapter 5). In this chapter we cannot hope to provide any detailed discussion or evaluation of the myriad changes that occurred over such a long period, and many aspects of change are either given discursive treatment or missed out altogether. However, the Industrial Revolution is very well documented, as is social change from the late eighteenth century through the nineteenth century, and some guidance for further reading is provided at the end of the chapter.

Our principal goal here is to examine the manner, rate and varied spatial impact of socio-economic change, and in particular to note the unparalleled and untramelled growth of towns and cities, and some of the major causes of such growth. Our concern is with urban population growth rather than the physical growth of towns. While the two are clearly linked, physical growth was held in check until the later decades of the nineteenth century and is examined in Chapters 5 and 6.

Urban development

What separates the eighteenth century from earlier periods in terms of both population and urban growth is the rate and spatial distribution of such growth. Also, from the middle decades of the eighteenth century until the later decades of the twentieth, overall population growth and urban growth were to be closely linked. Prior to the eighteenth century, population growth had been slow but steady. Although overall population totals remain a matter of some speculation at such early dates, in the absence of national censuses, it is broadly agreed that the population of England, for example, doubled from about 1551 to 1751 (from c. 3 million to nearly 6 million). As late as 1700 the great mass of the population was rural, both in terms of location and occupation. Also, most of the population lived in the southern and eastern parts of England — reflecting a better climate and more productive soils, and a map of population distribution which had evidently changed little from the Roman period.

Estimates of the urban component of the population by 1700 vary considerably, partly because of the basic difficulty of differentiating between a small town and a large village (see Clark and Slack, 1976, for a detailed discussion of this distinction). What was striking about the urban hierarchy of pre-industrial England was its extremely lop-sided nature. There were perhaps 600 very small market towns scattered over the land-scape, with populations of less than 5000 in 1700. Many of these were 'towns' only through their market function or administrative significance, not through their population size. A second tier of towns, perhaps 100 in all, had populations of perhaps 7000-8000 in 1700, while a much smaller third tier in the hierarchy had populations in excess of 10 000 in 1700. This third group included Norwich, York, Bristol, Exeter and Newcastle. They were all important regional centres. Only Bristol was a relative new-comer to this list, reflecting its growing trade with the Americas. The others had retained their position since the Medieval period.

At the head of the pre-industrial hierarchy came London. As early as 1500 London's population had been estimated to be as high as 60 000 — or at least six or seven times the size of the next towns in the hierarchy. Despite setbacks such as the Plague and the Fire in the seventeenth century, London continued to grow with what to contemporary observers was frightening rapidity, reaching 250 000 in 1600 and doubling that population to half a million by 1700. In 1700 London was the largest city in Europe, approached only by Amsterdam in size. Even before the clear onset of a new wave of population growth in the later decades of the eighteenth century, London was the object of suspicion and criticism. It certainly 'absorbed' people and killed them amidst its squalor. It has been described as an area of 'natural decrease in population' in the eighteenth century (Daunton, 1979, p.255), and its continued growth relied very heavily on in-migration from elsewhere in Britain. Indeed throughout the pre-industrial period, and well into the nineteenth century, urban mortality rates were twice those in rural areas, though urban birth rates were also significantly higher (Loschky, 1972). London also dominated the national economies of England, Wales and even Scotland. It was not only the focus of wealth and capital, its huge population required feeding. The influence of London and its need for food had effects on farming practices as far off as Scotland, while the growing consumption of coal in London involved some 650 000 tons being transported down the east coast from Tyneside and Wearside in 1750 (Wrigley, 1967). The importance of London as a focus of urban population growth has diminished in relative terms, though it remains well over twice the size of any other urban area in Britain. Its importance as a focus of urban problems and in determining urban policies has, however, continued into the twentieth century (see, for example, the deliberations of the Barlow Commission in Chapter 6).

It has been estimated that by 1751 the population of Great Britain as a whole was about 7.4 million, of which the majority (5.8 million according to Wrigley and Schofield, 1981) lived in England. The great majority still lived in villages. Less than 17 per cent lived in towns with populations of 10 000 or more, and nearly two thirds of this urban population were to be found in London itself which had a population in 1751 approaching 700 000. In 1751 the old hierarchy of urban centres under London still survived largely intact, though Birmingham was now the fifth largest town in England, and Liverpool the sixth, with about 23 000 people each. The new 'order' was beginning to emerge, though to most contemporary observers in the later decades of the eighteenth century the pace of change, both demographic and economic, would not have been particularly apparent, while the physical impact on the landscape of mining, industrial and urban development remained highly localized until well into the nineteenth century.

By 1801, however, changes were becoming evident. One of the most obvious was in population growth, particularly the surge in urban population growth which occurred from the 1780s onwards. Between 1751 and 1801 the population is estimated to have grown by no less than 45 per cent, compared with under 8 per cent from 1701 to 1751 (Law, 1967). This sudden surge in population seems to have been part of a complicated three-strand relationship involving demographic growth, agrarian change and economic development. The impetus for the dramatic growth in urban population in the nineteenth century lies in the nexus of this complex relationship.

Population growth depended in the first instance on increased yields from Britains's agricultural sector, since the surplus agrarian wealth from continents such as North America and Australia were to remain untapped until the end of the nineteenth century. The initial impetus towards population growth, and in particular urban growth, depended very largely on advances in our own agricultural economy. These advances in agrarian technology and efficiency are well documented by numerous authors, including Chambers and Mingay (1966), Darby (1973) and Walton (1978). These advances, coupled with a series of clement summers in the middle decades of the eighteenth century, certainly allowed scope for a more rapid increase in population, but cannot alone explain why the population began to surge in the later decades of the century. Agrarian advances were in some ways a fairly passive factor since the new population increase was spatially discrete: it occurred initially far more rapidly in those areas which were also experiencing the new tide of economic growth. The reasons for such localized population increases are complex and remain unclear. One factor was clearly a better, more reliable and balanced diet, though the impact of this on population growth can only have been marginal. Increasing medical knowledge and better control of some diseases may also have been a minor factor. Parish records from those areas that felt the early impact of more rapid population growth, e.g. South-East Lancashire and Staffordshire, certainly show a decrease in the average marriage age. This could have had considerable implications for the birth rate. Habbakuk (1971) has suggested that a reduction of one year in the mean marriage age might increase family size by 8 per cent, and the overall influence of fertility on population growth in this period is discussed in depth by Tranter (1985).

There is clear evidence that as job opportunities began to widen with the onset of economic change children left home earlier, became economically independent earlier, and the marriage age in turn began to fall. There has been considerable dispute about the *necessity* of population growth as a trigger to economic development, or even as a necessary adjunct, given that many of the inventions associated with the Industrial Revolution were labour saving rather than labour exploiting in nature. However, it is difficult to argue that the growth in population did not at least aid economic development, if only through increasing the market for goods produced by the new industries. The overall evidence concerning whether population growth stimulated economic development, or vice versa, is unfortunately both fragmentary and contradictory in nature. The relationship between those two strands of the nexus is succinctly summed up by Wood (1982): '. . . either might have caused the other, or each might have an entirely separate origin'.

Although the debate about the causes of population growth and its relationship with economic development remains unresolved, the rate of expansion and its localized, urban nature is becoming increasingly clear. Annual growth rates in England and Wales were less than 0.25 per cent per annum up to about 1740, but by the 1780s annual growth was averaging 1.45 per cent, and this continued through to the 1820s (Lawton, 1978). By 1801 the top of the urban hierarchy had drastically, and irrevocably, changed. In the top five towns by population after London, none of the older centres such as York or Norwich had survived. York only had 16 000 inhabitants in 1801 while nearby Leeds had over 50 000. Manchester was now second with over 80 000 people. London, which was in no sense a 'centre' of the Industrial Revolution, had nevertheless increased to nearly one million inhabitants by 1801. Urban population growth, coupled with economic growth and change, were beginning to rewrite the population map of Britain.

Economic change

The year 1760 is not a particularly satisfying date from which to begin to consider industrial growth and change in Britain. Some would consider the early success of Abraham Darby, who at Coalbrookdale in Shropshire in 1709, used coke rather than the traditional charcoal in the smelting of iron as a more fitting starting point for the number and range of inventions and innovations which laid the foundation for the Industrial Revolution. Certainly the pace of change in industrial technology accelerated as the eighteenth century advanced. However, it was in the manufacture of textiles, particularly cotton, that the most influential developments occurred. A series of innovations and inventions, beginning with Kay's 'flying shuttle' in the 1730s, through Hargreaves' 'spinning jenny' (1766), Arkwright's 'water frame' (1769) and Crompton's 'mule' (1779), led to the rapid mechanization and later the mass production of cotton. These inventions also led to a shift from the production of cotton as a 'cottage' industry, normally carried out at home, to large mills. Though at first waterpowered, early steam engines using coal were powering a few of the new complex machines by the late 1780s.

Most of this early development was centred on Manchester, and the demand for labour very quickly established South East Lancashire as the fastest growing urban area outside London, though the Clydeside area of Central Scotland, also favourably placed for the import of raw cotton from America, saw significant growth in this period. The movement towards mechanization and mills led in turn to larger, more concentrated labour forces, and then new, or larger, urban settlements. In Lancashire in particular, wherever a stream would provide enough power, cotton mills were quickly established. By 1801 towns such as Stockport, Bolton, Oldham and Blackburn all had populations of between 12 000 and 15 000, almost the same as York and

Exeter. In Scotland, the Glasgow area abounded in fast-flowing streams and the cotton industry developed from the beginning as a fully-fledged mill industry, imported from England. Between 1787 and 1834 the number of cotton mills in Scotland increased from 19 to 134; they were almost all in Glasgow or near to it and included the mill at New Lanark (see Chapter 4). Glasgow itself had a population of well over 60 000 by 1801, with Paisley, the second textile centre, already approaching 10 000.

The cotton industry represented the earliest example of a movement towards rapid mechanization and mass-organized production in mills, but those areas that lay outside the ambit of 'King' cotton tended to see a slower pattern of economic development and consequent urban population growth. On the east flanks of the Pennines innovation in the woollen and worsted industries, following the example of cotton, led to urban growth in a whole series of small settlements in the West Riding of Yorkshire, centred on Bradford. The great growth in demand, and therefore urban growth, associated with industries such as iron and steel, shipbuilding and heavy engineering, coalmining and chemicals lies mainly in the middle and later decades of the nineteenth century. Coal output, for example, equalled 16 million tons in 1816, rising to 50 million tons by 1850 and over 200 million tons by the end of the century when over a million people were directly employed in the coalfields.

Economic development on this scale depended on a number of factors. First of all there had to be a fundamental change in the nature of the market for such goods. One basic reason for the successful development of many new industries was the existence of a ready market in Britain, particularly in England. Although most of the English population prior to early in the nineteenth century still lived in rural communities, few were either self-sufficient or dependent on subsistence agriculture by the beginning of the eighteenth century. Most agricultural producers had a marketable surplus, and many more men worked for a money wage. Internal and overseas trade were well developed. Thus there was a pool of available purchasing power for the producers of new goods to tap. Here lay one of the reasons for the success of many of the early entrepreneurs — a willingness to cater for, and develop, a cheap mass market. This was particularly the case with both the cotton and woollen textile entrepreneurs who produced largely for the 'lower' classes. Similarly, the pottery industry of North Staffordshire concentrated on the whole on the mass market. As the nineteenth century advanced British entrepreneurs were thus well placed to make major inroads into overseas markets. The pattern of exports in some ways shows the varying importance of different industries as the nineteenth century progressed. In 1700, woollen yarn represented the most important export; by 1830 it was cotton, as it still was by 1900, though by now exports of iron and steel and coal and coke had increased significantly, pointing to the growth in the latter industries towards the end of the nineteenth century.

Entrepreneurship and the introduction of the factory system were both vital ingredients of the Industrial Revolution and important factors in the acceleration of urbanization. The factory or mill was usually consequent upon mechanical advances and the increasing reliance on water and later steam power, which required the housing of powered machinery under one roof near the power source. It brought other, organizational advantages to the entrepreneur. Division of labour, control of output and productivity, all became much easier under the factory system. But it brought no advantages to labour, except in some cases higher wages.

Increasing shifts to mechanization and factories brought unemployment to successive groups of workers in the traditional rural industries. Equally, areas that failed to introduce the factory system soon suffered high unemployment as they rapidly became uncompetitive, e.g. the traditional woollen manufacturing region centred in Wiltshire and Gloucestershire lost out to the more innovative West Riding of Yorkshire, leading to severe hardship in the 1790s. Labour did not always easily accept such change, and labour unrest, both within the factories and often against the factory system and mechanization, was a frequent feature from the 1780s onwards. Such labour resistance to the harsh, monotonous regime of the factory (and the mine) led some entrepreneurs to pacify and mollify their workforces by providing housing and community facilities for them (see Chapter 4).

The growth of the iron and steel and coal-mining industries owed much to the surge in demand for their products. Much of this new demand lay with the rapid expansion of the railways from the 1830s onwards and the movement towards building iron rather than wooden ships as the century progressed. Both industries developed on a spatially concentrated basis, wherever the raw materials were to be found. Often coal and iron were to be found in close proximity to one another (e.g. in South Wales, the 'Black Country' and Central Scotland). Both industries were extremely labour intensive, as was shipbuilding, and led to increasing levels of urbanization on and near the coalfields.

Population growth

We have already alluded to the upsurge in population growth in the latter half of the eighteenth century, and the problems involved in accounting for it. From 1801 a population census was held every 10 years. Table 2.1 shows the actual increase in population for the United Kingdom from 1801 to 1911. An increase from perhaps 11 million in 1801 to 20.8 million in 1851 shows an overall increase of 98 per cent, while the figure for 1901 of 37 million shows a further 78 per cent increase on 1851. The increase over the century is clearly very considerable, particularly when compared with population increases in the sixteenth and seventeenth centuries. The period of greatest growth was in the early decades of the nineteenth century, particularly from 1811 to 1821. But, as Table 2.2 shows, the annual rate of increase was not in fact so great; it was considerably less than the rates of increase experienced in numerous developing countries in the 1970s. However, if the overall increase in population was steady rather than spectacular during the nineteenth century, the pattern of growth was uneven in the extreme. The growing demand for labour in the developing industrial areas, with the continuing rapid growth of London, led to a number of complex migration flows that began to reverse the basic population map of centuries. Population grew rapidly in the Midlands and the North of England. But general regional shifts apart, by far the most outstanding characteristic of population growth was its urban character. By 1801 Manchester was already the second largest town in Britain with 84 000 people. Some industrial towns saw extremely rapid increases in population as their economic

Table 2.1   Population increase in England, Scotland and Wales from 1801-1911

Date	Population (000's)
1801	10,501
1811	11,970
1821	14,091
1831	16,261
1841	18,534
1851	20,816
1861	23,128
1871	26,072
1881	29,010
1891	33,028
1901	36,999
1911	40,840

Source: after 'Commerce and Industry', Vol. 2. W. Page (ed.) Constable 1919.

Table 2.2 Population increase in Great Britain at selected dates

Census date	Population	Average annual increase (%)
1821	21,193,458	1.40
1831	24,306,719	1.40
1841	26,916,991	1.02

Source: Danson, Statistical Journal Vol XIII (1850).

Table 2.3 Urban population growth, 1801 - 1851 (000s)

	1801	1831	1851
Birmingham	71	144	233
Bradford	13	44	104
Derby	11	24	41
Huddersfield	7	19	31
Leeds	53	123	172
Liverpool	82	202	376
Manchester	75	182	303
Nottingham	29	50	57
Oldham	12	32	53
Portsmouth	33	50	72
Sheffield	46	92	135
Wolverhampton	13	25	50

Source: from Burnett, J. (1978) A Social History of Housing, 1815-1970, David and Charles.

fortunes rose. The population of Liverpool, for example, rose from 34 000 in 1773 to over 200 000 in 1831, with an increase of no less than 43.6 per cent between 1821 and 1831. Table 2.3 provides some idea of the rapid population expansion of the new centes of economic growth. Even smaller urban centres saw quite spectacular population increases, e.g. Bolton rose from 4500 in 1773 to 12 500 in 1801.However, some of the older, established towns, if they lay outside the compass of the new industrial growth, saw little if any growth over this period. Some even declined. Worcester, for example, moved from 13 000 in 1779 to only 11 300 in 1801 (Corfield, 1982). Even allowing for some inaccuracy in the data, it is clear that not all urban centres necessarily saw growth in this early period of the Industrial Revolution.

By 1851 the 'urban' and 'rural' populations were roughly equal in size according to the national Census of that year, though after 1851 the population scales turned decisively in favour of urban areas, and some rural counties began to experience population decline. The urban population, however, was highly localized. Officially seven provincial towns in England had populations exceeding 100 000, with Liverpool and Manchester both nearing 400 000 each. The population of Greater London was approaching 2.7 million people and London's built-up area sprawled over nearly 700 square miles. By 1881 its population was 5 million and twenty years later over 6.5 million.

After 1876 the national birthrate began to decline, although in some cities it had already begun to do so in the 1850s and 1860s, e.g. Glasgow and Liverpool (Checkland, 1964). Also towards the end of the nineteenth century the death rate began to fall significantly from 22 per thousand in 1875 to less than 17 per thousand in 1901. In-migration to the larger urban centres slowed down, though as late as 1901 the birthrate was 28.5 per thousand, and urban growth continued largely through natural increase. In some areas, though, population growth continued to be quite high. New coal mines were being developed in Northumberland and Durham and in the South Yorkshire and Derbyshire coalfields, leading to sharp increases in population. Two new groups of towns also appeared, both linked to the development of the railways. The first of these consisted of the railway towns such as Swindon and Crewe — both the creations of individual railway companies. Other old, established towns such as Derby and York saw substantial population increases as they became important railway centres. Crewe had a population of 4500 in 1851 which had grown to 42 000 by 1901, principally because it became a major railway junction, and the location of the London and North Western Railway Company's workshops. The second group of towns to benefit from this later burst of population growth were the resort towns whose growth rested on the development of railway links with the main centres of population. Some resorts saw phenomenal rates of growth, e.g. Blackpool grew from 4000 to 63 000 between 1861 and 1911. Bournemouth had fewer than 700 people according to the 1851 Census but after the arrival of the railway in 1870 providing direct access to London, the town grew rapidly, reaching over 78 000 by 1911 (Coppock, 1973).

One final point concerning population growth is worthy of mention, particularly in the context of housing. A commonly held view of Victorian society is that family size was considerably larger than that of the late twentieth century. It is certainly true that the number of children born to families was, on average, considerably higher than today (in the 1820s it stood around 36-38 live births per thousand, roughly double the present rate). However, infant mortality rates were also extremely high and there is little evidence of particularly large families. As Burnett (1978) has commented, the range of family sizes in the Victorian period, though larger than today, paralleled those apparent in preindustrial families. Many families had no children, while in the 1870s 43 per cent had between 5-9 live births. However, life expectancy was often very short. A study of working-class households in Nottingham in 1851 suggests that less than 20 per cent of such households had four or more surviving children (Smith, 1970). Poor diets, overcrowded housing and lack of sanitation took their toll of urban children throughout the nineteenth century.

Social change

Population growth, and more specifically the attraction of more and more people away from the villages and the land into the growing towns and cities, led inexorably to a breakdown of the old, long established social order. This was but one of the many evils for which this foreign interloper — the large town — was to be blamed (see Chapter 4). The old social order consisted of a strict vertically organized society, dominated by landownership. At the top were the landed aristocracy and under them the gentry, squires and professional men — doctors and clergy. The lower levels were occupied by tenant farmers, artisans and tradesmen, with a mass of labourers, paupers and vagrants at the bottom. This intricate structure had survived intact for centuries, held together by patronage and dependence.

The stress engendered by economic development and the concomitant urbanization led to a slow breakdown of this order, though the process was nothing like as rapid as some commentators have suggested. The social structure in Britain in 1850 was closer to that of 1760 than 1900. With urbanization, however, there gradually emerged a different social order, one with horizontal rather than vertical linkages, and a set of 'classes' slowly crystallized out of the disruption; change and conflict went hand in hand with urban growth. This sense of 'class' was felt particularly in towns such as Birmingham, Manchester and Sheffield (Rose, 1981).

Quite how many classes emerged from the crucible of urbanization is still a matter of considerable debate among urban historians, with some suggesting three, others five and yet others as many as eight. Three broad groups may perhaps be recognized. The 'upper classes' consisted by the middle of the nineteenth century of the old landed aristocracy and the new, rich entrepreneurs and industrialists. It is too simplistic to suggest that these two groups were mutually antagonistic: many entrepreneurs were from the aristocracy, e.g. the Duke of Bridgewater owned coal mines in Lancashire and was involved in financing the canal named after him, which was opened in 1761. Much greater diversity attended those who, by the middle of the century, saw themselves as 'middle class', though this loose grouping only represented some 5 per cent of the population. An income of £100-150 per year and the ability to maintain at least one servant allowed entry into this new class. Such people were managers, shopkeepers and the growing band of clerks and professionals. Largely excluded from power, even through the Reform Bill of 1832, this group often became important in local urban politics and formed an aggressive, growing minority, often critical of the social system and the horrors which accompanied unchecked and uncontrolled urban growth. Many of the reformers mentioned in Chapter 4 came from the ranks of the middle classes.

The 'working classes' consisted of the great majority of the newly urbanized population and formed a particularly diffuse grouping with considerable stratification in a pattern which was still very clear in Edwardian Britain (see Chapter 5). Social stratification within the working classes was closely linked to wage levels, with artisans and highly skilled craftsmen earning perhaps 30s per week in 1851. Below them the majority of workers earned just over £1 per week, while at the bottom of the system the unskilled urban labourer (and the rural labourer) earned as little as 12s per week. The gulf between the top and the bottom was felt, and could be recognized, through the overt material differences in housing, clothing and diet.

All three (or more) classes shared no bond or trust with one another, but rather mutual suspicion and antagonism. For the working classes, the exploited proletariat of the Industrial Revolution, there was precious little of the material fruits of urbanization and economic advancement to be had. Gone was the paternalistic patronage and protection afforded by the old upper classes; in its place there was savage repression leading to the denial of organized protest (the Peterloo Massacre of 1819) and the denial of organizations to improve working conditions (the Tolpuddle Martyrs of 1834). For the working classes the utopian communities envisaged by Robert Owen remained a mirage: the reality was a squalid urban environment and overcrowded, insanitary housing.

As the nineteenth century advanced increasing social segregation and social distance between classes began to be translated into geographical distance and residential segregation. The upper classes, and by the Edwardian period the middle classes, sought to move away from the polluted, grimy and overcrowded inner residential districts. This process was slow, however, and even well-known upper class suburbs such as the Calthorpe estate in Edgebaston, Birmingham, were far more socially mixed than their contemporary reputations for exclusiveness suggested (Cannadine, 1982).

Transport and the Industrial Revolution

The scale of economic development and urban growth which characterized the Industrial Revolution would have been very considerably impeded without concomitant innovations and improvements in transport. Indeed the proverb 'necessity is the mother of invention' might be very usefully applied to the nature and timing of improvements in transport in the century spanning 1760-1860.

Prior to the onset of the Industrial Revolution, transport in Britain of either people or goods was a slow, tedious and often hazardous affair. The road system and 'horse power' provided the only means of inland travel, but the responsibility for the upkeep of roads lay in the hands of individual parishes. However, the growth of trade towards the end of the seventeenth century saw the beginnings of the 'turnpike' system, which was to lead over the next hundred years to dramatic improvements in the main roads, and consequent reductions in journey times. The turnpikes originated from the setting up of turnpike trusts by local magnates or entrepreneurs for the improvement of small sections of major roads, initially usually leading to London, which, as we have already seen, dominated the space economy of the country through the demands of its huge population. In return for the improvement and upkeep of roads, the turnpike trusts were empowered, by act of Parliament, to charge tolls on their section of road. Turnpiking spread rapidly during the eighteenth century with a particular surge between 1750 and 1770. By the latter date over 16 000 miles of road had been turnpiked. It is significant that the Post Office instituted its own mail coaches in 1783, and fast, reliable stage coach services became widely available from 1790.

Apart from roads, most movement prior to the 1760s was by coastal shipping and along navigable rivers. This mode of transport was particularly important for goods and materials, whose movement overland by either pack-horse or, later, waggon was both slow and expensive. Although some canals had been built in earlier times, the 'canal era' belongs properly to the early period of the Industrial Revolution, from about 1760 to 1830. Although the total mileage of canals was little more than one tenth that of the turnpikes — 2387 miles as opposed to nearly 22 000 miles (Moyes, 1978) — their far greater capacity for carrying bulky goods and materials made them much more influential in stimulating economic development.

The first two canals directly associated with the new period of economic growth were the Sankey Brook Navigation (1757) and the Bridgewater Canal (1761). Both were built to carry coal from the Lancashire coalfield to the river Mersey to the south, and thus provide cheaper coal for Liverpool and Manchester respectively. In itself this is highly significant: the need for cheap coal proved a stimulus for most canal construction. Shortly afterwards the 'Potteries' area of North Staffordshire was linked to the Mersey, forming the first part of a national canal system which formed a 'great cross', linking the four major river basins of the Mersey, Trent, Severn and Thames, and centred on Birmingham.

The canals were major feats of engineering, slow to build, and heavily capitalized. Such was the profitability of the early canals, however, that the 1790s became known as the period of 'canal mania', with no fewer than 51 canal acts being passed between 1792 and 1795 alone. By 1806 three separate canals crossed the difficult Pennine watershed, reflecting both the economic importance of the areas lying adjacent to the Pennines and the audacity, and optimism, of both the canal builders and investors. By 1830 the canal system was virtually complete, and indeed few canals built during or after the Napoleonic Wars proved a commercial success. They were all soon to be eclipsed, however, by a dramatic Victorian invention: the railway.

The railways had their beginnings in horse-drawn tramways but, with the opening of the Stockton and Darlington railway in 1825, the building of railways began in earnest. By the end of 1835 some 269 miles of track were open, and by 1841 only 14 of the 41 towns in England with populations of 25 000 or more were not rail connected (Moyes, 1978, p.415). Between 1845 and 1852 a period of 'railway mania' ensued, with hundreds of companies being set up and as many bills being passed in parliament. In 1850 some 6000 miles of track were already open, and by 1870 this had more than doubled to 13 400 miles. By 1890 the railways were carrying over 800 million passengers per year, and 300 million tons of freight.

The railways tended to reinforce the existing pattern of towns and cities rather than to provide the stimulus for new urban centres. They provided a fast, reliable and efficient means of communication. Their role in fostering the outward spread of cities and the growth of suburbia at the end of the nineteenth century is discussed in Chapter 5.

Conclusion

By the end of the nineteenth century the population map of Britain had been transformed. The population had risen by nearly 400 per cent over the previous century, but of greater significance was the very uneven distribution of the population by 1900. At the time of the first national Census in 1801 possibly one third of the population might have been justifiably described as 'urban'. By 1851 it was over 50 per cent and by 1901 at least 80 per cent. The transformation from a largely rural to a predominantly urban pattern of population had occurred in less than one hundred years. Moreover, an increasing percentage of the population lived in large towns and cities of over 100 000 inhabitants: in 1801, 11 per cent lived in large cities (in fact in one, London); by 1851 this had risen to almost 25 per cent, and by 1901 to 43.6 per cent (Law, 1967).

Urban population growth had followed in the wake of economic development and industrialization. The growth of the mill, factory and mine, with their need for large labour forces, had initially produced dense, urban populations. The lack of cheap, universal transport systems prior to the end of the nineteenth century ensured that the new industrial towns remained physically small and this added greatly to the density of the populations.

For the new urban populations, economic change had brought with it social changes, though for the great majority, not for the better. Although the tie with the village and the land had now been broken, it was replaced by dependence on an uncertain income to be gleaned from working in the factory or mine. For the urban masses food proved to be expensive and shelter difficult to find. Urban growth and economic development were not to be paralleled by political and social advance during the nineteenth century, and this was to lead to major problems for Victorian society, most obviously in the field of housing. Inevitably in an introductory survey of this nature there is a necessity to generalize. But this is not to suggest that all towns faced the same problems, nor reacted to them in a uniform manner. In the same way that the broad social groupings discussed above varied, so did the large towns which developed as a consequence of the Industrial Revolution (see Briggs, 1963). The Victorian period was one of great diversity rather than uniformity, and this should be borne in mind when reading the remaining chapters in Part One.

References

Briggs, A. (1963) *Victorian Cities,* Penguin Books, Harmondsworth

Burnett, J. (1978) *A Social History of Housing* 1815-1970, David and Charles, Newton Abbott

Cannadine, D. (1982) *Residential differentiation in nineteenth century towns: from shapes on the ground to shapes in society.* In J.H. Johnson and C.G. Pooley (1982) The Structure of Nineteenth Century Cities, Croom Helm, London

Chambers, J.D. and Mingay, G.E. (1966) *The Agricultural Revolution, 1750-1880,* Batsford, London

Checkland, S.G. (1964) *The Rise of Industrial Society in England 1815-1885,* Longman, Harlow

Clark, P. and Slack, P. (1976) *English Towns in Transition, 1500-1700,* Oxford University Press, London

Coppock, J.T. (1973) *The changing face of England: 1850-circa 1900.* In H.C. Darby (1973), A New Historical Geography of England, Cambridge University Press, Cambridge

Corfield, P.J. (1982) *The Impact of English Towns, 1700-1800,* Oxford University Press, Oxford

Daunton, M.J. (1979) *Towns and economic growth in eighteenth-century England.* In P. Abrams and E.A. Wigley (1979) Towns in Societies. Cambridge University Press, Cambridge

Darby, H.C. (ed.) (1973) *A New Historical Geography of England,* Cambridge University Press, Cambridge

Habbakuk, H.J. (1971) *Population Growth and Economic Development since 1750,* Leicester University Press, Leicester

Law, C.M. (1967) The growth of urban population in England and Wales, 1801-1911, *Transactions of the Institute of British Geographers,* Vol. 41, pp 125-43

Lawton, R. (1978) *Population and Society 1730-1900.* In R. A. Dodgshon and R.A. Butlin (1978). An Historical Geography of England and Wales, Academic Press, London

Loschky, D.J. (1972) Urbanization and England's eighteenth century crude birth and death rate, *Journal of European Economic History,* 1972, Vol. 1.1, No. 3, pp 697-712

Moyes, A. (1978) *Transport 1730-1900* In R.A. Dodgshon and R.A. Butlin (1978). An Historical Geography of England and Wales, Academic Press, London

Rose, M.E. (1981) *Social change and the industrial revolution.* In R. Floud and D. McCloskey (1981) The Economic History of Britian 1700-1860, Cambridge University Press, Cambridge

Smith, R. (1970) Early Victorian household structure, *International Review of Social History,* Vol. 15, Part 1, pp 69-84

Tranter, N.L. (1985) *Population and Society 1750-1940,* Longman, Harlow

Walton, J.R. (1978) *Agriculture 1730-1900.* In R.A. Dodgshon and R. A. Butlin (1978), An Historical Geography of England and Wales. Academic Press, London

Wood, A. (1982) *Nineteenth Century Britain 1815-1914* (2nd edn), Longman, London

Wrigley, E.A. (1967) A simple model of London's importance in changing English society and economy, 1650-1750, *Past and Present,* Vol XXXVII, pp 44-70

Wrigley, E.A. and Schofield, R.S. (1981) *The Population History of England 1541-1871: a reconstruction,* Edward Arnold, London

Further Reading

There is an extensive literature concerning the period covered in this chapter. Listed in the references are two historical geography texts, one edited by Darby (1973) and the other by Dodgshon and Butlin (1978). They provide an in-depth analysis of agrarian, economic, transport and population change. Corfield (1982) provides an excellent discussion of urban growth prior to 1800, and Waller (1983) covers the second half of the nineteenth century. Hobsbawm, E.J. (1969) *Industry and Empire,*Penguin Books, London, is an excellent source of information about economic change over the nineteenth century, and Briggs (1963) provides a series of detailed contrasts between the larger English provincial towns. Changing social structure and the emergence of social classes is well documented in Perkin, H. (1969) *The Origins of Modern English Society 1780-1880,* Routledge and Kegan Paul, London, and Thompson, E.P. (1963) *The Making of the English Working Class,* Penguin Books, London.

3   The nineteenth-century housing question and the failure of state intervention

In Chapter 2 we outlined the major parameters of change affecting British society from the advent of the Industrial Revolution to the latter decades of the nineteenth century. The effects of the changes that took place, though varied in their spatial distribution, were to have a growing and fundamental impact on the country's economic, social and political life. It is important to remember that these changes were visited upon a society that was ill equipped to meet them. The reaction of Victorian society to the results of these changes must be seen in the context of the novel nature of the processes at work.

In this chapter we focus on an examination of the nineteenth-century housing problem. This proved to be one of the immediate and enduring results of the increase in population which began in the eighteenth century and the concentrated nature of this increase in the centres of economic development — the new industrial towns. The promise of jobs attracted people to the towns, but little attention was paid to the need to provide shelter for the burgeoning urban populations. The housing problems that resulted from such rapid urban population growth proved to be both massive and intractable. There are a number of reasons for examining the nineteenth-century housing question in depth here, rather than considering the detailed nature of economic expansion and the impact of the factory and the mine on the newly urbanized landscape. First, the 'housing question' was a central issue from the 1840s onwards. It obviously dominated the lives of the new urban working classes, who had to endure the harshness of their new environment. It also became an issue for reformers and provided much of the ammunition for the philosophers, political thinkers and utopians who found the new growing urban agglomerations both distasteful and unnatural. Here lay the antecedents of the growth of the 'anti-urban' thesis on the one hand and the development of new economic and political theories on the other. Housing conditions also became a central concern for government, though mainly through alarm at the possible consequences. This alarm concerned both the real threat to public health which the working-class housing districts provided, and the potential threat that such appalling housing conditions might cause social unrest or even revolution. A second reason for studying the nineteenth-century housing problem is that it provides a vehicle for the examination of the attitudes of Victorian society towards its own massive social and economic inequalities.

We can also see, through analysis of the housing problem and the radical response to it, the beginnings of both the comprehension of the need for state intervention and, by the end of the century, the outlines of such intervention. In this way we can trace the background to the much wider process of state intervention in the urban environment which was to become first of all the town planning movement and eventually the modern planning system.

Housing and the urban poor

Rapid urban growth in post-1945 Britain, for example within the New Towns programme, has not always been free of problems, for example, in the provision of services. Population growth rates have often been quite high, but they have usually been foreseen and planned for. Equally, housebuilding has been undertaken by large-scale contractors using mass-produced materials. Though invalid in many respects, a comparison might reasonably be made with the problems that confronted many towns and cities in the late eighteenth and nineteenth centuries. As we have seen, while the overall population growth rate in the nineteenth century must not be exaggerated, a postulated return to such a national growth rate in the early 1960s through an unexpected upsurge in the birthrate led to something akin to panic among national planners.

Of course, for individual towns and cities in the nineteenth century, population growth rates could be quite phenomenal. The crucial factor then was that such growth was unprecedented and therefore unexpected. It is too easy to be over-critical of the failure of Victorian society in particular to plan for, and overcome, the numerous problems that high population increases inevitably left in their wake.

The building industry was ill equipped in the extreme to meet the sudden, and usually sustained, increase in the demand for housing. It is important to note from the outset that until the end of the period we are dealing with housebuilding and house ownership were almost entirely in private hands. Thus builders, principally concerned with the profit motive, only provided dwellings when and where there was an effective economic demand — they were not concerned with meeting the need for housing.

In medieval times, and into the Georgian period, houses were built primarily of local materials. Moving bricks or stone over long distances was prohibitively expensive for all but the very rich because of the poor state of the roads. Thus domestic dwellings were normally constructed of wood, though all kinds of local variations existed, from quarried stone, where this was locally available, through brick, to flint. During the Georgian period more buildings were built in brick, as improving technology allowed the use of more locally available clays. However, brickmaking was slow to move to mass production, a vital prerequisite if the enormous upsurge in demand in the early nineteenth century was to be met.

The nature and structure of the nineteenth-century building industry is well documented by Burnett (1978) and can only be dealt with very briefly here. Most building firms were local, small and vulnerable to bankruptcy. It was a precarious profession dependent on credit, and profit margins were often small. The major costs in building were materials, usually highly taxed. Taxation was estimated to account for up to one-third of the total cost of a cottage costing £60 in 1850 (Burnett, 1978, p.21). Land was comparatively cheap, as were labour costs, but the search for profits, allied to sudden changes in demand, led to builders 'cutting corners' and the advent of the term 'jerry' builders, suggesting 'something temporary, inferior' (Burnett, 1978, p.21). Although the standard of housing for the working classes was poor in the extreme, the design of such houses was usually left to the builders themselves. The architectural profession is conspicuous by its absence when it comes to the design of nineteenth-century working-class housing.

The poor housing standards experienced by the working classes throughout the nineteenth century were in the first instance a product of the inability of the urban poor to pay for decent shelter. Poverty lay at the root of poor housing, but the terrible over-crowding and disease which characterized urban life for the working classes can also be laid directly at its door. Poverty is a concept lacking in objective definition: it is relative to the norms of a particular society at a specific time. However, there can be little doubt that poverty was a regular visitor to most working-class homes in Victorian Britain. It was axiomatic to contemporary observers in the nineteenth century that one in ten of the population were officially 'paupers' without means of support. In many surveys the figures were far higher than this. For example, in Edinburgh in 1839 it was reported that over 21 000 out of a population of 137 000 were in 'a state of utter destitution', and figures of 15 per cent or more in such abject poverty were common for several Scottish towns. Whether the new urban poor were worse off than their pre-industrial rural predecessors is a debatable point. What is indisputable, however, is that there were more, many more, of them.

The basic cause of persistent poverty in the nineteenth century city was less the absolute level of wages (low though these were) and what they would pay for in the way of food and shelter than the uncertainty, irregularity and seasonal nature of many jobs. Until the middle of the nineteenth century there were no effective trade unions (the Tolpuddle martyrs were transported as late as 1834). The lack of effective organization of labour clearly left it vulnerable not only to low wages, long hours and terrible working conditions but also to being laid off or sacked without any protection whatsoever. The casual nature of many jobs, the seasonal nature of others, e.g. in the construction industry and in the docks, and the volatile nature of the economy, with alternate boom periods and slumps, left many working-class families in perpetual uncertainty as to their financial security. Henry Mayhew (1851- 1862) noted that three successive wet days in London could bring 30 000 people in London to the brink of starvation.

Official statistics concerning those in poverty, collected by the Poor Law Commission, later the Local Government Board, tended to suggest figures of about 5 per cent of the population. The seminal work of investigators such as Booth (1889) in London and Rowntree (1901) in York suggested that 28-30 per cent of the population 'had an income which was inadequate for their support' (Rose, 1972). Yet officially pauperism by the end of the 1880s was reduced to less than 3 per cent of the population.

Housing was not necessarily so expensive for working-class households; it often amounted to no more than one-quarter of total income. Indeed the failure of the poor to pay higher rents and thus improve their housing conditions was criticized by middle-class contemporaries, who understood neither the financial insecurity of the working classes nor the relatively high cost of other basic essentials such as food and coal. As Burnett has written:

Rent was necessarily second in priority to food, and when half or two thirds of all income went to this alone, a rent of 2/6d to 4/- a week for two rooms was all that most labourers and semi skilled workers could afford. (Burnett, 1978, p.67)

Burnett is referring here to London rents in the 1880s and to families renting two rooms. For many families throughout the nineteenth century such luxury was beyond consideration.

The literature concerning working-class housing in the Victorian era is particularly rich, and it is growing. The work of people such as Dyos (1961), Dyos and Wolff (1973), Tarn (1971, 1973), Stedman Jones (1971), Gauldie (1974), Wohl (1977) and Burnett (1978) has added immeasurably to our understanding of the nineteenth-century housing problem, particularly in London, while collected essays edited by Chapman (1971) and Sutcliffe (1974) have added to our knowledge of provincial towns and cities. Below we shall consider some of the more common types of working-class dwellings and attempt to provide an insight into the housing conditions and standards which prevailed in numerous working-class districts in the nineteenth century.

The worst dwellings, occupied by the poorest sections of the community, were the cellar dwellings. In most towns, cellars were not built intentionally for human habitation (though Liverpool was one exception to this) but were used as dwellings because of the intense overcrowding. They were often associated with the Irish poor, who, after an unsuccessful Irish rebellion in 1797, began to come to England in increasing numbers, particularly from the 1820s onwards. Liverpool, an obvious port of entry for the Irish, was estimated by Engels to have:

> Over a fifth of the population — more than 45 000 persons — living in the 7826 narrow, dark, damp, badly ventilated cellars which are to be found in this city. (F. Engels, 1845, translated by W.O. Henderson and W.H. Chaloner, 1971, p.43)

Many cellars lacked proper flooring, had ceiling heights of between 4 and 6 feet, were by definition normally below street level, and had no sanitation. Doctors, who as we shall see were among the foremost of agitators for housing reform, felt that many cellar dwellings were particularly evil in that they were very poorly ventilated and, being below street level were often open to the seepage of raw, untreated sewage from outside, from the rooms above or occasionally, from both.

In many of the newer, burgeoning provincial industrial towns the most common answer to the shortage of working-class accommodation was the 'back-to-back' (see Figure 1). These dwellings saved the builder in terms of both materials and land and were built in their thousands in the nineteenth century. They were particularly popular in some Midland towns such as Nottingham (perhaps they made up 75 per cent of the total dwelling stock in the 1840s) and in northern towns such as Sheffield (which had 38 000 in 1665) and Leeds where they comprised 71 per cent of the total housing stock by 1886. They were built at very high densities, often over 70 per acre (compared with the Tudor Walters Report recommendations of a maximum of 15 dwellings per acre in 1919). Normally they were built in double rows with the inner houses facing each other across a narrow 'court' while the outer dwellings faced onto a street. Thus there was a maximum number of shared or 'party' walls, and inner rooms lacked windows and ventilation. In their poorest form they lacked any internal sanitation, and often each court

Figure 1   Nineteenth-century housing layouts. A, back-to-back or court housing; B, by-law housing. (*Source:* Ordnance Survey 2nd edn., 1905)

shared a communal water pump at one end and an earth closet toilet or 'privy' at the other. Back-to-backs quickly acquired a bad reputation and were banned in many larger cities as the nineteenth century progressed — beginning with Manchester in 1844. However, they have had their defenders (e.g. Burnett 1978), who have pointed out that they did often provide more than one room per family and thus allowed some privacy. They certainly proved a very adaptable form of dwelling and were still being built in Leeds as late as 1937.

'Tenements' had a variety of both origin and form. In most English cities, and particularly London, they simply represented the multiple occupation of large houses — an inevitable response to the acute shortage of accommodation. Often they were originally built for, and occupied by, wealthy families and their servants. As the richer families moved on to more fashionable, modern dwellings, these large older houses were acquired by landlords and, through a complex series of leases and subleases, were rapidly subdivided for poorer families. This early form of 'filtering' of the housing stock often led to some of the worst instances of overcrowding. In view of the high profits to be gained by landlords from such houses, even when they were new, they were often acquired for immediate subdivision and letting to poorer families.

In the north-east of England, and in all the larger Scottish cities, the term 'tenement' had a rather different meaning. The tenement here was the normal form of dwelling for working-class households. Usually stone built and four storeys high, the Scottish tenements were divided into small flats, with access onto a communal stairway or 'close'. In most instances the resulting dwellings, though purpose-built, were extremely small and cramped, often consisting of no more than two small rooms within which families of ten or more would live, eat and sleep. Overcrowding was thus a much more widespread and persistent problem in Scotland than in England.

Although one result of poverty was very poor housing, other evils flowed from this. Overcrowding was endemic for many working-class households, and with poverty, overcrowding and totally inadequate sanitary arrangements, disease, debilitation and early death all too often followed.

Overcrowding was well documented. In 1838, within a poor district of Bristol, consisting of over 1000 people occupying 166 houses, no less than 123 out of 275 families occupied only one room each. Fifty-four of the houses had no toilet, and in 83 there was no water or an 'insufficient supply' (*Statistical Journal*, Vol. XIII, 1850). A report published in the same journal in 1847 noted that in Church Lane, St Giles, London — one of the worst slums — 30 houses housed 100 families and that there were no more than 90 'bedsteads' for 463 people. Many rooms, the report noted, had up to 22 people sleeping in them. The investigator added:

> In these wretched dwellings all ages and both sexes [. . .] swarms of children, the sick, the dying and the dead, are herded together with a proximity and mutual pressure which brutes would resist.

In the same Church Lane, during the cholera epidemic of 1849, it was noted that in a five-week period no less than 24 deaths occurred directly from cholera, 'independent of those (deaths) in the workhouse'.

Until the late 1850s there was no attempt to provide an integrated sewerage system. Even the middle classes tended to use earth closets in the garden. These were usually open cesspits, cleared on a regular basis. In working-class districts they were often shared between dozens or, occasionally, hundreds of people. Here sewage removal was infrequent and in many areas nonexistent. These conditions, aided by inadequate diet, damp, ill-ventilated dwellings, and the intense overcrowding, inevitably led to very high mortality rates. These were increased by regular summer epidemics of diseases such as typhus and cholera, the causes of which were but little understood. Medical care for the poor was in most cases nonexistent.

The social and political context

That such appalling housing conditions and their dreadful consequences were allowed to develop in the new, growing industrial towns might, perhaps, be seen as the result of a society overwhelmed by sudden and unexpected change. This in itself would scarcely excuse those in authority for allowing such terrible conditions to prevail for such a large section of the population, but the really damning evidence against Victorian society is that housing conditions actually deteriorated for many working-class households as the century advanced. The failure of Victorian society to alleviate the housing problem needs explanation, and in seeking that explanation we need to examine both the organization of Victorian society and the social attitudes that formed its approach to what was increasingly recognized as the major social problem of the day.

Power to improve living conditions for the urban poor was ultimately invested in Parliament. Unfortunately the constitution of the latter in no way represented society as a whole, let alone those of the lower classes. Parliament at the beginning of the nineteenth century was elected on the basis of a franchise already nearly five hundred years old. The right to vote depended on the ownership of the freehold of land worth 40s a year. Over the centuries, the increase in the value of land had inevitably led to a larger electorate, but it has been suggested that as late as 1831 the electorate consisted of no more than perhaps 400 000 men. Most of the male adult population, and all women, had no vote at all. The distribution of parliamentary seats was also medieval: each of the 40 English counties elected two MPs, and most of the other seats represented 'boroughs' whose size and importance bore no resemblance to the distribution of the population in 1700, let alone 1800. Many of these were the so-called 'rotten' or 'pocket' boroughs, most of which lay in the patronage of important landowners. The system was undemocratic, out-dated and corrupt, and everyone recognized it. Reform, however, when it eventually came in 1832, was not particularly significant. The electorate was 'enlarged' to 800 000 — less than 4 per cent of the population. The worst of the pocket or rotten boroughs lost their seats and were replaced by the new industrial towns (e.g. 'boroughs' such as Bere Alston in Devon and Dunwich in Suffolk lost two seats each, whereas Leeds and Birmingham each gained two seats for the first time). The urban poor, however, remained unfranchised and unrepresented. The nature of the 'interests' represented in Parliament was to have a profound influence on the attempts to reform housing later in the nineteenth century.

Within the growing towns themselves there was often no municipal organization or council, or, where the latter existed, again very limited and often idiosyncratic franchises operated which were clearly undemocratic. Following on the Reform Act of 1832 came a reform of local government by the passing of the Municipal Corporations Act of 1835. Although national reform of the political system brought no obvious relief to the poor, the reform of local government did mean for many urban areas at least the setting up of local councils, which eventually were to be very influential vehicles for the improvement of the urban environment.

Nineteenth-century society itself, and in particular that part of society which was in a position to institute reform, was arguably, until the middle of the century, less deaf to the horrendous living conditions of the poor than unaware of them. Another feature of society in this period is the apparent stoic acceptance of their lot by the working classes. Though protest did certainly occur from time to time, most notably through the Chartist movement, which sought among other things a much wider reform of the electoral franchise, there was no wider-scale serious unrest. The revolutionary tremors that unseated governments in Europe in 1830, and again in 1848, produced scarcely a ripple in Britain. Why was this the case?

There is no simple answer to this question, but one overriding social attitude that permeated Victorian society from top to bottom was the acceptance of a rigid class hierarchy, coupled with the notion that people should 'better' themselves by their own efforts. Thus the concept of state intervention to help the poor was almost universally detested. The poor associated the state with the workhouse, provided for paupers, while most of society accepted the principle of *laissez faire* or minimal interference by government and were extremely reluctant to see public money spent on social projects. Vested interests blocked reform at every turn — particularly where property was concerned, and property was central to the housing problem.

Housing reform

The attempts by Victorian society to solve or at least alleviate the appalling housing problem are important in a number of respects. First of all, it slowly became clear that neither the market approach nor *laissez faire* would solve the problem, any more than charity or philanthropy. Also it became equally clear that there was a need for a rational, planned approach to provide a good physical environment for the new urban populations. Finally, by the end of the century increasing sections of the population were coming to realize that the provision of decent housing for the poor would require the spending of public money. The seeds of municipalization of housing were thus sown amidst the wreckage of Victorian solutions to the problem, and the beginnings of twentieth-century housing policy may be seen quite clearly before the end of the Victorian era.

Victorian attempts to solve the housing problem took three forms: an indirect approach through concern for public health; a direct attack through a series of housing acts; and a much more acceptable Victorian solution — the philanthropy of private individuals. We shall consider the first two approaches here. Philanthropy will be examined in Chapter 4.

Public health   To the wealthy classes of society the housing and living conditions of the urban poor were *terra incognita*. Since there was little knowledge of the actual environment in which the working classes lived, there was, not surprisingly, little concern. This widespread ignorance and apparent lack of interest or curiosity was in many respects paralleled by an equal ignorance of the terrible working conditions to be found in factory and mine.

However, during the 1830s an increasing number of articulate, literate and influential investigators began to examine the worst working-class districts. In some cases these men were doctors visiting the sick; in others they were people interested in the moral and religious well-being of the poor. No matter what the motive, evidence began to appear in learned journals, newpapers and even government reports. This evidence was extremely disturbing, and two aspects of the overcrowding in working-class residential areas caused particular concern: the moral damage that might result from children being brought up in such appalling surroundings, and the intolerably high mortality rates to be found in such districts. Neither could be accepted by a nation that was at the same time setting itself up as the most civilized, Christian society the world had seen. Many investigators linked overcrowding — particularly the sharing of beds by five or more individuals of both sexes and various ages — with potential moral depravity. One investigator, noting the high rate of shared beds in Hull, commented that it was 'a signal proof of destitution and discomfort, but a fruitful and certain source of evil' (*Statistical Journal*, Vol. V, 1842, p.215).

It was the work of perhaps the greatest of the reformers, Edwin Chadwick, that led to the first attempts at intervention and reform. Chadwick was born in Longsight, then a village near Manchester, in 1800. In the early 1830s he acted as personal secretary to Jeremy Bentham, the first of the Utilitarians, whose ideas were to influence many reforms of the twentieth century. In 1838 all local Registrars (representing some 553 districts for England and Wales) were asked to send in statistics on deaths in each district. The results were disaggregated and analyzed by Chadwick, who was both horrified and staggered by the extent of mortality and the variation between social classes. Deaths from zymotic (infectious) diseases amounted to 56 000 per year. Chadwick's analysis also showed that life expectancy variations were unacceptably high (see Table 3.1).

Table 3.1   Average life expectancy by class

Town or district	Class		
	Gentry and professional classes	Tradesmen	Labourers
Leeds	44	27	19
Bethnal Green	45	26	16
Derby	49	38	21

Source: After Lewis R.O., A.O., (1959) 'Edwin Chadwick and the Public Health Movement' Longman.

Chadwick also linked the incidence of disease with the worst slums by the production of 'sanitary' maps of Liverpool and Bethnal Green in London. The results were a shock to the nation and clearly something had to be done. By also linking the frighteningly high mortality rate among the working classes to the possibility of social unrest, Chadwick skilfully ' drew his respectable hearers to the edge of the pit, and made them observe the monsters they were breeding beneath their feet' (Lewis, 1959, p.46).

In the early 1840s Chadwick's efforts began to bear fruit. In 1844 a Royal Commission was set up to investigate sanitary arrangements in the towns. In 1846 the corporation of Liverpool, 'the unhealthiest town in England', had a private Act of Parliament passed known as the Liverpool Sanitary Act. This gave the corporation responsibility for drainage, sewerage and paving in the city. The following year the city appointed a Medical Officer of Health.

In 1848, no doubt helped by the news of the imminent arrival in Britain of yet another cholera epidemic, Chadwick succeeded in having Parliament pass a Public Health Act. Typically of Victorian legislation this was an 'enabling' Act — the new local authorities could adopt its measures, but there would be no coercion. So much legislation in this era would prove to be permissive rather than mandatory — clearly reflecting the Victorian dislike of government interference with the private affairs of individuals.

The 1848 Public Health Act was important, however, despite its permissive nature. Local authorities could appoint their own Medical Officers of Health to be responsible to local Boards of Health. Slowly but surely most towns acted on the measure, and during the 1850s and 1960s more and more local laws (or bye-laws) were enacted to provide sewers, fresh water pipes, paved streets etc. Slowly sanitation improved, but often in a rather chaotic, uncoordinated manner. Various other acts were passed, and in 1875 a second major Public Health Act was enacted. This attempted to rationalize and codify existing legislation. More importantly, it laid down general guidelines for new building, e.g. minimum street widths, lighting, window sizes for rooms, ventilation, provision of proper sewerage systems and fresh water. All this led to a slow but definite improvement in the standard of working-class housing in the later decades of the nineteenth century. Its physical legacies are the regimented rows of straight terraced houses which still survive in many inner-city areas. Although these areas are often now a cause for concern, and a focus for current housing policy, they provided a significant landmark in the provision of better housing conditions for the urban working classes.

The housing acts   Reform in the matter of public health was slow but steady, and there can be little doubt that conditions began to improve in matters of sewerage, the provision of pure drinking water and, after 1875, in the building standards for new dwellings. Public health, was, however, of concern to all. The frighteningly high mortality rates among the urban working classes were seen as an affront to the Christian morals of Victorian society; but they were also seen as responsible for producing a debilitated, inefficient labour force. Direct reform of housing shows the dilemma that faced Victorian society, and in many respects illustrates, in a microcosm, its totally inadequate approach to any kind of social policy.

Such was the nature and extent of the housing problem that any realistic reform would have required either the general relief of poverty through such measures as raising wages and improving security of job tenure, thus raising income, or the direct subsidization of housing for the working classes. Neither solution appealed to the establishment. The first would have required intervention in the free market economy and recognition of the role of trade unions, while the second would have been equally unpalatable — the spending of public money. Despite the Reform Act of 1832, the electorate, still consisted of the monied classes, and this was inevitably reflected in the general make-up of Parliament. Public money was raised principally through taxing the electorate, and to subsidize the poor in this manner was seen as not only wrong but both unprofitable and unnecessary. This view was, moreover, supported by the church and indeed by many of the urban poor themselves. People should better their lot through their own efforts — if the state were to provide cheap, subsidized housing for the poor, it would stifle enterprise and encourage sloth. These essentially Victorian views are not without echo in our own society a century later.

This long preamble to housing reform through direct legislation is necessary in order to understand the failure of the reformers to pass any housing legislation that would have made tangible inroads into the housing problem until the last decade of the century. The housing acts can be dealt with fairly briefly. The first such act, while normally seen as an attempt to alleviate overcrowding, has usually been interpreted as an example of social control rather than housing reform. In 1851 Parliament passed the Common Lodging Houses Act, under which the common lodging houses would have to be both registered and open to inspection by the recently formed police forces. Although part of the Act was aimed at reducing the appalling overcrowding found in the worst lodging houses (each lodging house was given a maximum number of residents it could legally accommodate), it was in many respects an Act aimed at increasing police powers in order to clean up, in a moral sense, the worst abuses found in the more infamous lodging houses.

By the mid-1860s agitation for further housing reform was increasing, as indeed was overcrowding. Originally introduced in 1866, but withdrawn and amended twice, the Artisans' and Labourers' Dwellings Act was passed in its final form in 1868. It had a very rough passage through Parliament, and the Act, when passed, bore precious little resemblance to the original Bill. As Burnett has written:

[. . .] the manner in which the original clauses were torn apart one by one and the entire emphasis and thrust of the bill changed, reveals both how far advanced of its time the bill was, and how bitter and united was the opposition to municipal ownership of working class dwellings. (Burnett, 1978,p.84).

The Bill was introduced and guided through Parliament by William McCullagh Torrens, and the resulting Act is known generally as the 'Torrens' Act. In brief the bill aimed both to legislate for the demolition of the worst of the existing slum housing and, more importantly, to allow for the building of new, decent housing for the working classes. Those who drafted the Bill were clearly concerned at reducing levels of overcrowding. It had a very stormy passage through the House of Commons, and the amended Bill, when it went to the House of Lords for consideration, laid far more emphasis on the demolition of unfit dwellings through reason of their being 'insanitary'. It started as a 'housing measure' but finally it became largely 'a sanitary bill' (Burnett, 1978, p.86).

It was in the Lords, however, that the Bill was to become thoroughly emasculated in that the remaining clauses concerning the rebuilding of houses by local authorities were removed. In essence the Bill wanted demolition *and* rebuilding. The Act provided for the former, but not the latter. The Act was therefore effectively unworkable as a means of housing reform — local authorities could evict the poor and demolish their housing, but not rehouse them.

In 1875 a second attempt was made to introduce a workable measure of housing reform. The Bill on this occasion was introduced by Richard Cross, the then Home Secretary, and the resulting Act is again known after its author as the 'Cross' Act. The actual title of the Act is the Artisans' and Labourers' Dwellings Improvement Act. Cross expected much the same opposition as Torrens had encountered, and the bill was indeed subject to many changes. Cross insisted from the outset that the resulting Act should be permissive, whereas the original 'Torrens' Bill had tried to insist that its provisions be forced upon all local authorities. Also Cross did not envisage that new housing for the working classes should be 'municipal', but that the increasingly important model dwelling companies (see Chapter 4) should provide new housing for the poor evicted through the demolition of slums.

The basic problem surrounding the 'Cross' Bill was financial. Owners of property for demolition would require compensation which would inevitably fall on the local rates. Equally, if the philanthropic model dwelling companies were to build on the cleared sites, they could not be expected to pay the full commercial value for them. The problem of the level of compensation to be awarded to the slum landlords was finally to be left to government arbitration. This favoured the landlords. In essence the Act was to become unworkable since the cost to the ratepayers in compensating owners of slums led to massive charges on the public purse. Like the Torrens Act before it, the Cross Act was a victim of the attitudes of the Victorian establishment as reflected in parliament. Both Acts remained virtual deadletters.

Although further acts were passed in an attempt to improve the 'Torrens' and 'Cross' Acts, the next significant piece of housing legislation did not arrive on the statute book until June 1890, with the passing of the Housing of the Working Classes Act. There was little opposition to this Act — a measure of the recognized failings of the emasculated 'Torrens' and 'Cross' Acts. The 1890 Act sought to strengthen the existing legislation, but also, in Part III, gave local authorities the right to erect dwellings, though without any central exchequer subsidy. By 1914, 179 local authorities had taken advantage of this Act to build municipal houses, and the 1890 Act can be seen as 'a qualitative turning point [. . .] and [. . .] a quantitative watershed' in the history of public housing (Merrett, 1979, p.26).

Conclusion

Government attempts to overcome the Victorian housing problem can only be seen as a qualified failure at best. Intervention in the area of public health did result in a slow but measurable increase in sanitary standards as the century progressed, and after 1875 basic building and sanitary regulations were laid down which were quickly adopted by the local authorities. In the broader areas of health, however, gross irregularities between social classes remained, and general access to medical care was to remain beyond the working classes until well into the twentieth century.

Attempts at legislation in the field of housing, however, were effectively destroyed by the combination of forces against reform. These included the property-owning classes, who dominated both Parliament and the electorate and clearly had a vested interest in blocking reform. Intervention in what was seen as part of the free market also went against the widely accepted views of free trade and *laissez-faire*. Housing was a commodity from which profits were legitimately to be made. Attempts to interfere in the market were to be resisted. The sad tale of the 'Torrens' and 'Cross' Bills and their emasculation in Parliament bear ample testimony both to this view and its power. By the late 1880s it was becoming clear that an amelioration of housing conditions for the working classes could only come about in one of two ways: a considerable increase in the incomes of the working classes or the eventual widespread provision of subsidized, municipal housing. The 1890 Act did see the beginnings of a movement towards the latter, but it was no more than that. Although successive governments during the later Victorian period and through the succeeding Edwardian era groped their way through legislation towards the acceptance of the need for subsidized state housing, it required the social and economic upheaval of the First World War to produce a legislative framework for effective housing reform.

References

Booth, C. (1889) *Life and Labour of the People* (17 Vols) Williams and Norgate, London. [Booth's mammoth work is succinctly summarized in A. Friend and R.M. Elmon (eds) (1969) *Charles Booth's London*, Hutchinson, London]

Burnett, J. (1978) *A Social History of Housing 1815-1970*, Methuen, London

Chapman, S.D. (ed.) (1971) *The History of Working Class Housing*, David and Charles, Newton Abbott

Dyos, H.J. (1961) *Victorian Suburb: a study of the growth of Camberwell*, Leicester University Press, Leicester

Dyos, H.J. and Wolff, M. (1973) *The Victorian City: images and realities* (2 Vols), Routledge and Kegan Paul, London

Engels, F. (1845) *The Condition of the Working Class in England in 1844*, translated by W.O. Henderson and W.H. Chaloner (2nd edn) (1971) Blackwell, Oxford

Gauldie, E. (1974) *Cruel Habitations: a history of working class housing 1780 - 1918*, Allen and Unwin, London

Lewis, R.A. (1959) *Edwin Chadwick and the Public Health Movement 1832-54*, Longmans, London

Mayhew, H. (1851-62) *London Labour and the London Poor* (4 Vols), republished 1969, Dover Productions, London

Merrett, S. (1979) *State Housing in Britain*, Routledge and Kegan Paul, London

Rose, M.E. (1972) *The Relief of Poverty 1834-1914*, Macmillan, London

Rowntree, B.S. (1901) *Poverty, A Study of Town Life*, Macmillan, London

Stedman Jones, G. (1971) *Outcast London*, Oxford University Press, Oxford

Sutcliffe, A. (ed.) (1974) *Multi-storey Housing: the British working class experience*, Croom Helm, London

Tarn, J. (1971) *Working Class Housing in Nineteenth Century Britain*, Lund Hampshire for the Architectural Press, London

Tarn, J. (1973) *Five Per Cent Philanthropy*, Cambridge University Press, Cambridge

Wohl, A.S. (1977) *The Eternal Slum*, Edward Arnold, London

Further reading

Undoubtedly the best contemporary account of working-class housing conditions is provided by Engels (1845) and of poverty by Booth (1902-3); Burnett (1978) provides the most complete source of overall housing conditions. Of the other sources listed on p.24 Wohl (1977) on housing in London is to be particularly recommended. Daunton, M.J. (1983) *House and Home in the Victorian City*, Edward Arnold, London, provides a graphic account of working-class housing in London in the later nineteenth century.

4 Victorian attitudes to the city: philanthropy and the origins of the town planning movement

Introduction

Victorian society had to face a bewildering variety of changes, but none had so immediate or great an impact as the growth of the 'great towns'. At the beginning of the nineteenth century British society was still largely rural, but by the end it was clearly urbanized. In 1801 less than 1.5 million people lived in towns with more than 50 000 inhabitants; by 1901 the figure was 15.1 million. The previous two chapters have traced some of the reasons for this dramatic change, and one of its most enduring problems — the question of housing for the new urban working classes. In Chapter 3 the failure of both market forces and government legislation to overcome even this one consequence of urban growth is made manifestly clear. Yet while Victorian society grappled, or sometimes failed to grapple, with these unexpected problems which appeared in the wake of urbanization, views of the nature of the new urban agglomerations, their advantages, their rather more obvious disadvantages for society as a whole, and possible alternatives, became widely debated.

Debates surrounding 'the city' emanated from a variety of sources throughout the nineteenth century (see, for example, Coleman, 1973). The 'great towns', and London in particular, provided immediate and obvious vehicles for the airing of contrasting views on the nature of the new urban society. These views covered not merely political thinkers such as Engels, Disraeli, Morris and Arnold, or economists such as Marshall and Hobson, but social reformers such as Owen, Octavia Hill and Booth, novelists such as Dickens and Mrs. Gaskell, and even poets such as Wordsworth. All these writers and their disparate views shared one thing in common: they were drawn from the professional or emerging middle classes. The views of the vast majority of urban dwellers, the working classes, remain unknown since they were largely illiterate and wholly without influence. However, this stream of opinions on the new urban environment, albeit that it came from a restricted group of the population, was to have an enormous subsequent impact on the English psyche (Williams, 1973). In this chapter some of these views will be reiterated, and examples of them looked at in some little detail, in order to trace the development of the reformist tradition in social and economic conditions and housing in particular. This will lead on to an analysis of the origins of the town planning movement, which was to have such a decisive influence on twentieth-century urban growth in Britain.

An awareness of the very different environment to be found in large towns, not only physical but social, cultural and economic, did not need to await the advent of the Industrial Revolution and the spread of large urban centres over the face of Britain. Before 1800, however, the discussion 'had been less about cities than about London' (Coleman, 1973, p.3), already approaching 1 million inhabitants. Also eighteenth-century views of urban life were not necessarily critical or hostile. Samuel Johnson, a native of Lichfield in Staffordshire, found London in the later eighteenth century a stimulating environment, so much so that he could say: 'A man who is tired of London, is tired of life.' On the other hand. William Cobbett, a radical journalist and politician, spoke often and with evident feeling of London in the early nineteenth century as 'the great Wen' (meaning a wart or blemish). Such extreme views are to be found throughout the nineteenth century.

Coleman (1973) has suggested that attitudes tended to vary somewhat as the nineteenth century advanced. Initially, views were largely focused on London as 'the one great city in a predominantly agrarian society' (Coleman, 1973, p.3). In the first period, up to the 1820s, the city was on the whole treated with suspicion and alarm, as an alien intrusion into the 'form' of rural life. Already writers such as Cobbet were seeing towns as unnatural and evil, spreading into the countryside which stood for moral virtue and order in society. The period from the 1820s to 1848 Coleman sees as one in which writers began to take sides rather more clearly. Some were critical of the evils of the new towns, whether in terms of their squalor, disease, housing conditions or lack of sanitation, their potential threat to public order, their vice and lack of religion, or the extremes of wealth and poverty which they increasingly produced. Others, however, began to see the possibilities of a new society and new wealth emanating from the cities, provided they could be controlled and directed. Here we have the beginnings of civic pride and 'municipal socialism', as exhibited in the attempts made after 1848 to attack sanitary problems in cities such as Liverpool and Manchester.

From 1848 to the 1880s Coleman identifies a third phase in the image of the town as reflected by contemporary writers. The year 1848 was significant in that it saw the passing of the first Public Health Act; and in the following decades many civic improvements were made. There was a growth of local civic consciousness and pride, nowhere so evident as in Birmingham under Joseph Chamberlain where 'civic pride was the driving force of a whole civic philosophy' (Briggs, 1963) that led to wholesale reorganization of the local government of the city and municipalization of services in the 1870s. Although writers in this period were still painfully aware of the many shortcomings of the Victorian city, there was a growing feeling of optimism that progress was being made. The squalor of overcrowding and unfit dwellings remained, but there was growing evidence of the positive effects of economic progress, philanthropy, and self help, all of which would eventually lead to a better environment for all. This acceptance of the town, and the hope of a better future, did not last however, and Coleman believes that there was a clear sense of growing disillusionment by the 1880s. Again housing seemed to be at the centre of growing bitterness and doubt. The evident failure of housing legislation, the continuing spread of poverty, and the increasingly desperate housing conditions in central London epitomized this sense of gloom and betrayal which the working classes clearly felt. This view was encapsulated in the publication of a pamphlet in 1883 entitled 'The Bitter Cry of Outcast London', written by a group of nonconformist clergymen. It received considerable attention, and in addition to describing the all too familiar circumstances of the filth, squalor and degradation of the slums it castigated in caustic terms the indifference of the wealthy and those in authority. A sense of despair about the urban environment was also now increasingly linked to the search for alternatives. Philanthropy by this period was clearly no solution; the example of the attempts to improve housing conditions by private means had clearly shown this to be the case. Some writers believed that much stronger government intervention was the only way to improve conditions. J.A. Hobson was typical of those advocating greater public intervention, both to improve the overall environment and to allow for decentralization of the population by the 'firm public control in the common interest over the steam and electric railways of the future' (Hobson, 1894).

Not all observers in the later decades of the nineteenth century placed such faith in public intervention, however, particularly in the light of the fate of the reformist housing bills of 1868 and 1875. Some saw the future in terms of a revolution of the oppressed poor and then the replacement of the existing capitalist urban society by a cooperative society based on smaller, egalitarian communities. This rather romantic and unrealistic view was put forward by William Morris in 1891 in the form of a fanciful novel entitled *News from Nowhere*. In this novel the author dreams that London and all the large towns have been swept away by a revolution of the masses:

[...] the centres of manufacture [...] have [...] like the bricks and mortar desert of London, disappeared [...] since they were centres of nothing but "manufacture", and served no purpose but that of the gambling market [...] (Morris, 1891).

Rather less extreme in their political views, but equally clear in their dislike of London and the 'great towns', were social reformers like Ebenezer Howard. Howard attempted to combine a dislike of private landlords with an attraction for municipal collectivism. Although in some ways his concept of the 'garden city' seems to have a nostalgic rural ring to it, appearing to lead full circle to the early writers such as Cobbett, Howard combined abstract ideals with a strong sense of what was practical.

Coleman's analysis is invaluable not only in emphasizing the range of ideas and attitudes concerning the Victorian city and in showing that contemporary writers were both extremely interested in and disturbed by their environment, but also in suggesting that as the nineteenth century advanced there was a growing sense of alienation from the city. This was to prove fundamental in moulding the strong anti-urban bias that has permeated much twentieth-century thinking in the context of urban issues and possible solutions. The importance and persistence of this anti-urban ideology in British culture is discussed in detail by Mellor (1982). Mellor provides a stimulating exposition of both our images of urban and rural life and the extent to which these images in many cases become self-perpetuating myths. Mellor illustrates the diffusion and longevity of the anti-urban ideology, and the early age at which we are inculcated into it by the use of literature for children. From *Alice in Wonderland* to *The Wind in the Willows* in prewar children's books and through the *Ladybird* reading schemes of the 1950s and 1960s to the more modern *Mr Men* series,

[...] the text and illustrations make it quite clear that a happy childhood is to be spent in a picturesque home, in a small town, with unrestricted access to the country and with frequent visits to the sea. (Mellor, 1982, p.68)

Mellor relates both the development and prevalence of this anti-urban, pro-rural imagery to the differing reactions of the various social classes that experienced the nineteenth-century city. For the working classes, whose views are largely unrecorded, one can only conclude that the city must have been an awful, grimy, monotonous environment. Their 'life experience' of the town meant enduring the harsh reality of capitalism — low, often irregular wages, noisy and often dangerous working conditions, long and usually unsocial hours at work. The entrepreneurs and capitalists clearly saw in the city business profits, possibilities, civic pride and progress, though quite whose progress is open to debate. For what Mellor describes as the 'intellectual' class, whose writings Coleman's analysis is based on, the city was increasingly seen as destructive of civilized behaviour and decency. It is in the writings of this latter heterogeneous but very influential class that the seeds of the anti-urban legacy may be found.

From the foregoing discussion it should be clear that the Victorian city unleashed a variety of responses, in the main hostile, though in differing measure. One stream of thought, broadly emanating from such writers as Cobbett, Ruskin and Morris, tended quite simply to be openly hostile to the industrial town, which was clearly considered to be the creature of capitalism. All three writers yearned for a return to a nobler, craft-oriented, ordered rural society, which existed very largely not in the past as such but rather in their image of the past. This set of ideas need not detain us here since their authors had little to say about how the great socio-economic 'leap backwards' was to be achieved. In essence they offered no immediate or remotely realistic cure for the numerous ills of the Victorian city. Two other streams of thought also emerged. One, in line with the then current spirit of *laissez-faire*, suggested that improvement and reform should come from private means, providing a necessary support for market forces and not engaging or requiring the services, or interference, of the state. This school of thought embraced both philanthropy, in which the rich could help the poor, which was acceptable on both social and religious grounds, and self-help, which again in the spirit of the age, was to be applauded. The third stream of thought suggested reform of the system, either directly through greater state involvement or through the use of private capital and cooperatives to provide for a better, planned environment for the population. Here lay the beginnings of the town planning movement. In the rest of this chapter we will examine the efforts of some of the philanthropists and the antecedents of the town planning movement.

The philanthropists

The widespread acceptance in Victorian society of the ideology of *laissez-faire*, with an almost religious belief in the ability of the unfettered processes of market forces to ultimately solve problems, has been mentioned briefly in Chapter 3. Concurrent with this belief was an historical mistrust and dislike of government legislation of almost any kind, particularly in areas where such legislation might be seen to restrict the free play of market forces. Housing was seen in the nineteenth century as a simple, widespread commodity for which there was a fluctuating though on the whole growing economic demand; it could be, and was, bought, sold or rented in the marketplace. Despite the glaring disparities in housing provision between different social classes and the appalling housing conditions of the poorer groups in society, interference by government legislation in the housing market was strongly resisted, as we have seen from Chapter 3. Housing, in the view of many, and in particular the numerically large, politically influential and economically powerful urban landlords, should not be subject to legislation. If the lot of the urban poor could not be remedied quickly or effectively by the forces of the free market in housing, then the philanthropy of private individuals or groups was a much more acceptable and in the end well-tried solution. This philanthropic approach to the housing problem took three very different forms: the 'model' village, the 'model' dwelling company, and the individual philanthropic landlord.

The 'model' village

One novel but widespread phenomenon that followed in the wake of the Industrial Revolution was that of the 'model' village. These settlements were essentially purpose-built, often to an overall plan by individual entrepreneurs or companies to house their own workforces. They were 'models' in that they provided housing layouts, designs and standards which were normally well in advance of the housing conditions of contemporary working-class families within the growing towns. There was usually strict control both of rents and, that curse of the Victorian poor, overcrowding. These settlements were usually quite small and often located away from existing centres of manufacturing and population — hence the term 'villages'. But this was not always so, and in all cases these were industrial settlements, not rural communities.

Model villages were built in numerous locations from the late eighteenth century through to the end of the nineteenth century. In some cases they consisted of rows of artisan cottages and little else, in others they were provided with communal facilities, and in some they represented pioneering attempts to develop new cooperative communities.

A very early example of a model village was that of New Lanark in the valley of the Upper Clyde in Central Scotland. Apart from being one of the earliest examples of such a venture, New Lanark was also the venue for one of the most interesting of the philanthropic attempts to introduce a new spirit of cooperative enterprise under the auspices of one of the best-known social and economic reformers of the whole period, Robert Owen. New Lanark was in fact founded not by Robert Owen — though it is always associated with him — but by a Glasgow merchant, David Dale. Dale visited the site of the famous Falls of Clyde near the old county town of Lanark in 1784 with the English inventor and cotton entrepreneur Richard Arkwright, himself responsible for the founding of a model village at Cromford in Derbyshire. At this time steam engines were only just beginning to become practical sources of power, and most cotton mills relied on water power. Such was the potential in the flow of the Clyde over the falls that Arkwright suggested that Lanark might in time become the 'Manchester of Scotland'. Dale immediately purchased the site and began building a mill. The site was narrow, cramped and difficult of access as the Clyde flows through a narrow, deep valley at this point, but the presence of the waterfall determined the location.

Robert Owen was a successful cotton mill manager in Manchester in the latter decades of the eighteenth century, and he came to New Lanark in 1799 when he married Dale's daughter. Owen saw in New Lanark an opportunity to improve the working conditions of the mill workers and to put his revolutionary ideas on social and economic welfare into practice. Owen argued that a healthy and happy workforce would be more productive and was genuinely horrified by the awful working conditions of the workforces of the cotton mills. In particular the young children were seen by Owen as both vulnerable and exploited. Many young children were sent to work in the mills as almost slave labour, either by their parents, or by the parish authorities as paupers or orphans. In New Lanark up to 300 of these children worked, and slept, next to the mill machines. Owen moved quickly to build a nursery to house these children, a school, and ensured that no child under 10 years of age should work in the mill. Later he built his New Institute for the Formation of Character, which was provided with a library and used for community activities. The village shop was developed on cooperative principles and New Lanark and Owen soon acquired fame throughout Britain and overseas. Owen offered an alternative to capitalism — 'villages of coopera-tion'; though a second such community near Motherwell and called Orbiston failed in the 1820s. Many of Owen's ideas were taken up by other philanthropists, though rarely with the success of the New Lanark venture, which remained unique.

Other model villages were usually much less advanced in their social and economic objectives. Some were the creation of companies rather than individual entrepreneurs and were built out of necessity rather than for philanthropic reasons (e.g. Swindon where railway workers needed housing). Towards the end of the nineteenth century two model villages received particular attention and were built to very high standards — Port Sunlight, begun by W.H. Lever in 1887 on the south side of the Mersey estuary to house the workers in his soap factory; and Bournville, developed by George Cadbury the chocolate manufacturer in the 1890s on a then greenfield site south of Birmingham. In Bournville

> great attention was paid to house design and the provision of open space and sunlight and environmental conditions as a whole. Suitably sized gardens, tree lined roads, and parks and recreation grounds made for worker's living conditions quite different from anything that the rest of Birmingham could show. (Cherry, 1972, p.105)

Model villages such as Bournville showed quite clearly that a decent residential environment could be provided for working-class households. Though the quantitative impact of such settlements was inevitably tiny in terms of the needs of the millions of working-class families, they did show what could be done. It is interesting to note that the philanthropic showpieces of Lever and Cadbury influenced Howard and his followers, and there is a direct link between these later model villages and the first garden city of Letchworth.

Model dwelling companies

As Coleman and others have suggested, the mid-Victorian age from the 1840s to the 1880s represented a period of quiet optimism that the new industrial society was capable of solving the numerous problems which beset it. It was a period of faith in the strength of economic progress through market forces, aided and abetted where necessary by municipal improvements and the philanthropy of the rich. This belief extended itself naturally to housing, and from the 1840s onwards much philanthropic effort in housing, particularly in London and the larger provincial cities, was concentrated in the form of semi-charitable trusts and companies, known collectively as the model dwelling companies. There was a bewildering variety of charities set up during the Victorian era, echoing and matching an equal number of causes. But while most of these efforts were of a straightforward charitable nature, the model dwelling movement was distinct in that 'unlike most of the other endeavours, it solicited not gifts but investments' (Wohl, 1977, p.142).

The generosity of many affluent Victorians in matters of charity was often quite extraordinary, matched though it was by such a powerful reluctance to engage the forces of the public purse in favour of the poor. However, in the context of housing this philanthropic zeal was tempered by that other singularly Victorian trait of encouraging self-help in others. It was seen by many potential benefactors as morally wrong to provide housing for the less affluent either free or through a subsidy: such actions would only encourage increased sloth among the 'destructive classes' who would thus lose the powerful incentive to improve their own material and housing situation. Attitudes such as this permeated the debates in Parliament over the modest housing legislation put forward by reformers such as Torrens, and were clearly quite widespread. The philanthropists who were concerned with housing reform through the building of decent or 'model' dwellings for the poor sought to overcome such prejudices, and widen their net of potential investors, not by asking for donations, but by offering dividends as returns for investment in such a worthy cause. Most of the companies aimed at a modest return of about 5 per cent per annum and very quickly this form of philanthropy earned the somewhat derisory soubriquet of 'philanthropy at 5 per cent'.

The earliest of these model dwelling companies was the Metropolitan Association for Improving the Dwellings of the Industrious Classes, and its first meeting was held in 1841. The model dwelling companies aimed on the whole at providing housing in central, accessible locations, where the majority of the poorer classes lived and where the worst living conditions were generally to be found. The high cost of land in such locations, particularly in London, forced the companies to build upwards if they were to accommodate a reasonable number of households at realistic rents. Thus the developments associated with the companies were, with few exceptions, large monolithic blocks of flats, usually 3 - 4 storeys high. They were built to high standards, particularly when compared to the contemporary working-class housing in areas to which they were adjacent. Size and number of rooms per dwelling were comparatively generous and subletting of rooms, the normal expedient available to working-class households to meet the rent throughout the nineteenth century, was not allowed. Thus sanitary conditions were good and overcrowding much reduced. The managers of the companies were often at pains to point out the low death rates to be found in their developments when compared to working-class districts generally, e.g. for the Metropolitan Association, between 1867 and 1875 the death rate among its tenants did not exceed 14 per thousand compared to 24 per thousand in London as a whole.

Most of the companies laid down a set of regulations which were usually strictly enforced. Such regulations, while covering obvious items such as rent, repairs, sub-letting etc., also tended to lay down strict rules concerning washing days, children's play areas, and tenants' rights, or the lack of them, concerning interior decoration of the flats. It all suggests a dreary, regimented existence compared with the laxity and freedom with which most working-class families were familiar. The few written accounts of tenants' opinions of such a life-style tend to confirm the somewhat stifling regime which operated in such buildings, though some tenants were clearly appreciative of the improved physical environment they offered.

The often stated aim of these companies was to provide better housing for the poorest groups in society. The preferred choice of expensive, central sites confirms this. However, in seeking to provide profits from such schemes the companies inevit-ably found that this aim could not be met. In essence the rents required to generate even a low yield on the investors' money put the model dwellings beyond the reach of the poor. Equally the stringent scrutiny of potential tenants to ensure that they were sober, thrifty people with regular incomes also ruled out many of those in greatest need of better housing.

George Peabody, the American banker, donated £150 000 in 1862 to be spent on the poor of London. It was decided to set up a model dwelling company with the money, called the Peabody Trust. Peabody appears to have had a genuine desire to aid the very poor, but, as Wohl points out,

it is safe to say that the Peabody buildings were generally housing members of the regularly employed and better paid labouring class and many artisans and clerks. (Wohl, 1977, p.156)

In 1887, Charles Booth defined the poor as those earning less than 21s per week, but a survey in 1885 showed that only 910 Peabody dwellings were let to households with an income of 20s or less, compared to well over 3000 tenants earning 20-30s per week. The record of the other companies appears to be even less generous in terms of providing homes for the very poor.

By 1905 the nine largest model dwelling companies operating in London between them housed some 123 000 people. But by this time the population of London was approaching 7 million, with an annual increase of some 70 000-80 000. It was clear that the model dwelling movement was providing but a small fraction of the dwellings needed. It was not a measure of the lack of interest or even of investment in such ventures, but rather the size of the housing problem itself. Philanthropy had clearly proved by the turn of the century that it was no answer to the housing needs of the population, and equally therefore that capitalism and the forces of the marketplace could not even begin to solve the housing problem. The model dwelling companies did leave some positive legacies. They were, in central London at least, almost the only source of new accommodation for the working classes as a whole from the 1860s onwards. They also showed that high-density accommodation need not necessarily mean overcrowding and insanitary conditions. But as a solution to the urban housing problem they were a clear failure, and with their failure capitalism and private enterprise were also seen to have singularly failed to solve this vexing and persistent problem. The necessity of large-scale municipal enterprise was recognized by many housing reformers before the end of the 1880s.

Individual philanthropy

In contrast to the large philanthropic model dwelling companies there was a minority of individual improving philanthropic landlords. The great majority of landlords, usually through intermediaries such as factors or agents, were interested solely in extracting the maximum rents, and therefore profits, from their properties; they were entirely oblivious of the terrible conditions which their tenants had to endure. Philanthropic landlords were clearly the exception; and they tended to be exceptional people. By far the best known of these was Octavia Hill, who gave her name to a style of housing management.

Octavia Hill, who was born in 1838, was the granddaughter of a famous public health reformer. She grew up in a reformist atmosphere and indeed it was a family friend, John Ruskin, the art critic and reformer, of the romantic school, who started her career in housing through a gift of some £3000. This was in 1865 and gradually Miss Hill expanded her ownership of dwellings. By the 1880s she owned, or managed on behalf of others, some £70 000 worth of property, involving perhaps 3000-4000 people. Her direct impact on the housing problem was therefore meagre, but her real influence lay in her methods and her writings. She was above all concerned with encouraging the very poor to improve their own lot. In the words of Wohl she 'epitomized, almost personified, the "self-help" approach to social problems' (Wohl, 1977, p.180), and in many ways should be categorized along with her band of female helpers and co-workers as an early social worker. She matched an interest in improving housing conditions for the poor with a zeal to reform and educate them. Octavia Hill's tragedy was that she failed to appreciate the enormity of the housing problem. She disliked the idea of municipal enterprise in housing and ridiculed the work of the model dwelling companies. In her view the need was to renovate and improve existing housing; yet in London in the latter half of the nineteenth century there was an obvious and desperate need for more housing in quantitative terms. Her work and example failed to galvanize landlords as a group and her contribution in some respects was a negative one: by rejecting the concept of subsidizing housing and municipal house-building she was out of step with the real needs of the urban population and 'became an anachronism among housing reformers, even in her own time' (Wohl, 1977, p.199).

The origins of the town planning movement

In some ways the third stream of ideas that emerged from the ferment of Victorian agonizing and debate on the desirability and direction of urban growth and the possible solutions to the problems apparently engendered by it lay between the ideas of those like Morris who explicitly rejected the city and those of philanthropists who believed that communal social problems could be overcome by individual action. On the one hand, the adherents of the third stream could recognize the need for, and benefits of, state or municipal involvement in solving urban problems, given their scale — particularly as far as housing was concerned — and the evident failure of capitalism and philanthropy to solve them. Equally, though, there was a strong feeling of alienation against large cities in the writings of people like Unwin and Howard and a wish to move to a more human scale of urban size — the garden city.

'Municipal socialism' is a term given to the increasing involvement of the town corporations from the middle decades of the nineteenth century onwards. Beginning with the need for municipal intervention to improve sanitation through sewage and fresh water schemes, this movement led to the growth of civic pride and intervention in all services for the community. As a result, by the end of the century there was normally municipalization of gas, electricity and the new means of mass transport — the tram and the omnibus. Although often strongly attacked, the benefits of 'municipal socialism' could not be denied.

However, a revulsion against 'the city' as it had developed by the later decades, its size, filthy environment, disease and social disorder, ran deep in those reformers who sought a realistic alternative and even today the town planning movement remains thoroughly imbued with an anti-urban ideology that clearly owes much of its origins to nineteenth-century roots. In fact many of the measures proposed then to control the city can only be seen now as of marginal or historical importance. Some conservative reformers, such as Wakefield and Marshall, argued that the poor should be removed, forcibly if necessary, from the cities to planned colonies in the country or abroad. Radical contemporary observers such as the Chartists proposed cooperative or community-based settlements beyond the influence of the capitalist city. Other, perhaps more romantic, Utopians such as William Morris looked to the demise of the city and its replacement by a rurally based, craft-orientated society. This vision, expounded in *News from Nowhere* in 1891, was oddly enough to prove hugely influential. This was not because of Morris's idealistic view of a nonurbanized world but because of the impact of his writing on Raymond Unwin.

Unwin was to become one of the leading figures of the incipient town planning movement in the earlier decades of the twentieth century. He was a member of the Tudor Walters Committee of 1918, which set physical standards in public housing, and he was to be heavily involved as a civil servant in housing and planning issues for many years. As Mellor (1982) points out, Unwin was directed towards socialism and medievalism by writers such as Morris. In practice he

> sought to re-achieve the apparent harmony of the self-contained village or medieval town in which each detail blended into a serene landscape. (Mellor, 1982, p.83).

In furthering these ideals, in 1912 Unwin published *Nothing Gained by Overcrowding* in which he argued for much lower residential densities than had prevailed under bye-law housing built in the later decades of the nineteenth century. Unwin argued in effect that lower-density housing laid out in environmentally attractive estates could prove as profitable to a developer as would higher-density developments because of savings on road construction and other benefits that would accrue as a result of construction being spread over a greater area. Whatever the truth of these assertions, Unwin's influence was to prove formidable in both the private and public housing sectors. In the former, enormous numbers of suburban semi-detached dwellings were constructed in the interwar period in estates not at all dissimilar to those advocated by Unwin. And in the public sector the whole ethos of the Tudor Walters report revolved around the assumption that working-class housing should be constructed at densities of no greater than 12 dwellings an acre. Certainly the appearance of the contemporary British city owes much to Unwin's ideas. His advocacy of lower-density, semi-detached housing laid out in planned estates with large productive gardens and a green outlook was to be widely practised for decades and still represents for many the ideal residential environment.

Although Unwin's main impact was undoubtedly as an advocate of lower-density housing, his direct influence as a planner and architect should not be ignored. He was, for example, partly responsible for that most elegant of suburban developments, Hampstead Garden Suburb, and the now somewhat less than elegant Wythenshawe in Manchester. The former, now an exclusive North London enclave, is unmistakably of the garden city movement. An intimate estate design and sylvan setting provide the backcloth for a tremendous variety of individually designed, low-density dwellings ranging from small artisan-type cottages to some of the largest and most expensive houses in Britain. The unity of design and purpose of the Suburb may be unequalled anywhere in the country, but its attempt to recreate a medieval, intimate village atmosphere has been the aspiration of many public and private developments initiated in the interwar and postwar periods. Unwin was to prove influential in another obvious manner. He it was who with Barry Parker designed the first of the garden cities at Letchworth in 1905. However, the idea of the garden city did not come from Parker and Unwin. This belonged to an altogether greater figure in the history of the town planning movement.

Ebenezer Howard was born in London in 1850. He travelled to America in the 1870s, published one book, *Tomorrow: a peaceful path to real reform*, in 1898, which was reissued in 1902 as *Garden Cities of Tomorrow*. He died in Welwyn Garden City in 1928. Although frequently described as a Utopian, Howard was to devise a view of society which was profound, detailed and practical. His ideas have in fact often been misunderstood and, ironically, they were to prove more influential after rather than before his death. But post-1945 British society — and certainly the role of the city within it — cannot even remotely be comprehended without invoking Howard's work.

Howard openly admitted that many of the details for his overall scheme were borrowed from other writers. The list of commentators, aspects of whose work proved relevant to his futuristic vision, is formidable (Fishman, 1977; Hall, 1983). They included Alfred Marshall's concept of moving workers and their employment to new towns in the country, Herbert Spencer's proposals for land nationalization and Thomas Spence's suggestion that new communities should purchase land at agricultural values and retain the surplus accruing as a result of new developments. Edward Bellamy's novel *Looking Backward*, published in America in 1888, affected Howard profoundly. In it Bellamy in effect foresaw a centrally planned, cooperatively organized, technologically based society eventually replacing the corrupt inequalities of nineteenth-century society. In some respects this was clearly to prove a model for Howard's concept of the garden city, except in one obvious respect: Howard was eventually to reject the idea of a centrally planned society and opted instead for a more decentralized, libertarian, individualistic vision, probably as a result of the work of Kropotkin, the Russian anarchist whose articles were published in London in the 1880s.

Inevitably Howard's book, published at the end of the nineteenth century, reflected his own varied experiences and complex intellectual development. It might be seen in general as a radical programme of action, a counterbalance to the appalling weight of late Victorian inequality. But it was also an idiosyncratic view, the statement of a man fully aware of the need for practical as well as ethereal prognostications. It was this practicality, this determination to implement ideas, that was to prove so important in the eventual acceptance of at least some of his ideas in the wider political arena. We can perhaps distinguish between the impact of his ideas in his own lifetime and their longer-term influence.

Howard and the development of the garden city movement

Howard argued that the new communities he envisaged, the garden cities, would combine the advantages of town and country while at the same time avoiding the drawbacks of both. In the famous Three Magnets diagram he indicated that a town-country, or garden city, environment would synthesize the benefits of the cities, notably social and economic opportunity, with the best features of the rural areas, especially cheap land and a good environment. The social and physical disbenefits of both would be avoided. The physical manifestation of this idea would occur in the proposed garden cities. Each of these was to consist of about 32 000 people, most of whom would exist in a central core of about 1600 acres. The town would be surrounded by a green belt owned by the community and would be designed according to quite grandiose principles, including the construction of boulevards dividing the city into six wards, the development of a central recreational and municipal core and the building of a wide glass arcade around the central park. Howard specifically rejected the gridiron pattern, with which he was familiar as a result of his American experiences, as a basis for the layout of garden cities. The circular pattern he instead advocated would avoid the monotony of byelaw housing, would allow for the easy division of the garden city into wards, or, as such residential enclaves were to be called after 1945, neighbour-hoods, and would ensure a finite size for the garden city. This last point is crucial but often neglected. Howard argued that once the garden city had reached 32 000 its growth must cease and other similar sized communities should be constructed nearby. Up to six such communities would be constructed in a circular form with a central city of about 58 000. The overall grouping of the seven towns was to be called the Social City (see Figure 2)

In an interesting reassessment of Howard, Hall (1983) indicates that attention is too frequently directed towards his physical proposals to the detriment of other issues. Several aspects of Howard's total vision have indeed tended either to be ignored or undervalued. The land question was for instance a crucial ingredient. Howard argued that because of the increase in rental values that would occur as land was transformed from agricultural to urban uses the community would initially be able to borrow capital, repay it later and provide for communal needs out of increased rents. Collective landownership would thus ensure abundant resources for necessary services while at the same time avoiding the problems of landlordism. This was crucial to

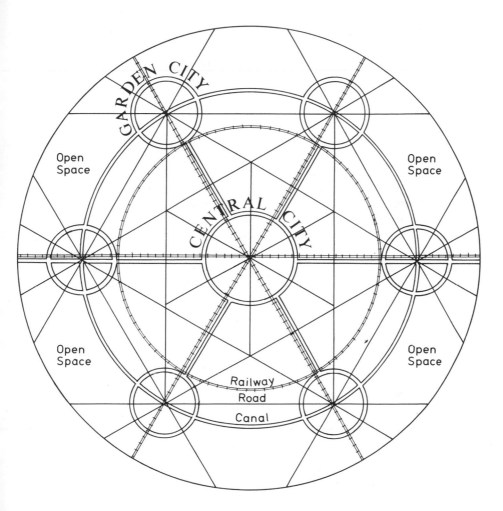

Figure 2   Howard's social city: an idealised interpretation. Each of the six garden cities and the central city would contain residential and employment areas and open spaces. The population figures for each would be 32 000 and 58 000 respectively. (*Source:* Ebenezer Howard *Tomorrow: A Peaceful Path to Real Reform*, Sonneschein, 1898)

Howard's perspective. Collective wealth would allow for the introduction of a local welfare support system and also for various forms of local experimentation, notably the construction of homes by individuals. Hall (1983) indeed perceives the proposed garden cities as a kind of urban homesteading. Control of land would, moreover, create a community-based, decentralized, cooperative society which Howard saw as the inevitable and desirable result of his ideas. Older values were to be replaced by a new social order of an altogether more humane nature. The very building of the garden cities would provide jobs, thus helping to overcome mass unemployment. Communal landownership and hence community profits would relieve poverty, stimulate innovation and enhance municipal benevolence. Freedom from landlords would breed independence, vitality and variety. The physical form was in essence the means to a better society.

From theory to reality: Howard's ideas in the twentieth century

Howard was no academic recluse. He was determined to carry out his ideas. In 1899 he founded the Garden Cities Association, later to become the Garden Cities and Town Planning Association. By 1902 a garden city company had been established and a year later nearly 4000 acres in Hertfordshire had been acquired from 14 separate owners, purchases made that much easier as a result of catastrophic agricultural rents. Some fifteen years later over 1200 acres were purchased for the development of what was to become Welwyn Garden City. Ostensibly at least Howard's ideas appeared to be bearing fruit. In retrospect it can be seen, however, that many of his original proposals were trimmed and that the garden city movement as a whole was by no means a dominant voice in dealing with the urban question.

The very design of the first garden city, Letchworth, was to differ in important respects from Howard's original intentions (Fishman, 1977). Densities adopted by Unwin and Parker were lower than Howard envisaged. Glass arcades and boulevards were abandoned. Howard's assumption that industry might prove a liberating factor in social change was not shared by the appointed planners, who allotted a subordinate role to industrial land in the physical plan. Although some manufacturers, notably publishers and some light engineering firms, did move to the town, many unskilled workers employed by the new industrialists could not afford to live in Letchworth and had instead to commute from communities beyond its agricultural belt. Howard's vision of the garden city as a physical reflection of a social movement was only marginally fulfilled in the early garden cities.

On the broader canvas too, Howard's influence was to prove far from crucial in the early decades of the century. In terms of urban development as a whole, as mentioned earlier, Unwin and Parker's Hampstead Garden Suburb, designed with what Hall has described as a 'feel of domestic English cosiness' (1983, p.46), was to prove altogether more influential in pre-1939 suburban England than was Letchworth. The design of individual dwellings in the Suburb was in some respects similar to those created in Letchworth. But in other respects, its suburban location and its economic and social integration with the city, the Suburb was in total contrast with what Howard had

promoted. Yet it was quite evidently the suburban, rather than the garden city movement, that held sway throughout the pre-1914 era and in the interwar decades. Indeed,
even where more formal attempts were made to establish a legal basis for the town
planning movement there was little to indicate that Howard's thinking had permeated
national political circles.

The first piece of legislation mentioning town planning was the 1909 Housing,
Town Planning etc. Act. Its evolution has been discussed by a number of
commentators (Ashworth, 1954; Minett, 1974; Miller, 1984) and need not detain us
greatly, partly because the Act's impact was so limited. But in essence it emerged
largely as a result of a widely held sentiment that suburbanization could make a substantial improvement to congestion in the older urban areas. Provided healthy and
well-designed suburban expansion occurred, physical and social problems in the cities
would apparently be moderated. However, the tools granted to local authorities to
control suburban expansion were in practice very limited. Schemes were voluntary,
not mandatory; agreements had to be reached between councils and landowners for
the implementation of planning schemes which might only apply to land about to be
developed; approval of central government's Local Government Board had to be
obtained; and the procedures for approval, which included widespread consultation
with landowners, were very complex. Not surprisingly only a handful of schemes was
ever approved. But what is important here is that virtually all commentators at the
time, and most notably John Burns, the government minister involved, saw
possibilities inherent within the Act of replicating throughout the country suburban
developments undertaken at Hampstead and elsewhere. Suburban, not garden city,
development was the government's objective.

Bearing in mind the problems associated with any practical implementation of the
garden cities and their relatively limited role on the national scene it might be imagined
that Howard's influence would steadily decline. However, this was to prove far from
the truth. His ideas were in fact to gather greater political momentum after his death.
In part this was because of the proselytizing impact of followers such as F.J. Osborn
and the New Townsmen, who advocated the construction of a hundred new towns.
Such sentiments gained little momentum in ruling political circles in the 1920s and for
much of the following decade. However, one crucial convert was bagged. Neville
Chamberlain, elected to parliament in 1919, had in his early life been heavily involved
in town planning and related issues in his native Birmingham and was fully aware of the
extent of urban congestion and allied social and economic problems. By 1920 he was
chairing a committee into unhealthy areas which argued for the planned movement of
population and industry to garden cities. Although this Committee's findings and those
of the 1935 Marley Committee (which in many respects were very similar) were not
acted upon, they clearly helped change public and political attitudes towards planning
in general and planned decentralization in particular. Certainly by 1937 Chamberlain,
then Prime Minister, was able to establish the Barlow Commission whose findings were
to prove so crucial to the development of post-1945 Britain in that, amongst other
policy recommendations, garden cities, or new towns, were to be formally
implemented by central government.

It is important of course to point out here that in some key areas the new towns (discussed in greater detail in Chapter 11) differed from Howard's vision of the garden city. Osborn and other new town advocates of the interwar era were to modify some of Howard's concepts, at times fundamentally. For example, whereas Howard had lobbied rich, paternalistic, often Liberal sympathizers such as Cadbury and Lever at the turn of the century, convinced that they would provide the initial capital for the garden cities, Osborn had different ideas. He was prepared to use the emerging welfare state as a mechanism through which garden cities could be implemented. He lobbied the Barlow Commission extensively and proved a tireless new town campaigner throughout the 1939-45 conflict. For Osborn it was simply unrealistic to imagine that Howard's ideal of a massive proliferation of community or voluntarily implemented garden cities would ever occur. Instead Osborn argued that by embracing the reforming sentiment that was clearly coming to permeate political circles during the war a national consensus could be achieved with regard to planning issues which would allow for the construction, by the welfare state, of far more new towns than the private or voluntary sectors could ever begin to contemplate. Even then nothing like enough new communities would be constructed to challenge the primacy of the major cities. Howard's conception of a multicentred settlement pattern breaking down the dominance of the larger cities was simply naive, Osborn believed. The new towns would remain, to some degree or other, satellites of the older cities. In many respects this proved to be the case.

How then should we evaluate Howard? It is clear that he proved to be far the most influential of the Victorian Utopians. Many of these thinkers adopted programmes that were far too idealistic, convoluted, or impractical. Howard's broader vision was, however, to survive. Some observers of the planning scene (Eversley, 1973) argue that Patrick Geddes, whose main contribution was published in 1915, should be perceived as an equal and complementary figure because of his systematic approach to planning and his determination to adapt the physical environment to changing societal needs. But in the context of the impact of visionary thinkers on post-1947 urban development there can be little doubt that Howard was an altogether more dominant figure. It is true that his determination to press for a complete social and physical transformation of society was a failure. His promulgation of community and cooperative enterprise, of shared rural-urban economies and of a decentralized and democratically structured society were largely to be forgotten. Neither should we ignore the fact, as Eversley (1973) points out, that other philosophical influences prevalent in the nineteenth century were to impose formidable constraints on post-1947 Britain. Utilitarianism for instance and its concern for regulation, order and control proved hugely influential in governing the operation of post-1945 town planning, which in recent decades has often been perceived as a bureaucratic device for preventing or moderating development through various statutes and orders. But ultimately here it should be stressed that many aspects of Howard's humane vision, particularly — and perhaps unfortunately - the physical strategy, were implemented by the 1945-51 Labour government and succeeding administrations. Urban growth was controlled; decentralization of socially mixed populations to working garden cities was adopted; protecting green belts were introduced around the cities and new communities; and his suggestion that the garden cities or new towns could make a profit because of rising rental returns proved accurate.

Conclusion

In this chapter we have attempted to explore some of the reactions of Victorian society to urbanism and also to examine, through a study of attempts at housing reform, the failure of private efforts, either by companies or individuals, to solve the many problems which urbanization brought. We have touched on housing specifically, but numerous other problems would have served equally well, e.g. crime, social welfare, medical facilities and disease, working hours and conditions. As we have seen, the reactions to the rapid urbanization of society were varied in the extreme. However, two important themes were emerging by the end of the nineteenth century.

The first of these themes was the growing recognition of the very magnitude of the problems facing society and the increasing complexity of life in the cities. The pessimism of the 1880s and the complete rejection of the city by romantics such as Morris was paralleled by a deepening sense of disillusion that capitalism and market forces could in any sense ameliorate the environment and markedly improve living standards for most of the population. It was obvious that while capitalism had indirectly, and often directly, caused many of the problems facing society it was utterly incapable of solving them. Philanthropy too was seen as hopelessly inadequate for the scale of the task involved. There seemed to be only one possible way forward. Slowly, and with great reluctance, Victorian and then Edwardian society groped towards a grudging acceptance that the issues confronting our cities, and therefore the great majority of the populace, could only be solved by direct government intervention. The tentative movement along this path is exemplified by the contrast between the emasculation of the reformist 'Cross' housing Bill in 1875 and the 1890 Housing of the Working Classes Act which gave limited permission for municipal house building. The undeniable success of 'municipal socialism' in most of the large cities was also evidence that further state involvement at both central and local level could not be avoided if improvements were to be initiated.

The second theme to emerge from this chapter has been the influence of that reformist stream which reacted in a positive fashion to Victorian urbanism — the town planning movement. Rather than attempting to ameliorate current ills, visionaries like Howard and Unwin looked to the future to ensure that previous errors would not be compounded. In essence they argued for higher-quality, lower-density housing in smaller, more human-scale towns, where all the population would have easy access to the town centre on the one hand and the open countryside on the other. Above all, these reformers argued passionately for a *planned* environment, in clear opposition to the large urban agglomerations which had grown up over the previous century. These latter cities stood for the negation of planning and a good environment with their hopelessly mixed land uses with factories, spoil heaps and houses standing cheek by jowl and the insensate environment which prevailed. Unfortunately the early town planners failed to separate urban problems, and lack of planning, from the large cities which seemed to exhibit the worst of each. Thus the town planning movement became inextricably bound up with the anti-urban thesis. Even Howard, who was not in fact anti-urban in his ideas, can be easily taken out of context by such statements as 'London must die'. He was in fact shrewdly foreseeing the slow decline of London as employment and people would eventually move away to smaller communities — Howard's garden cities. He was thus forecasting a process which has indeed occurred in the last 30 years. However, the planning movement stood for more than anti-urbanism and its ideas were to have their triumph, though much later than the visionaries imagined.

References

Ashworth, W. (1954) *The Genesis of Modern British Town Planning*, Routledge and Kegan Paul, London

Briggs, A. (1963) *Victorian Cities*, Pelican, London

Cherry, G.E. (1972) *Urban Change and Planning*, Foulis, Oxford

Coleman, B.I. (ed.) (1973) *The Idea of the City in Nineteenth Century Britain*, Routledge and Kegan Paul, London

Eversley, D. (1973) *The Planner in Society. The Changing Role of a Profession*, Faber and Faber, London

Fishman, R. (1977) *Urban Utopias in the Twentieth Century*, Basic Books, New York

Hall, P. (1983) Ebenezer Howard: Has his time come at last? *Town and Country Planning*, Vol. 52, No. 2, pp 42-47

Hobson, J.A. (1901) *The Evolution of Modern Capitalism: a Study of Machine Production*, 2nd ed., Sion, London

Mellor, R. (1982) *Images of the city: their impact on British urban policy*, Unit 2, D202, Urban Change and Conflict, Open University Press, Milton Keynes

Miller, M. (1984) The roots of planning, *The Planner*, Vol. 70, No. 9, pp 11-15

Minett, J. (1974) The Housing, Town Planning Etc. Act 1909, *The Planner*, Vol. 60, No. 5, pp 676-680

Morris, W. (1891) *News from Nowhere*, Reeves and Turner, London

Williams, R. (1973) *The Country and the City*, Chatto and Windus, London

Wohl, A.S. (1977) *The Eternal Slum*, Edward Arnold, London

Further reading

Coleman (1973) provides an excellent digest of the attitudes of contemporary thinkers towards the nineteenth-century city. Wohl (1977) is first-class source for the work of the philanthropists in London.

In terms of the Utopians and their impact, Fishman (1977) is readable and Eversley (1973) provides a trenchant critique of town planning's origin. The relationship between planning and urban development is examined in Cherry (1972).

5   Edwardian Britain and the urban transport revolution

Queen Victoria died in January 1901 after a reign of nearly 64 years, having given her name to the period of the most intense industrialization and urbanization in Britain's history. The country inherited by her son Edward was very different from the Britain Victoria found when she became Queen in 1837. In the latter year, the process of urbanization was well underway, but over half the population of England and Wales still lived in settlements of fewer than 2500 people while less than one in five of the population lived in communities which exceeded 100 000 inhabitants. By 1901 the total population of England and Wales had more than doubled from under 16 million in 1837 to 32.5 million. By 1901 four out of ten lived in towns of 100 000 or more people, and nearly 80 per cent lived in settlements of more than 2500 inhabitants. In 1837 Britain's population was in the process of urbanizing; by 1901 it was unquestionably urban, and most of the people now lived in large towns. By 1911 over 41 per cent of the population were concentrated in London, South-East Lancashire, Merseyside, Tyneside, West and South Yorkshire and the West Midlands. In Scotland over half the population was now crowded into the Central Lowlands, and two-thirds of these around Glasgow in the west.

By 1901 London boasted a population of some 4.5 million, with a further 2 million people living in the growing outer surburban ring. The'great towns' such as Liverpool, Manchester, Birmingham and Glasgow all had populations approaching or in excess of three-quarters of a million each, while a medium-sized town such as Sheffield had seen a population increase of over 300 per cent in the six decades of Queen Victoria's rule, from under 100 000 in 1837 to over 450 000 by 1901.

The end of the long reign of Victoria was seen at the time as the opening of a new chapter for the nation — the advent of a new, modern era. However, well before the end of the nineteenth century the processes of change were at work, if largely unperceived by contemporaries. The population in 1901 was essentially young — over 42 per cent were under twenty years of age. But already the long period of rapid population growth that characterized the Victorian era was coming to an end. Between 1901 and 1911 the overall percentage increase in population fell below 11 per cent for the first time since the Census began in 1801. The birthrate began to decline, though so too did the death rate. The hectic growth of the large urban agglomerations, which had seen such spectacular population increases during the preceding century, was slowing down rapidly. Between 1891 and 1901 the average rate of increase for urban areas in England and Wales was 15.2 per cent; but while the smaller towns of 20 000-50 000 people recorded an average growth rate of 20.3 per cent, the four largest cities all recorded less than 10 per cent - London 7.3 per cent, Liverpool 8.5 per cent, Manchester 7.6 per cent and Birmingham 9.2 per cent (Hall, 1973). Some small towns still experienced spectacular rates of growth, e.g. Clydebank, west of Glasgow, saw a population increase of 79.9 per cent between 1901 and 1911, the highest percentage increase of any town in Britain in this decade.

Despite the increasing alienation of many intellectuals, and the grimy, squalid environment in which many people were born, lived and died, Britain was clearly now very much an urban country. This is neatly illustrated by a cartoon by Max Beerbohm where 'Industrial System' addresses 'Civilization' as follows:

> No, my dear, you may have ceased to love me; but you took me for better or wuss in younger and 'appier days, and there'll be no getting away for you from me, ever. (Cecil, 1969, p.43)

In this chapter we shall seek to describe the life and environment of the urban population of Edwardian Britain, and to examine the forces which were to lead to the great physical expansion of our cities in the interwar period — the urban transport revolution.

Economic, political and social change

In Chapter 2 we examined briefly the outlines of the various technological innovations which together led to the massive growth of Britain's industrial economy, without which the development of the 'great towns' would not have occurred. The pace and spatial pattern of economic growth largely determined that of population growth, and economic development was the underlying cause of the massive social changes which were wrought on British society during the Victorian period. In the first half of the nineteenth century, as first in the field of industrialization, Britain could, and did, have a dominant share of world trade, aided by a huge merchant fleet and a growing overseas Empire. However, by the 1880s rivals were appearing on the scene — notably Germany and the United States of America. It is increasingly recognized that the late nineteenth and early twentieth century was

> an important turning point in British economic history, when the British dominance of the world economy won in the early nineteenth century began to be steadily eroded. (Thompson, 1975, p. 183)

This erosion of Britain's dominant position was disguised for some time, and the inevitable economic problems which would result from it were both fatally delayed and in some ways made much worse by the First World War and the accompanying temporary boom for a number of terminally sick export industries such as textiles, coal and shipbuilding. The case of shipbuilding in Glasgow serves to make the point. Checkland (1976) graphically describes how the growth of naval contracts for ships from the Clydeside shipyards hid the demise of orders for merchant ships from the 1880s onwards. The naval race between Britain and Germany during the Edwardian period, coupled with the commercial race between the Cunard and White Star shipping companies to build larger, faster and increasingly luxurious passenger liners, all helped to keep the Clydeside yards busy: the world preeminence of the Clyde seemed unchallenged. Yet Checkland succinctly traces the beginnings of Glasgow's long decline as an industrial city from this very period. Thus, as Checkland states:

> [...] it was possible to ignore the erosion of the fundamental basis of the Clydeside economy brought about by changes in demand, the rise of foreign rivals, and the refusal of other nations to continue in a state of dependence upon British suppliers. (Checkland, 1976, p.10).

The misplaced confidence of Glasgow in the true level of demand for her ships was repeated elsewhere in other sectors of the national economy. By 1900 the United States was producing more coal, iron and steel than Britain, and Germany too outstripped British production of steel.

This fundamental and irreversible shift in the position of Britain as a dominant industrial power, which was clearly occurring as the nineteenth century drew to a close, was not apparent to most contemporaries who were concerned with economic matters only at the most immediate level: their employment, wages, prices and rents. How were these changing during this period? Although the Edwardian period was scarcely one of full employment, there was a marked diminution in the numbers of casual employees in all the large cities, particularly in London's dockland where dockers were becoming increasingly employed on a regular basis. Gradual shifts in occupations were also beginning to appear, shifts which were to become more marked in the interwar period. Agriculture, a major source of employment in 1837, had shrunk and was employing less than 10 per cent of the working population by 1901. Manufacturing and mining employment, though it had grown massively in numerical terms, had only increased in percentage terms from 40.8 per cent in 1831 to 46.4 per cent in 1911. Other changes were beginning to occur, in particular the growth of jobs in transport, retailing, the public services and the clerical professions.

Wages, however, stagnated during the Edwardian period and, for the working classes, failed to keep pace with rising prices. One benefit for working-class families was a general fall in most food prices from the 1880s onwards, principally due to the import of cheap food from America. Although this had a disastrous effect on prices for Britain's farmers, and led to a prolonged agricultural depression, the poor were undoubtedly better fed as a result. In particular, luxury items such as sugar, milk and fresh fruit became more widely available. However, even food prices increased towards the end of the Edwardian period. Coal too, despite a massive expansion in production in the twenty years up to 1914, particularly in South Yorkshire and the East Midlands, became an increasingly expensive, though necessary, item for urban households. Fortunately rents rose slowly, except in those centres still experiencing rapid urban growth. Coventry, the centre of the new motor manufacturing industry, saw rents rise by as much as 18 per cent between 1905 and 1912 (Taylor, 1964). Rents as a whole, however, tended to rise quite slowly during the Edwardian period, though they still absorbed between a quarter and a third of most families' weekly budgets. Unlike most other outgoings, rents were a fixed and regular item which had to be paid. The items working-class families spent least on were clothing and furniture. These were luxury items which inevitably lay at the margin of the weekly budget. They were also in many respects, along with housing, the most obvious and overt measures of social class. As far as furniture was concerned, most working-class families as late as 1914 could still put all the household possessions on a single cart.

If Edwardian Britain broadly coincided with the beginning of the long decline of the country as a world economic power, it was also a time of increasing political ferment. Although the franchise had steadily spread downwards as the nineteenth century had progressed, at the dawn of the Edwardian era the country was still largely governed by members of the old landed aristocracy. The Conservatives had held power since 1886 and continued to do so until halfway through Edward's reign. Those men with the franchise either voted Conservative or Liberal, though the Liberal party in 1901 was badly split over issues such as the Empire and free trade.

A new force had arrived on the scene — socialism — though it was slow to become a popular movement. Most workers, and their trade unions, sought the support of one or other of the two major political parties. In July 1901 a court ruling (the Taff Vale judgement) threatened the whole existence of trade unions by making trade unions legally and financially responsible for strike actions by their members. This judgement, repealed in 1906, had the effect of galvanizing the Labour movement and in the historic 1906 general election no less than 29 Labour MPs were returned.

The trade union movement during the Edwardian period only represented a minority of workers — about 2 million members representing perhaps one in six of the organized labour force. During the early 1900s the movement remained weak, reflecting high rates of unemployment (often quoted as averaging 5.5 per cent though the real figure is unknown). The most strongly unionized workers were the miners, shipbuilding workers, cotton workers and engineers. They were amongst the better paid. The poorer working groups, however, were the least well organized. The unions, relatively weak though they were, nonetheless were blamed for Britain's declining position in the world trade by demanding shorter working hours and higher wages. But, as Thompson (1975) points out, the most strongly unionized industries such as coal mining and shipbuilding 'were exactly those whose export performance was best maintained before 1914'. Indeed Thompson argues that the relative weakness of trade unionism in Britain, and thus the low wages paid to workers, fatally delayed the movement towards greater mechanization which was already occurring in the United States, our greatest commercial rival.

If trade unionism remained relatively weak, the tide of change was beginning to turn in favour of the less affluent. The Boer War (1899-1902) had savagely shown up the maladministration of the Conservative government and, while the war was won amidst a furore of jingoism and national fervour, foreign criticism and ridicule of the inadequacies of the British army soon turned many against the Conservative regime. It was clearly time for a change, and the Liberal party put forward a radical programme of reforms for the election of January 1906. The result, to the surprise of most contemporary observers, was a huge Liberal landslide. In the next five years the new government laid the basis of the Welfare State, setting up local labour exchanges, introducing the first, admittedly parsimonious, old age pensions, and the first state insurance scheme; it also passed acts to enforce both minimum wages in some industries and to fix working hours for adults. Although by modern standards many of these schemes seem excessively cautious and restrictive, the whole programme undoubtedly marked a major step forward for the well-being of the working classes.

The Liberal programme was mandatory in character, not enabling, and in this respect it marked a growing recognition of the necessity and inevitability of increasing government intervention in the lives of the people. The growth of 'municipal socialism' in the 1870s in particular, coupled with the physical expansion and growing economic strength of the new industrial towns, had placed increasing strains on the outmoded jigsaw of small local government administrative units, each of which had separate functions. Local government in the early decades of the nineteenth century was in no sense equipped to meet the needs of a growing, sophisticated and complex urban society. The Municipal Corporation Act of 1835 marked the first attempt to rationalize the chaotic system of boroughs and to establish elected councils. As the century advanced it became increasingly clear that the system needed a drastic over-haul, both in terms of the powers of local government and the location and size of the administrative units, which were increasingly out of step with the sociogeographic realities of the day. Various minor amending acts were passed, but the major overhaul did not come until 1888 with the passing of the Local Government Act for England and Wales. The basic provisions of this Act laid out the pattern of local government which was to survive until 1972, nearly 90 years later. In essence the Act gave autonomy and representation to the historic counties and, under the county councils, a lower tier of boroughs and urban districts.

The 'great towns' were to have a separate autonomy, on a par with the new County Councils. At first ten towns with populations of 150 000 or more were proposed as County Boroughs, but political pressures in parliament reduced the population threshold to 50 000 and 61 County Boroughs were incorporated in 1888, rising to 81 by 1914 (Waller, 1983, p.247). What the Act did enshrine was an obvious urban - rural dichotomy, which at the time represented the balance of political interests, but which increasingly in its turn became divorced from geographical reality as urban populations spilled over their county boundaries as the twentieth century advanced. This was to prove a fatal handicap for planning in the post-1945 era.

The reorganization of local government in 1888 led to the disappearance of many of the small urban districts that had developed in the lee of the various large cities, while in the ensuing decades, up to the 1930s, many of the larger county boroughs successfully extended their boundaries to incorporate their growing suburban populations. Birmingham, for example, in 1838 covered approximately 12 square miles. In 1871 it absorbed three urban districts, Saltley, Balsall Heath and Harborne to increase its area to 20 square miles; its population thus became nearly half a million. In 1911 the boundary was extended again, absorbing adjacent urban and rural districts; and the area of the city was more than trebled to 67.5 square miles. In area Birmingham was now three times the size of Glasgow and twice as large as Manchester or Liverpool (Freeman, 1966).

The activities of the new local authorities were overseen by a central government body, the Local Government Board, which had developed from the ineffectual Poor Law Commission, which had concerned itself with the main task of earlier local authorities — dealing with paupers. The Local Government Board proved to be an unpopular body with the more enterprising local authorities.

Sheffield Council, along with many other urban local authorities, was concerned at the lack of control over the layout and density of the surburban development that was taking place on the outskirts of the town. Sheffield tried to purchase land in the suburbs in order to control such new urban development but was prevented from doing so by the Local Government Board. Under pressure from similarly minded authorities, the Board grudgingly passed the first town planning act in 1909 — officially the Housing, Town Planning, Etc. Act. Under the new Act local authorities were empowered to prepare schemes for controlling the development of new housing areas. By 1913 Sheffield had ten separate areas in hand which were to be subject to overall town planning. These covered nearly 5000 acres (Keeble Hawson, 1968). In all, some 74 local authorities had 105 schemes covering 167 571 acres approved by the Board by 1915 (Waller, 1983, p.183). The Act itself, however, gave local authorities few powers; and it insisted on detailed discussions with all interested parties — a recipe for procrastination and delay. The term 'town planning' was now at least on the statute book and a recognized, if weakly defined, part of the work of the new local authorities.

Urbanization in the nineteenth century had brought in its train, along with many other changes, a major shift in economic and social relations. The increasing range of occupations, the accumulating wealth produced by the industrial system and its grossly unequal distribution, all led to the development of a society which was at once both very sharply divided into an increasing number of social classes, yet within which the opportunity of upward social mobility existed and was evidently sought after. In his account of working-class life in Salford in the Edwardian period Robert Roberts neatly points to the importance of status and its many overt forms even within working-class society:

> Division in our own society ranged from an elite at the peak, composed of the leading families, through recognised strata to a social base whose members are damned as "the lowest of the low", or simply "no class". (Roberts, 1980, p.17)

Most households strove not to increase their status but simply to maintain it, and social acceptance and position in society showed in myriad ways from spoken accents to clothes, sobriety, furniture, a 'clean' rent book etc.

Thompson (1975) shows the gross inequalities in wealth and income that characterized the Edwardian period. In terms of wealth 87 per cent of the population had capital of less than £100 (reflecting in part the fact that nine out of ten households rented their homes rather than owned them). Only 1 per cent owned capital of £5000 or more. The 87 per cent of the population owned a total of 8 per cent of the total national capital, while the 1 per cent owned 67 per cent. Incomes too showed gross inequalities. The average income was about £80 per year. But a High Court judge earned £5000, a charwoman less than £30. Women, who made up a third of the total labour force, were grossly underpaid compared to men — another dimension of inequality. The wealthy in this society were not merely extremely rich but conspicuously so. After the stifling conformity and sobriety of the Victorian period, the Edwardian age was one in which the affluent ensured that their wealth was on display. The vulgar, overt wealth of the rich contrasted sharply with the poverty of the poor. This and the lack of compassion for, or interest in, the latter until the Liberal reforms were noted by the more observant contemporaries. C.F.G. Masterman, a member of the reformist Liberal government, called it 'public penury, private ostentation'. The rich had little need and even less reason to venture into slums where half the population lived. Young Winston Churchill, while walking through a Manchester working-class district, was moved to comment: 'Fancy living in one of these streets, never seeing anything beautiful, never eating anything savoury, never saying anything clever!' (quoted in Cecil, 1969). What was it like to live in one of these districts?

In many respects the working-class districts or neighbourhoods resembled 'villages' in terms of their size and their sense of community. They were normally defined in physical terms by other land uses: factories, canals or railway lines demarcated the edge of a district and provided a hard physical boundary. The community in which Robert Roberts grew up was typical:

> Our own (community) consisted of some thirty streets and alleys locked along the north and south by two railway systems a furlong apart. About twice that distance to the east lay another slum which turned on its farther side into a land of bonded warehouses and the city proper. West of us, well beyond the tramlines, lay the middle classes, bay-windowed and begardened. We knew them not.
> (Roberts, 1980, p.16)

Roberts's community was served by fifteen public houses, about twenty shops, two pawnbrokers, two chapels, one theatre and eight bookmakers. The people who found themselves in such communities struggled to retain respectability in the eyes of their contemporaries, and to keep hearth and home clean despite the all-pervading filth and rubbish which threatened to overwhelm the back entries or 'ginnels' which separated the rows of small brick houses. It was a harsh environment, and for the poorest classes 'life in a late Victorian working-class slum too often meant death' (Meacham, 1977). Social cohesion and economic dependence were certainly traits of these communities, but the evidence of contemporaries portrays a tough environment in which self-reliance played a much greater part than neighbourly help. The image of such urban working-class communities portrayed by sociologists in studies such as those of Ship Street (Kerr, 1958) and Bethnal Green (Young and Willmott, 1957) provides a somewhat romanticized view of the inner strengths and social networks of such neighbourhoods. The reality in Edwardian Britain seems to have been altogether a more grim struggle for survival.

Housing and suburban growth

The housing problem facing Edwardian Britain was in essence the same as the one that had plagued the country throughout the previous century — there simply were not enough houses being built. In the later decades of the nineteenth century there had been a spectacular housing boom, particularly of 'byelaw' housing. In broad terms population growth and housebuilding appeared to keep in step, but the latter was subject to violent fluctuations in time with short-term business cycles. Equally, rates of building varied locally. Thus, while in Sheffield housebuilding rates fell from a peak in 1900 to less than 20 per cent of the 1900 figure by 1915, only 15 miles away the mining towns of Barnsley and Doncaster saw an active housebuilding period right up to the outbreak of the First World War. In most towns, however, there was a decline in new housing 'starts' after 1904.

Overcrowding was the inevitable consequence of the housing shortage and was, equally inevitably, at its most acute in the poorest districts. Levels of overcrowding varied enormously between towns, reflecting differing building methods and population pressures. Thus a survey in 1908 found that four-fifths of the population of Derby lived in houses with five or more rooms, two-fifths in Bradford and only one-fifth in Jarrow (Burnett, 1978). Overcrowding was particularly severe on Tyneside, but it was worst of all in Glasgow where 85 per cent of the population lived in tiny flats in four-or five-storeyed tenement blocks. By 1914 central Glasgow had the highest population density of any city in Europe — some 700 000 people living in three square miles. A 1917 survey showed the levels of overcrowding in the slums of Glasgow still to be horrendously high, and widespread:

In 1917 there were more than four persons per room in 10.9 per cent of Glasgow's houses, over three persons in 27.9 per cent, and over two in 55.7 per cent; the figures for corresponding English cities were 0.8 per cent, 1.5 per cent and 9.4 per cent. (Checkland, 1976)

Most of the new housing built at the end of the nineteenth century and in the Edwardian period was terraced; it was built within the broad framework of the regulations introduced in the 1875 Public Health Act. The standard, size and appearance of such housing, however, varied enormously, and slight variations in style, from the provision of bay windows to the amount of ornamentation of lintels and porticos, in themselves reflected subtle but real divisions of social class. The great growth of the white-collar professions, particularly in London, and the growing social awareness of the better-off artisans led to the development of middle-class suburbs, and even in some cases to the development of whole estates of houses for purchase rather than renting.

The rapid growth of new residential districts on the edge of the existing towns, which helped to stimulate the passing of the 1909 Housing, Town Planning Act, affected all cities. In Birmingham the once wealthy suburb of Handsworth grew from 11 000 in 1861 to 70 000 by 1911 (Freeman, 1966). The most persistent and numerically largest growth rates were to be found, not surprisingly, on the outskirts of London. As the capital city, London had a disproportionate share of the nation's wealth and was the centre for the rapidly burgeoning array of clerks required to run both the nation and the Empire. Commerce was also booming, swelling the ranks of white-collar workers who sought an Edwardian villa away from the squalid working-class districts, as befitted their higher social station. Social class differences were quickly being reinforced by residential segregation. Most of the rural districts adjoining the existing built-up areas of London provided desirable 'rural' locations for the emerging middle classes. Between 1901 and 1911 many of these areas saw rapid population increases, e.g. Hendon 73 per cent, Finchley 78 per cent, Wealdstone 102 per cent, Wembley 137 per cent, Coulsdon and Purley 128 per cent, and Merton and Morden no less than 156 per cent (Jackson, 1973). Nearly all these phenomenal increases were associated in part at least with improvements in public transport during this period.

Some of these suburbs appeared on the map very rapidly indeed. One such example, that of Golders Green, is well documented by Jackson (1973, pp 70-89). As late as 1906 Golders Green was a small rural crossroads surrounded by a few houses and cottages.

It lay north of the main built-up area, though it was already surrounded by new suburban extensions. Its survival owed much to the presence of Hampstead Heath to the south, and the absence of railway lines. In 1906, however, the Underground Electric Railways Company acquired a site next to the crossroads for a new station: it was planned to extend the line from Hampstead northwards. On 22 June 1907 the first trains left Golders Green for Charing Cross, in the heart of the metropolis. The journey time was a mere 24 minutes. Before this momentous event the journey would have taken as much as 2 hours. Even before the railway opened the speculators had moved in. Land which had been valued at between £150 and £250 per acre now sold at eight times that figure, often changing hands on several occasions before building began.

Golders Green was to be a distinctly and exclusively middle-class suburb. Many of the houses were given a 'cottage' style appearance, being half-timbered with gables. To complete the sense of the rural idyll, road names were to be 'view', 'rise', 'drive' or 'way' in contrast to the more common 'road' or, even worse, 'street'. Many houses were given individual names, again aimed 'to impart a rustic tone: Beech Dell, Pine Glade, The Glen, The Vale' (Jackson, 1973, p.128). House prices varied from c. £450 leasehold to c. £600 freehold. Housebuilding activity was frenetic up to and into the early years of the First World War, reaching a peak of nearly 750 in 1911. By 1915 the new station at Golders Green saw over 10 million passengers; the population had grown, in less than a decade, from next to nothing to over 20 000 people.

While Golders Green was an exception in its rate of growth and also in its development as an owner-occupiers' suburb, this general pattern of residential development was occurring in all the larger towns in the late Victorian and Edwardian periods. Such new housebuilding was inevitable, given the growth in population. Housing densities were beginning to fall: houses themselves tended to be larger, with more room; also the new middle classes demanded gardens rather than backyards, to complete the semi-rural image they sought. All of these factors led to the physical dispersal of the Victorian city, the beginnings of suburbanization and urban spread which were to dominate the period from 1919 to 1939. Such loosening of the shackles on urban growth required a commensurate improvement in public transport, amounting indeed to a revolution. It is to this transport revolution that we must now turn.

The urban transport revolution

Urban growth, urban form and transport have always been inextricably linked together and current patterns of urban development reflect past forms of transport to a surprising extent. With a few notable exceptions, most cities prior to the advent of the nineteenth century were limited in size to perhaps 50 000 inhabitants by the absence of an effective urban transport system. These 'pedestrian' or 'foot' cities reflected this slow and limiting mode of movement in the spatial organization of land use, the narrow streets, the tendency to build up wherever possible, and the severe overcrowding which inevitably followed on the need for people to live within easy access of their places of work, shops and leisure. The Industrial Revolution was itself initially held back by the lack of adequate means of bulk transport; but it proved to be the catalyst for a series of transport innovations in the nineteenth century which were to culminate in the Edwardian period and have a massive influence on twentieth-century urban growth: '[...] the golden era of urban transport evolution was undoubtedly the nineteen century'. (Daniels and Warnes, 1980, p.1.)

As discussed in Chapter 2, overland transport by road improved in the 1780s through the development of a widespread system of mail coaches, making efficient use of regular changes of horses and taking advantage of the road improvements brought about by the 'turnpike' trusts. This system was gradually superseded in the 1830s with the rapid development of the railways as a superior form of interurban transport. Within the growing urban centres transport of goods was mainly by cart, while most people moved about on foot. The ownership and upkeep of a carriage was only available to the privileged upper classes, while horse-drawn taxis, or hansom cabs, were a very expensive alternative to walking. The expense of urban transport was to prove to be a major impediment to the development of an effective means of public transport until the advent of the Edwardian period.

The first successful attempt to introduce public transport into the towns involved horse-drawn 'omnibuses'. The first of these was introduced in central London in 1829 by an entrepreneur called George Shillibeer. The name 'omnibus' (meaning 'for all') had first been used by a French entrepreneur in Nantes in 1826, and the name soon gained general acceptance (McKay, 1976). The first London omnibuses were long coaches with a capacity of 20 passengers, who faced each other on the long benches inside. The first route was from Paddington Green to the Bank of England in the City. The five-mile journey was scheduled to take one hour, and the fare was a shilling. Soon rival companies were set up and the fare fell to sixpence, Shillibeer himself being driven out of the market by 1834. By 1850 there were nearly 1300 horse omnibuses plying their trade in central London (Joyce, 1967). Soon other large towns had their own omnibuses: they started in Glasgow in 1845 and Manchester had more than 60 by 1850. The early horse-drawn omnibuses were not, however, the much needed cheap and efficient public system. The passengers were mainly businessmen and the routes themselves often reflected the linkage between commercial districts. By the 1850s, when most towns had received their gothic cathedral-like railway stations, omnibuses often linked the railway terminals with the town centre. They remained, however, prohibitively expensive for the great majority of the population and were only used by the masses on special occasions such as the great Exhibition in London in 1851.

Horse-drawn omnibuses had the disadvantage of having to pull their loads along often uneven streets, and extra horses had to be hitched up to help navigate hills. Tramways had obvious potential advantages: they gave the passengers a smoother, safer ride, and the reduction in friction involved in the wheels being pulled along tramlines meant faster journey times and the opportunity to increase passenger-carrying capacity. Horse-drawn tramways had been in existence well before the middle of the nineteenth century, but they were used to transport coal both underground and to the nearest river or canal. The increase in the ability of a horse to pull loads of coal once the waggons were on rails was well known — from about 17 hundredweight on an ordinary road to 42 hundredweight on a tramline. It seemed logical to apply the same potential economy to urban roads for the purpose of carrying passengers.

In the United States early experiments began in the 1830s. Initially the iron rails were raised above ground level, which meant that the tracks interfered with other road traffic, but the invention of grooved, flat rails in 1852 overcame this potentially serious problem. Despite their obvious advantages, horse trams were very slow to develop in Europe. In 1860 an American entrepreneur, inappropriately named Train, introduced the first horse-drawn trams to Britain by opening a line in Birkenhead which ran between Woodside and Birkenhead Park. Train opened further lines in London and the Potteries. Those in London had raised rails, which proved extremely unpopular with other road users, while the Birkenhead line experienced a series of accidents which led to adverse publicity. Despite its potential, the horse-drawn tram was not therefore an immediate success, and the London lines closed within a year. In 1869, however, trams appeared in Liverpool; and they reappeared in London in 1870. In 1870 Parliament passed the Tramways Act, in theory to facilitate the construction of new tramway lines. However, the Act forced companies to maintain the road surface 18 inches either side of the tramlines and gave local authorities the right of eventual compulsory purchase of lines running through their area; in addition it compelled companies to gain the consent of owners whose frontages the trams would pass, as well as that of the relevant local authorities.

In effect this Act stultified the growth of the tram network and slowed down the introduction of innovations. The tram companies found themselves hostage to the local authorities who 'tended to exact tribute' (Jackson, 1973, p.26) by insisting on major road-widening, bridge-strengthening and improvement schemes which made opening up new routes very expensive. Also the thought of possible enforced municipalization of lines made companies reluctant to invest in new technology.

The 1870 Act was suggested as the major cause of the slow adoption of electrification for the tram system in Britain. The invention of the electric tram was beset by numerous technical problems, but these were successfully overcome by pioneering engineers and entrepreneurs in the United States. The first really successful electric tramcar system was opened in Richmond, Virginia, in 1887. By 1890 nearly 1000 miles of electric tramway were in operation in the United States (McKay, 1976, p.50) using overhead wires to carry the electricity. By 1903 nearly 30 000 miles of electrified tramlines were in use in the United States. Europe was curiously slow to adopt this new innovation, which was safer, faster and dramatically cheaper than the horse-drawn tram and offered the first really cheap mass transit system for cities.

Britain proved particularly slow to adopt the electric tram. There had been an innate hostility to trams from their inception in the 1860s. The 1870 Tramways Act had held back the diffusion and technological advance of trams, while the prospect of overhead wires to carry the electric current evoked open and widespread opposition. In 1897 a group of councillors from Birmingham visited a number of European cities to examine their tramways. Their report to the city council strongly recommended 'that no consent be given for the erection of overhead wires in any part of the city' (quoted in McKay, 1976, p.86). The comparatively slow adoption of electrification of the tramway system in Britain is often seen as further evidence of the beginning of economic decline (discussed earlier in this chapter). In Germany the innovation was accepted much more quickly. In 1895 only 6 per cent of tramways in Britain were electrified, compared to nearly a quarter in Germany. However, the turn of the century saw a final and decisive shift in favour of electrification and its 'unsightly wires': by 1902 nearly 40 per cent of tramways were electrified. In London the first electric tram service was inaugurated in April 1901. It was run by a private company, the London United Tramways Company. One of the major reasons for the rapid spread of electrification in most British cities, however, was the municipalization of the trams — yet another example of the 'municipal socialism' which had already seen the takeover of the water and gas companies by city corporations. The Sheffield Tramways Company's lease ran out in 1896 and the corporation took over, inheriting 44 tramcars, 310 horses, 4 omnibuses, 9 miles of track and 182 employees (Vickers, 1972). As with the case of Birmingham, in 1897 a group of Sheffield councillors visited various European cities to examine their tram systems. Unlike their Birmingham colleagues, however, the Sheffield group enthusiastically recommended the adoption of the overhead system of electric wires and the first electric trams ran in Sheffield in September 1899. In Glasgow a similar pattern was followed: the private Glasgow Tramways and Omnibus Company, formed in 1870, was replaced by a municipal service in 1894. Once again there was doubt placed on the desirability of overhead electrification, which led to delay. In October 1898 the first electric tram line opened, from Springburn to Mitchell Street in the town centre, followed in 1899 by a decision to electrify and extend the whole system.

By the turn of the century most medium and large British cities were adopting, albeit reluctantly in some cases, the overhead system of electrification. The sudden spread of the electric tram in Britain was based on one simple fact: it was very cheap. Thus in Sheffield the cheapest horse-drawn tram fare was 1d, but the introduction of the electric tram allowed this to be halved. In Glasgow in 1894 you could travel 1.1 miles for a penny; by electric tram in 1904 you could travel 2.3 miles for 1d, and a new $\frac{1}{2}d$ fare was introduced (McKay, 1976, p. 183). Running costs were dramatically cheaper for electric trams, and reduced fares led to massive increases in patronage. In Sheffield receipts rose from just over £30 000 in 1900 to £286 000 in 1908. With the advent of the electric train came the first cheap public transport system, which all sections of society could afford to use. The tram proved to be particularly important for the working classes, not merely because it enabled them to live further from their places of work but because the tram enabled them to increase their mobility dramatically and to widen their horizons. Trams have been described as 'representative working-class vehicles, the gondolas of the people' (Hoggart, 1969, p.145). Because of their cheap fares, trams were instantly, and permanently, seen as vehicles for the working classes, unlike the buses which were quickly to rival and eventually replace them. The new trams proved a liberating force for the poor, allowing them to move among their towns with a new freedom. It is difficult to overestimate the importance of this breakthrough in urban transport. As Roberts put it:

> Except for war itself, this revolutionary new form of transport contributed more than anything else to breaking down that ingrained parochialism which had beset millions in the industrial slums of pre-1914 England. (Roberts, 1980, p.147)

No sooner had the electric tram established itself as the prime provider of public transport within urban areas than further technological innovations saw the emergence of a new 'omnibus', powered by the internal combustion engine. The bus was destined to supplant the tram in the interwar period and completely eclipse it in the 1950s, but in the Edwardian period its widespread adoption was only beginning. The first municipal bus 'fleet' (consisting of four single deckers) was operational in Bournemouth as early as 1903, since the fashionable resort had rejected the overhead wires required for electric trams. Towards the end of the Edwardian period the bus became a more common urban vehicle; though only in 1910 did the number of motor buses in London equal the number of horse-drawn buses. In its early days the bus proved more attractive and more successful in country areas, which could not justify the heavy capital costs of installing a tram system.

The steam railway system, almost completely developed by the 1870s, played a curiously patchy role in the provision of urban public transport. The train was initially seen as a means of travelling between cities, and railway companies were very slow to realize the potential of urban or surburban short-haul services. For the middle classes of most large cities, who could also afford the comparatively high fares, the railway did provide the opportunity to live in the country with good access to 'town'. However, it was only in London that the railway companies had a major part to play in the provision of mass public transport and the development of new suburbs.

The nature of the steam railway locomotive and its slowness in the initial development of speed made it unattractive and uneconomic to have stations much closer than two miles apart. This compared very poorly with trams in densely populated areas. Railways therefore tended to come into their own about six miles out of the centre of cities, where they took over from the tram or the omnibus. But for most cities radii of continuously build-up land remained only 2-3 miles wide until the Edwardian era. Thus the potential passenger traffic for railways remained very low. Railways did play a part in developing outer, middle-class suburbs from the 1860s onwards and their role in the major cities of Glasgow, Liverpool, Manchester and Birmingham is well documented in Kellett's (1969) seminal work on railways and Victorian cities. Kellett's conclusion is, however, that, with exceptions, the railway was not a major causal factor in the development of suburbs in these cities.

London was different. At the beginning of Victoria's reign, and even earlier, London had experienced some suburban growth, while the more affluent had already moved out of the metropolis to small country towns. Apart from its physical size, London also became the centre of the national railway network with no less than 15 major railway termini. Thus outer London was carved through by a considerable number of railway lines with potential for suburban growth. In 1864 the Great Eastern Railway accepted an obligation to run one cheap train in the morning and evening between Liverpool Street and Walthamstow and Edmonton. This was done as an alternative to rehousing those displaced by the railway company's new terminus. This cheap fares policy was undertaken to concentrate the working-class clientele on one route, not for reasons of philanthropy nor, initially, for profit. Nevertheless, it did lead to the successive development of working-class suburbs in North and East London and led to a general Cheap Trains Act being passed in 1883. This Act did not prove very effective except on the routes served by the Great Eastern Railway itself.

The overall role of the railways in suburban development, even in London, remains questionable. There is certainly little evidence that the railway companies as a group sought to generate demand by the building of suburban stations, even less branch lines. If it could be proved that the railway companies had positive policies towards encouraging suburban growth and hence generating more traffic

> then there would be some justification for describing the railways as an important *cause* of suburban growth in the period up to 1900. (Kellett, 1969, p. 376)

Even in the case of the Great Eastern Railway the policy of cheap fares was initially based on a desire to keep the working classes *away* from most of its routes.

Indeed the hostility towards trams and their perceived role as transport for the working classes suggests that the links between transport and social class in this period would be worthy of further investigation.

One other mode of public transport needs mentioning: the development of the underground railways. The first of these, the Metropolitan Railway, built its first line in London in 1863. This was quickly followed by the Inner Circle line which linked the major surface railway termini and at the same time eased congestion in the central area of the metropolis. The early underground lines were 'cut and cover' lines in that they followed the routes of the main streets; the tunnels were laid in huge trenches which were filled in again. The trains were initially pulled by steam engines, but later the lines were electrified. Similar, though much smaller underground systems were developed in Glasgow, Liverpool and Newcastle. Rather more obviously than in the case of the surface railways, the underground companies did play a role in encouraging and anticipating demand by building stations in sparsely populated areas, and by successful advertising campaigns exalting the rural charms of new suburbs such as Edgeware.

It is often tempting to link the rapid physical expansion of British cities from the 1880s to the end of the Edwardian period directly to the technological advances in a variety of modes of transport. After all, the mid-Victorian city remained compact, physically small and desperately overcrowded largely because an efficient, cheap and ubiquitous public transport system was not extant. One must inject a note of caution, however, in that the relationship between transport and suburban growth is a complex one, and certainly not one which should be seen in simple 'cause and effect' terms. As Jackson has written of London's surburban growth:

> [. . .] there is a temptation to over-emphasise and oversimplify the part played by public transport in the growth of the suburbs [and it is] not difficult to find cases where builders went ahead in a transport desert, confident that services would be quickly provided. (Jackson, 1973, p.213)

Conclusion

In some texts which seek to examine urban growth and change in Britain, comparatively scant attention is paid to the late Victorian period and the Edwardian period. The latter is often seen as a simple extension of the nineteenth century, with the social, economic and political upheavals generated by the First World War as a fitting, if catac-lysmic, ending of the nineteenth-century period of urban growth. In some respects 1919 does form an important watershed, e.g. in housing styles, densities and tenure patterns. In many other ways the Edwardian period is deserving of separate treatment. In political terms it saw the beginnings of the breakup of the hegemony of the Conservative and Liberal parties: the reformist administration of 1906-11 proved to be the swan song of the old Liberal party. The period also saw the continuing growth of trade unionism — exemplified by major industrial unrest in 1912 — the growing political strengths of the working classes and the emergence of socialism through its electoral arm, the Labour party. By the Edwardian period the social segregation and class structures which were developing in the preceding century were confirmed and given new kinds of cement to strengthen their rigidity. The growth of white-collar employment, with increasingly subtle but important nuances of class distinction, were to be reflected in patterns of residential segregation on a scale unimagined 50 years before. Such patterns have largely survived and have indeed been magnified in the later years of the twentieth century. Economically the Edwardian period confirmed to the informed observer the beginnings of the relative decline of the British economy. The decline was both delayed and disguised by the war, but from 1921 onwards it became a recognized and potent force that was to have a dramatic and overriding impact on the social, population and, above all, economic geography of the nation and its cities, an impact still very strongly felt today. The influence of this decline, and its varied spatial impact, cannot be overestimated in examining urban and regional change and public policies from the interwar period to the present day.

Suburban growth and urban sprawl are normally associated with the interwar period from 1919 to 1939. However, it is clear that the crucial advances in transport technology were achieved well before 1919, and the slow dismantling of the compact, overcrowded Victorian city was already underway before 1914. The interwar period, with the lower residential densities imposed by the 1919 Housing, Town Planning Act, merely endorsed and extended a process of physical expansion which had begun well before the end of the nineteenth century.

References

Burnett, J. (1978) *A Social History of Housing 1815-1970*, Methuen, London

Cecil, R. (1969) *Life in Edwardian England*, Batsford, Norwich.

Checkland, G.S. (1976) *The Upas Tree, Glasgow 1875-1975*, University of Glasgow Press, Glasgow

Daniels, P.W. and Warnes, A.M. (1980) *Movement in Cities*, Methuen, Cambridge

Freeman, T.W. (1966) *The Conurbations of Great Britain* (2nd edn.), Manchester University Press, London

Hall P. (1973) England circa 1900 *A New Historical Geography of England*, in H.C. Darby (1973) Cambridge University Press, Cambridge

Hoggart, R. (1969) *The Uses of Literacy*, Penguin Books, London

Jackson, A.A. (1973) *Semi-Detached London,* George Allen and Unwin, Chatham

Joyce, T. (1967) *The Story of Passenger Transport in Britain,* Ian Allen, London

Keeble Hawson, H. (1968) *Sheffield: the growth of a City,* Northend, Sheffield

Kellet, J.R. (1969) *The Impact of Railways on Victorian Cities,* Routledge and Kegan Paul, London

Kerr, M. (1958) *The People of Ship Street,* Routledge and Kegan Paul, London

McKay, J.P. (1976) *Tramways and trolleys,* Princeton University Press, Princeton, New Jersey

Meacham, S. (1977) *A Life Apart,* Thames and Hudson, London

Roberts, R. (1980) *The Classic Slum,* Penguin Books, Harmondsworth

Taylor, A.T. (1964) *The Economy.* In *Edwardian England,* S. Nowell-Smith (1964) Oxford University Press, London

Thompson, P. (1975) *The Edwardians,* Weidenfeld and Nicolson, London

Vickers, J.E. (1972) *From Horses to Atlanteans,* JEV Publications, Sheffield

Waller, P.J. (1983) *Town, City and Nation, England 1850-1914,* Oxford University Press, Oxford

Young, M. and Willmott, P. (1957) *Family and Kinship in East London,* Routledge and Kegan Paul, London

Further reading

This chapter covers a reasonably narrow time span but a broad spectrum of issues. For insight into political, social and economic life in the Edwardian period either Thompson (1975) or Cecil (1969) may be recommended. The best narrative of working-class life in the period is undoubtedly that by Roberts (1980), while a broader view is provided by Meacham (1977). Kellett (1969) is the classic source for information on the role of the railways in suburban growth, while Joyce (1967) may be recommended for a relatively simple but informative source on the role and development of public transport in general. Finally, Jackson (1973) is an excellent reference for case studies of suburban growth around London.

Acknowledgement

The quotation from Roberts on p. 59 is reproduced by permission of Manchester University Press.

In the previous chapter the relationship between urban development and transport innovation in the Victorian and Edwardian periods has been explored. In some respects the interwar era, the focus of interest here, can similarly be perceived as illuminating that complex tension between urban expansion and the widespread introduction of new forms of communication, in this case the motorized vehicle. However, these decades merit separate analysis for, although transport technology, with its attendant impacts on the built environment, was to prove a consistent theme between 1919 and 1939, other issues such as the sheer scale of housing construction, the incipient development of formal town planning and the increasing affection with which these years are held by some national politicians in the 1980s substantiate the claim that these twenty years, although frequently neglected, were profoundly important in the evolution of cities and the means of controlling them.

In dealing with the period it is vital to emphasize the extent of social and economic change and the degree of heterogeneity that characterized Britain between the World Wars. Post-1945 analyses tend often to highlight the scale of economic demise and unemployment that certainly typified extensive regions of the country during these decades. But the picture was far more varied than this simplistic categorization would suggest. Certainly in terms of urban development — which must remain the focus of interest here — the scale of suburban expansion was formidable. Between 1929 and 1939 there was a 25 per cent addition to the housing stock of England and Wales, and in the twenty years after 1919 over 4.3 million dwellings were constructed in Britain (Glynn and Oxborrow, 1976). What was the socio-economic context within which this sort of change occurred?

The interwar years: the social and economic context

Contrary to what is frequently imagined, the British economy grew substantially, particularly during the second decade of the period. Between 1927 and 1937 the economy expanded on average by more than 3 per cent per annum. Widespread technical progress occurred in many industrial sectors; for example by 1937 electrical engineering and vehicle manufacture were collectively employing almost 900 000 people. This expansion was achieved during a period of very conservative national economic policy. Immediately after the First World War unsuccessful attempts were made to boost economic output, but these soon gave way to generally deflationary policies. For instance the return to the gold standard in 1925 and rigidly orthodox budgeting between 1929 and 1937 certainly dampened demand and helped sustain unemployment. Not that governments proved totally unwilling to intervene in the economy. In a number of cases central government encouraged the creation of cartels in return for tariff protection (Glynn and Oxborrow, 1976). But on the other hand the more expansionist demand management policies advocated by Keynes in his *General Theory of Employment, Interest and Money* published in 1936 were to find little support in the Treasury before 1939.

The merit or otherwise of interwar economic policy is a far from dry historical debate. Rigid orthodox budgeting certainly fell into disrepute during much of the post-1945 period. Instead demand management approaches intended to boost demand, output and employment in times of economic recession came to dominate the thinking of many postwar chancellors. However, after 1976, and especially after 1979, the older dispensations of reduced public expenditure, tight monetary control and constant vigilance against inflation rather than unemployment came again to the fore. This partly reflected the political vision of Conservative politicians, notably Mrs. Thatcher, who publicly praised the social changes and economic stringency typical of the interwar period. It is important, however, here to recall that the interwar period is not remembered so wishfully by everyone.

Social conditions between the wars in fact varied considerably from class to class and region to region (Stevenson, 1977). Most people improved their material status during the period. But for a substantial minority conditions were bad. Between 1921 and 1938 unemployment rates averaged about 14 per cent. In the depression years of 1931 to 1933 unemployment levels exceeded 20 per cent. Unemployment tended to be higher for the old, for the unskilled, for those in textiles and the heavier trades, and in what are now seen as the 'older' industrial regions of Scotland, Wales, the North and Northern Ireland. In some towns unemployment rates were incredible. In January 1933, 91 per cent of the insured labour force of Saltburn was unemployed. Partly this unemployment was due to cyclical trends affecting the world economy, but certainly in the regions this was accentuated by structural unemployment as the older exporting staple industries lost markets due to an overvalued pound, high unit costs and the loss of protected overseas markets.

Inevitably, high rates of unemployment accentuated the scale of poverty within the country. Forms of relief were available during the period, but not all workers were eligible for standard unemployment benefit and various forms of extra payment were subject to means testing. Moreover as Rowntree when exploring poverty in York in the mid-1930s pointed out, unemployment was only one factor; old age, illness and low wages were often equally important in explaining the total distribution of deprivation. In turn, such poverty accentuated ill health. Standards generally rose throughout the period but there remained marked regional and intra-urban variations. Infant mortality revealed marked regional and intra-urban variations; for instance in 1933 rates in Wigan were almost four times those in Oxford. In the same year infant deaths within one year of birth were over 20 per cent higher in central Birmingham than in its suburbs. As with so many aspects of social and economic change, general advances were coupled with marked social and regional inequality. Some fifty years later this pattern was to re-emerge within administrations in the 1980s eager to apply the economic doctrines of conservative, if not always Conservative, interwar governments.

Interwar urban development

Massive suburbanization changed the outlook of many British cities in the interwar period, but it was transport innovations that allowed this to happen. As Cherry (1972) has argued, changes in communications in the 1920s and 1930s allowed for a marked loosening of urban spatial structure and a steady weakening of workplace-residential links. In London the underground allowed for extensive suburban development; here, and in one or two other places, electric trains augmented steam provision, thus creating a more efficient and reliable service to the burgeoning commuter zones. Indeed in London the proliferation of tram, omnibus, underground and train services encouraged the formation in 1933 of the London Passenger Transport Board to coordinate passenger transport in the capital. Elsewhere, however, it was not so much an increase in transport modes that was the real issue for in some respects — with the decline in tram mileage for instance — choice of services perhaps declined. But the impact of the mode that came increasingly to dominate movement within and between towns and city, the motorized vehicle, was to prove profound.

The growth in motor vehicle production in Britain in the period was extraordinary. From 1923 to 1937 annual production rose from 95 000 to over half a million, of which more than a fifth was exported. By the late 1930s Dyos and Aldcroft (1969) indicate that, directly and indirectly, the industry employed more than one and a half million people. Of course there were offsetting employment losses elsewhere. Horse-drawn carriages virtually disappeared by the early 1930s for instance. A third of tram mileage disappeared between 1924 and 1933, by which time buses were carrying more passengers. Train services too suffered acute competition, particularly on shorter journeys, as both freight and passenger business declined relative to road provision. In retrospect none of these changes can be seen as surprising. Road transport was simply more attractive for a whole range of manufacturers, distributors and retailers. It was more convenient, it allowed for greater contact between different industrial sectors, it was quicker, and it encouraged personal contacts.

The vertiginous growth in road transport was both a cause and a consequence of an expanded interwar road construction programme. After the First World War a new Ministry of Transport was established which, with funds raised from a vehicle duty tax, began to help improve old roads and construct new ones in association with local authorities. Between 1920 and 1930 more was spent on road improvements than was collected from motor taxation. During that decade new urban roads were constructed in a number of cities, substantial improvements were made to existing trunk roads such as the Great North Road and some new trunk roads were built. However, the following decade saw a marked decline in road improvements and construction, and throughout the period it is clear that the road programme never kept pace with the increase in road traffic. Very few roads were constructed relative to needs, congestion increased in and around the major cities, and, in London at least, average speeds at the end of the 1930s were probably lower than had been the case with horse-drawn traffic thirty years earlier. Financial stringency, the inability to implement a national road programme and political disinterest all combined to leave the country with a totally inadequate road system at the outbreak of hostilities in 1939.

Nevertheless, despite the failure to implement a national road-building programme, it is evident that profound social and economic changes occurred as a result of the liberalizing effect of the motorized vehicle. Journeys of all kinds were simpler to make either by car or by bus than had been the case with other forms of transport. Permanent relocation to the suburbs was made that much easier. The inner areas of the seven largest urban centres, London, Manchester, Birmingham, West Yorkshire, Glasgow, Merseyside and Tyneside, lost more than 2 per cent of their populations between 1921 and 1938 whereas their suburbs expanded by almost a third (Dyos and Aldcroft, 1969). Of course not all this expansion, especially that around London, was due to the freedom engendered by car or bus. In some places trains or the underground ensured easy commuting to the metropolitan core from suburban locations which might be located 10 to 15 miles from city centres. But the drive to the station, the local trip, the shopping and entertainment journey became a prerogative of the car or the bus. However, although the motorized vehicle certainly stimulated suburban expansion, it is by no means the only factor that needs to be invoked if the scale of interwar residential development is to be understood.

Housing expansion in the interwar period

There was a formidable housing shortage by the end of the First World War. Glynn and Oxborrow (1976) suggest that because of factors such as high household formation rates, which continued into the 1930s, and the cessation of house building during the war there was probably a quantitative shortfall of several hundred thousand dwellings by the early 1920s. By 1921, for example, about 15 per cent of the population of the country were living in dwellings with more than two persons per room — startlingly high overcrowding statistics. Of course much available housing was of a poor standard. This was a reflection of the poor construction and maintenance standards pertaining throughout the nineteenth century; also it was because of slow replacement rates in the pre-1914 era. This was due to a number of factors. Much Victorian development was owned by small landlords unable even if they so desired to redevelop individually in what were often large interdependent tenements. In addition, the depreciation of dwellings against taxation was not allowed. Dwellings thus appeared as nondepreciating assets when the reality was very different.

The scale of residential development in the interwar period must therefore be perceived in the context of both quantitative and qualitative failures of the market characteristic of the pre-1918 era. It is, however, worth noting that in some respects the demographic framework within which interwar house construction was undertaken was not entirely unfavourable. For example, there was a marked change in the pattern of births and deaths in the 1919 to 1939 period compared with what had occurred previously. Between 1921 and 1941, for instance, a natural increase in the population of about 3.6 million was recorded — substantially less than had been the case in the ten years ending in 1911. Indeed throughout the interwar period the rate of increase in population averaged just 0.4 per cent per annum compound. In effect lower birth rates and much lower death rates replaced the very different patterns characteristic of the nineteenth century. One other demographic feature of the interwar period probably helped ease the situation. Although some regions of the country enjoyed a considerable expansion in their populations, internal migration was not as great as might have been imagined, bearing in mind variations in the spatial distribution of jobs. It is true that the South-East in particular grew faster than the national average, but nevertheless internal migration was much lower throughout the period than had been the case in the later decades of the previous century. Pressures on accommodation attendant upon economically determined movements of population could have been far greater.

Nevertheless, it was clear by the beginning of the 1920s that there was a severe housing problem which justified governmental intervention. Small-scale capitalism which had provided so much pre-1914 accommodation was simply proving inadequate to cope with demands. This reflected in part the peculiarities of the taxation system already alluded to, in part market concern that rent controls introduced in 1915 presaged a wider intervention by central government which would diminish profits in housing, and in part alternative investment possibilities. But whatever the reasons, after 1914 the proportion of the national housing stock in the private rented sector declined sharply from fully 80 per cent to only 58 per cent by 1939. In this same 25-year period local authority accommodation rose from a virtually negligible figure to about 15 per cent, and owner-occupation, of which more later, rose from 10 per cent to 31 per cent.

This last statistic, that is the rise in owner occupation, is surprising bearing in mind the determination of the government in the immediate postwar period to charge local authorities with the responsibility for housing the working class by introducing subsidies to encourage the provision of housing at less than market price. The history of housing subsidy in the interwar period is in fact complex. One or two key developments ought, however, to be mentioned. The 1919 Addison Act allowed housing authorities to construct dwellings and to let these at prevailing working-class rents with any shortfall being largely met by central government. This generous provision quickly gave way to the Chamberlain and Wheatley Acts of 1923 and 1924. The former was intended to subsidize the private sector, the latter to subsidize local authorities. Both lasted to 1934 and collectively assisted in the construction of nearly one million dwellings. The subsidies provided amounted at most to about 20 per cent of the weekly costs of a typical three-bedroom dwelling and were thus unable effectively to assist the very poorest families to rent. After the Addison Act was effectively scrapped in 1921 total subsidies to housing were small, amounting to no more than a few per cent of total local and central government expenditure on public social services. Increasingly, however, local authorities raised capital on the market. Indeed, about one-third of total capital expenditure on housing in the interwar period was raised by local authorities.

However, although local authorities were responsible for the construction of about 1.1 million dwellings in the 1919-39 era, almost three million were built by private enterprise, some with subsidy but the vast proportion without. What accounted for this formidable programme? Glynn and Oxborrow (1976) highlight the factors that must have been influential. In terms of demand for housing some issues appear incontrovertible. Building society assets increased more than six times between 1923 and 1938 and borrowers from half a million to 1.4 million between 1928 and 1937. Societies, working in tandem with builders, were, moreover, able to offer loans of up to 95 per cent of purchase price. Social pressures no doubt also encouraged many aspirant white-collar workers to seek out pleasanter suburban environments, which were increasingly available as a result of new forms of communication. Average wages and the proportion of salary earners rose and taxation levels remained low.

The possibility of house purchase was made all the more realistic, especially in the 1930s, because of the happy coincidence of a number of factors affecting the supply of new housing. Private housing was probably cheaper in the 1930s relative to average wages than it has ever been since. Land was cheap and abundant and was not subject to planning controls in most cases. Rates of interest were low too and the index of building costs actually declined after 1924. For many in permanent, better paid occupations who had gained from the slight redistribution of wealth towards the middle classes that occurred in the interwar period and who were able to drive or ride to commercial or service jobs in the cities a suburban villa became a necessity, not a dream.

Nevertheless, while the extent of residential development in the interwar period should be applauded — it reached almost 350 000 dwellings in 1936 for instance — it would be a mistake to imagine that all housing problems had been solved. Old difficulties remained and some new ones were created. There was, for instance, still a very real housing problem at the end of the period. The national overcrowding survey of 1936 called for in the 1935 Housing Act established that some local authorities considered that a substantial proportion of their working-class families lived in overcrowded conditions. Sunderland cited a figure in excess of 20 per cent (Cherry, 1972). Perhaps a third of Manchester's total accommodation was still unfit for human habitation as late as 1939. Nationally, perhaps half a million houses were scheduled for slum clearance. In some cities standards had, it is true, improved as a result of extensive demolition. The 1930 Greenwood Act introduced by a Labour government had provided subsidies for slum clearance and rehousing, and almost 300 000 dwellings were demolished or closed as a consequence. This, nevertheless, represented a drop in the ocean compared with the real need to redevelop extensive areas of older nineteenth-century housing.

Even when new housing was constructed certain shortcomings were apparent. Partly as a result of the 1919 Tudor Walters Report, standards within public accommodation had been substantially improved. The size of most dwellings increased, and there was a widespread diffusion of electric light and gas cookers, although heating of bedrooms remained rare and the availability of hot water inadequate. In other respects the construction of much public housing left a great deal to be desired. Many estates were constructed on the outskirts of towns and cities without any real appreciation of the economic and social needs of new communities. Becontree, for example, built for over 100 000 by the London County Council in the interwar period in Essex, is often seen to epitomize the planning mistakes of large publicly developed estates: too many three-bedroomed units for an increasingly heterogeneous population, few social or educational facilities, little if any retailing and no local jobs. These dormitory towns were clearly totally different in conception to the garden city ideal which had found increasing political and intellectual favour in the pre-1939 era.

Not that developments in the private sector were always that much better. Many suburban developments were undertaken in a piecemeal fashion without any thorough integration of nonresidential functions, especially employment. However, more shops were provided than was usually the case in public schemes, dwelling design was more varied, often reflecting the idiosyncratic designs of a myriad of small builders, and private — though not often public — open space provision was more generous. But often the overall aesthetic impact was depressing. Cherry (1972) identifies an impressive array of interwar planners and philosophers expressing disappointment, sometimes disgust, at the standards and scale of suburban design. Joad, the popular philosopher, talked disparagingly of a single dispersed suburb from Watford to the south coast. Thomas Sharp, a leading exponent of planning, decried the sprawling suburban waste. John Betjeman the poet invoked 'the friendly bombs to land on Slough'. One of the many converging impulses which eventually culminated in the introduction of comprehensive land-use controls in 1947 was undoubtedly a widespread dismay at the aesthetics of interwar suburbia and the concomitant problems of loss of agricultural land, sterile and uniform residential design, and enforced commuting.

Obviously a great deal of suburban development was intended for professional or white-collar workers. Some public estates it is true were constructed on suburban sites, but most housing constructed on the outskirts of cities and towns was intended for owner-occupiers. Inevitably, therefore, the cities experienced more clearly than ever before a marked spatial differentiation between the better-off, who were able to live in more attractive areas, and the bulk of the working population, who were still confined to private — and sometimes public — housing largely located in the older, congested areas. Ashworth (1954) uses socio-economic groupings and rateable values to point out the degree to which some local administrations in places such as Surrey and Cheshire were to become markedly more affluent than inner urban councils. Of course, as the richer people left local revenue was lost to the cities since the better-off paid their lower rates to rural, not city, authorities. This weakening of the demographic and hence of the economic and political power of the cities was to prove a major theme in postwar Britain.

The failure of planning in the interwar period

It is not surprising in retrospect to see the marginal impact that planning was to have on development in the interwar period. State intervention of all kinds was still opposed until the late 1930s by many powerful business and political interests. Although Labour governments held power twice during the period they did little to further town planning. In many respects such state intervention that was introduced proved more effective in industrial and employment issues than it did in terms of controlling housing. This tendency reflected official disquiet at the marked regional disparities that existed in economic opportunities and a growing realization that the locational needs of industrial firms were changing rapidly. In parts of London and the South-East, in Slough and Park Royal for instance, new industrial estates were springing up divorced from traditional locational requirements. Access to new roads and electricity provided by the newly formed national grid system liberated many light engineering plants from historic industrial zones. Once freed from specific locational requirements new industrial concerns might, it was increasingly realized, be coerced or persuaded to locate in totally different regions where unemployment remained high.

Initially, to try to reduce regional economic disparities the Industrial Transference Board was created in 1928. It helped move about 200 000 from the depressed areas to more affluent regions. In 1934, however, the Special Areas Act defined four regions, South Wales, Northumberland and Durham, Scotland and West Cumberland, to which additional forms of financial assistance would be available. The powers of the Special Area Commissioners were in practice limited (Ward, 1982). But one thing they did do was to construct industrial estates in places such as Gateshead, Hillington in Scotland and Treforest in Wales. By 1939 about 12 000 were employed in state-owned factories in the Special Areas. This was a small figure in relation to total unemployment in the regions, but the estates nevertheless helped imbue some confidence in the areas concerned. In retrospect they must also be seen as forerunners both of industrial estates generally, of which there was to be a marked proliferation in both public and private sectors after 1945, and of the state's increasing determination to moderate the scale of regional economic and employment imbalance. For many years after the Second World War governments of all political complexities implemented policies designed to encourage the relocation of industry to the depressed areas of the country. The origins of this approach clearly lie in the realities of interwar economic inequalities.

The very gradual development of state intervention in the industrial arena was mirrored in the town planning field. Two major planning acts and other pieces of supplementary legislation were passed in this period. The 1919 Housing and Town Planning Act was introduced partly as a response to the very evident failure of the 1909 Act discussed in Chapter 4. Only 13 planning schemes had been submitted under the earlier Act (Cherry, 1974). The 1919 Act attempted to remedy this inactivity by obliging local authorities with a population of more than 20 000 to prepare town planning schemes, initially by 1926. However, many authorities failed to prepare a scheme, no action was taken, and in 1932 compulsion again disappeared from town planning law (Ashworth, 1954, p.200). In other respects the 1919 Act introduced certain slight advantages compared with its 1909 predecessor. In particular, greater opportunities were provided for the inclusion of land already occupied by buildings to be included in schemes, and the Act also allowed neighbouring authorities to prepare joint town planning schemes. Nonetheless, the practical development of town planning as a result of the 1919 Act was minimal in relation to the real problems of the cities and their sprawling suburbs. By 1930 only 38 schemes had been approved for the development of about 60 000 acres which, as Ward (1974) suggests, differed little if at all from other unplanned developments. However, with the election in 1929 of a Labour government it appeared for a while as if truly interventionist planning legislation would be passed. But with the rapid return in 1931 of a Conservative-dominated National Government all thoughts of any substantial intensification of the 1919 Act disappeared. Instead the 1932 Town and Country Act was passed and this did little to enhance public powers of development control. For the first time there was an indication that land might permanently be free for building in planning schemes, but complex and punitive regulations governing the compensation that local authorities would have to pay as a result of such intervention effectively negated that idea. The Act also allowed local authorities to prepare schemes for any land, not simply peripheral housing projects. In practice this made little difference to the operation of planning. No real attempts were made to plan cities or towns as integral unities or to integrate highways and land-use issues (Ashworth, 1954). Indeed, where peripheral residential development along major roads appeared to need some form of control, separate legislation, the 1935 Ribbon Development Act, was to prove more appropriate. The concept that town planning required the sympathetic integration of a variety of physical, social and economic forces was not a sentiment widely held in the 1930s.

In one respect, however, the 1932 Act proved more successful than its 1909 and 1919 predecessors. By 1939 almost half the country was subject to some form of planning control. Such control might be limited it is true. Frequently it resulted in developments that were no different from the many unplanned schemes that were being implemented elsewhere, because the 1932 Act removed mandatory elements contained within the 1919 Act. Nevertheless, once an authority had made a resolution to prepare or adopt a town planning scheme it received powers of interim development control. In effect those wishing to undertake a development within the area covered by the resolution needed permission from the authority concerned, or else the building could be removed without the payment of compensation if it conflicted with the planning scheme subsequently introduced. Such a provision was a long way removed from the comprehensive land-use legislation to be introduced some fifteen years later by the 1945 Labour government. But it was an indication that wider state intervention was becoming more evident in planning and other social policy areas. There were other indications of this trend.

One important factor in the gradual acceptance of greater state intervention in town planning was the emergence of what Ward (1974) has called 'distinct political species'. Some groups, such as diehard Tories, continued to express total hostility to any form of intervention. But their importance was fading by the end of the decade. Other groups, such as Labour social democrats, enlightened Tories, and rationalist planners (focusing, for example, around Political and Economic Planning, founded in 1931) perceived for varying reasons and to varying extents the need for state intervention. This was not simply a British phenomenon. Fascist and Russian dictatorships in Europe and Roosevelt in America were implementing extensive programmes of planned public expenditure, partly to moderate the acuity of economic depression and partly to prepare effective war machines. This last point was certainly not lost in Britain. The 1937 Barlow Commission was charged with defining the most effective interregional and intraregional distribution of the industrial population, partly in response to perceived strategic considerations. By 1937 the Spanish Civil War had given an early foretaste of the realities of total conflict.

Nevertheless, it would be wrong to imagine that the introduction of comprehensive planning legislation during and immediately after the Second World War was simply a reflection of the inevitably widening state power generated by conflict. Perhaps, as others have argued (Hall *et al.*, 1973), the 1930s saw a dovetailing of certain social inventions and certain social changes that collectively heralded the arrival of town planning. In this perspective social inventions, such as the planning idea, are seen by reformers as processes through which social problems can be alleviated. This was true of the late 1930s. Howard and the garden city ideal were still hugely influential within planning circles; some planned communities and suburbs had been constructed; the Town Planning Institute had become an active lobbying body; and, as we have seen, town planning was becoming a formal, if still incipient, local government activity. However, although ultimately these pressures may of themselves have stimulated a more comprehensive approach to economic and physical planning, the more interventionist planning articulated in the Barlow Report's findings of 1940 reflected not simply the reformist mood of the age but also the clear determination of governments of the time to implement social change through policy innovation. In part this highlighted central government's concern at the physical and aesthetic problems of uncontrolled suburban expansion. But, more than this, persistent economic depression in the regions, the worrying spread of political extremism throughout Europe and the looming threat of war all pointed the government of the late 1930s towards a degree of state intervention that would have been quite unimaginable twenty years earlier. By the formulation of the Barlow Commission in 1937 it was clearly apparent that comprehensive land-use legislation was going to be introduced. In succeeding chapters we shall trace the legislative evolution of planning after 1940 and will attempt a critical review.

References

Ashworth, W. (1954) *The Genesis of Modern British Town Planning*, Routledge and Kegan Paul, London

Cherry, G.E. (1972) *Urban Change and Planning*, Foulis, Oxford

Cherry, G.E. (1974) The Housing, Town Planning etc. Act, 1919, *The Planner*, Vol. 60 pp 681-684

Dyos, H.J. and Aldcroft, D.H. (1969) *British Transport, An Economic Survey from the Seventeenth Century to the Twentieth*, Leicester University Press, Leicester

Glynn, S. and Oxborrow, J. (1976) *Inter-War Britain: A social and economic history*, George Allen and Unwin, London

Hall, P. *et al.* (1973) *The Containment of Urban England*, George Allen and Unwin, London

Stevenson, J. (1977) *Social Conditions in Britain Between the Wars*, Penguin Books, Harmondsworth

Ward, S. (1974) The Town and Country Planning Act, 1932, *The Planner*, Vol. 60, pp 685-689

Ward, S. (1982) Inter-war Britain: a study of government spending, planning and uneven economic development, *Built Environment* Vol. 7, No. 2, pp 96-108

Further reading

The period tends to be unexploited academically, at least from the planning point of view. Cherry (1972) is probably as good as any on urban development. Glynn and Oxborrow (1976) are excellent on the socioeconomic context. Richardson, H.W. and Aldcroft, D.H. (1968) *Building in the British Economy Between the Wars* Allen and Unwin, London has obviously been used widely by many interested observers, including ourselves.

Part Two Urban development in the post-1939 era: The planning framework and socio-institutional constraints

An outline of postwar town planning

The drift to state intervention in town planning which was to receive such a substantial boost in the 1940s has been alluded to previously. The system that was to emerge after 1945 clearly reflected both the intellectual vision of Utopians such as Howard and the growing dissatisfaction with the scale of physical despoilation and economic inequity characteristic of interwar Britain, which have been discussed previously. Nevertheless, in retrospect the transformation in official attitudes towards state intervention in town planning was truly dramatic from, say, 1939 to 1945. Obviously the war and its physical and political impacts was the major influencing factor in all of this, although some form of planning would have been introduced even had peacetime conditions been perpetuated. Aesthetic distaste at the scale of suburban expansion alone would probably have stimulated more interventionist land-use controls. More significantly here, however, the Barlow Commission, so central to the intensification of physical and economic intervention in the postwar era, was established as early as 1937. Its conclusions, while relevant to wartime activity, held implications of a profound nature that would remain as pertinent to peacetime as they were to war-shattered Britain. It is to the Barlow Report that we now turn our attention.

The Barlow Report

The Barlow Commission represents the fulcrum around which twentieth-century planning revolves: it crystallized the disparate pro-intervention forces developing in Britain in the first forty years of the century, and it in turn laid down many key post-1945 principles. In some respects it was unable to make recommendations on all the issues it considered essential, and there remained clear differences of opinion within the Commission as to the most appropriate form of administrative machinery for the interventionist policies all considered necessary. But nevertheless the conclusions of the Report were to prove immeasurably significant in the postwar reconstruction.

The Royal Commission on the Geographical Distribution of the Industrial Population under the chairmanship of Sir Anderson Montague-Barlow was established in 1937. Its brief was threefold: to inquire into the present and possible future distribution of the industrial population; to consider what social, economic or strategic disadvantages arose from the concentration of industrial populations in certain towns, cities and regions; and to indicate what remedial measures should be taken in the national interest. In terms of the first two of these issues, the Commission, reporting in 1940, was in general agreement. It appeared that industrial development, if left to market forces, would continue to concentrate in the relatively prosperous regions of the Midlands and the South-East and this would aggravate social and economic conditions in the older industrial regions, to say nothing of the obvious strategic implications in times of extensive urban bombing (HMSO, 1940). In terms of the third aspect of the brief, remedial action, the Commission was, however, divided. Although all 13 members agreed that the urgency of the problem required national action, the extent to which controls should be introduced on the location of industry was a contentious issue. In retrospect the minority report produced by, among others, the influential planner Patrick Abercrombie was to prove at least as important as the majority report in that it advocated national controls on the location of industry, an approach in the event favoured by the Labour government elected in 1945. In other respects, however, the overall conclusions and recommendations of the Commission were to prove central to the development of postwar planning legislation. In particular the Commission appreciated that government control of land and industry would need to be enhanced in order to moderate regional economic decline and urban congestion and that positive measures, such as the construction of garden cities, would prove crucial in any strategy aimed at reducing such congestion. In essence, therefore, the Commission argued — and this was largely to be implemented after the War — that the state needed to intervene both interregionally, in that jobs should be diverted to areas of economic stagnation, and intraregionally, in that urban congestion should be moderated through policies of planned decentralization. As such the Barlow Report was to lay down the major alignments of post-1945 planning that were to remain central to governments of all political persuasions until the late 1970s. The succinct and comprehensive nature of the Report, its determination accurately to identify the true consequences of economic decline and urban congestion and its conjoining of national economic issues with urban physical problems have rightly encouraged observers to evaluate it as a classic of its kind.

It is important to stress, however, that the final Report published in 1940 synthesized ideas from a range of sources of both a nineteenth-century and a twentieth-century vintage. As Hall *et al.* (1973) have established, the conceptual bases of the Report lie with earlier thinkers, notably Howard. His vision, developed forty years earlier, argued that the cities needed to be controlled within an overall strategy that decentralized both individuals and industry from the congested cities. This framework, perceived through the realities of regional economic depression characteristic of much of the interwar period, produced powerful formative impulses that were to guide the findings of the Commission. In substantiating the need for, and direction of, postwar planning, the Barlow Report reflected the intellectual stirrings of the time. Many of the ideas expounded by the Commission were in effect unoriginal, but its holistic approach, linking economic and physical planning within different national-to-urban spatial scales, was certainly original.

Although the Barlow Report was to provide a major motivating force in the formulation of postwar intervention in land and regional development, the detailed exposition of policy was still in 1940 some way off. Two sets of forces were to mould the ultimate articulation of planning: the immediate impacts of the war and the wartime reports and plans.

The impact of the war

The war held two obvious consequences for the development of town planning in Britain: national reconstruction became an absolute necessity rather than an inspired ideal, and the degree of state intervention required to win the war undoubtedly encouraged many to believe that the peace might equally effectively bring forth the planned destruction of want.

As Cullingworth (1975) has made clear, as early as 1941 the Cabinet accepted the principle that the physical destruction of cities, due to enemy bombing and economic decline in the regions, would require strong central and local government intervention in terms of both economic and physical planning. Indeed throughout the war there was a steady intensification in the degree to which town planning was perceived by the government as an emerging political necessity. By February 1943 an independent Minister of Town and Country Planning had been appointed. He was charged with the duty of securing consistency and continuity in the framing and execution of a national policy with respect to the use and development of land throughout England and Wales. In that year too, the Town and Country Planning (Interim Development) Act brought all land in England and Wales under interim development control, thus ensuring that all those wishing to undertake development had first to obtain permission. If they did not do so such development might be removed without compensation when it did not accord with a subsequent planning scheme. Of much greater importance was the 1944 Town and Country Planning Act. This authorized local authorities to acquire, compulsorily if necessary, not simply blitzed land but also land suffering from obsolete development or bad layout. This Act in effect for the first time allowed authorities to undertake extensive redevelopment of older congested areas.

The war proved crucial for the development of planning, not only because of the gradual intensification of legislation but also because of the powerful sentiment of the time that a new peacetime Britain could be forged out of the enthusiasm and social unity characteristic of the period. Planning in this sense was clearly but one aspect of a national determination to conquer want and inequality. What the Beveridge Report (HMSO, 1942) did for social welfare Barlow and the plans, acts and reports that followed in that ferment of activity between 1940 and 1947 were to do for physical and economic planning. The war became a prelude for widespread social and economic reforms that so many clearly anticipated and desired.

The post-Barlow reports and plans

Although the Barlow Commission laid down the strategic framework within which planning was to be implemented, there still remained a great deal of detail that needed to be fleshed out. In terms of land, for example, two centrally important reports were to be published in 1942. The Scott Report on Land Utilization in Rural Areas argued strongly for the development of a planning system which would embrace rural as well as urban localities and which would, as generally proved to be the case in post-1945

Britain, protect rural land from other forms of development. This blanket anti-development attitude was enshrined within the majority report despite the farsighted suggestion of the economist Stanley Dennison who argued that 'the true criterion should be the value of the land to the community in different uses' (Hall, 1976, p. 101).

The second Report published in 1942 on land and development, that of the Uthwatt Committee on Compensation and Betterment, will be discussed in greater detail in Chapter 9. But in essence the substance of the Committee's inquiries lay with the perennial problem of compensation and betterment. In effect its brief was to examine how owners should be compensated for land purchased compulsorily by public agencies and the extent to which compensation should be paid to owners for potential developments not allowed by the local planning authorities. In addition the Committee was to make recommendations on the even more contentious issue of betterment: the extent to which those benefiting from planning decisions made by the community should pay for such increases in the value of their land. As will be developed later, the radical proposals adopted by that Committee were in the event watered down in the first of many complex political struggles on this the most controversial of planning issues.

Just as detailed proposals governing rural development and the land issue were needed to complement the overall approach developed by Barlow, so specific recommendations were also required to guide city-regional development in the postwar era. It was obvious from the Barlow Report that there would be a strong disposition towards controlling urban growth and industrial development throughout the country and that urban congestion would be relieved through programmes of planned decentralization to the garden cities and similar communities. Two administrative developments were to solidify this still somewhat amorphous vision. In 1946 the Reith Committee on New Towns was published. Like Howard, the Committee argued for socially mixed and economically independent communities of between 30 000 and 60 000. Unlike Howard, however, this Committee considered that special development corporations appointed by central government would be needed to implement the new communities. These recommendations were to be adopted in the New Towns Act of the same year.

But where were the new towns to be built? Perhaps the first indication came with the publication in 1945 of Patrick Abercrombie's Greater London Plan. Using the recommendations of the Barlow Report as guiding principles, Abercrombie argued that about one million people would need to be rehoused as a result of the impending redevelopment of London, and that rather than housing these in suburban estates new development should be undertaken beyond a green -belt cordon about five miles wide to be created around the city. Of the million to be relocated in this fashion, about 600 000 would go to existing communities some distance from London, but almost half were to be accommodated in eight new satellite towns. In the event not all of the sites proposed by Abercrombie were selected for new towns in the post-1945 era, but the principle of containing the growth of cities through green belts and of decentralizing overspill populations to new communities was to prove the central theme behind the replanning of London and eventually other major cities such as Manchester, Liverpool, Glasgow and Birmingham. Twenty years after the death of Howard his

Utopian ideal was in many respects to be executed. This became apparent within the lifetime of the 1945-51 Labour government, which, in a series of historically important pieces of legislation, substantiated the administration and direction of postwar town planning.

The synthesizing legislation

In effect the legislation introduced by the postwar Labour government and central government advice emanating from that administration and its successors can in retrospect be seen to have governed the evolution of the city regions in five ways. First, the 1947 Town and Country Planning Act imposed a duty on county councils and county borough councils to produce a development plan, thus initiating the vexed question of the mechanics of planning. Secondly, the 1946 New Towns Act and 1952 Town Development Act laid the basis for planned decentralization from the cities. Thirdly, the 1947 Act grappled with the complex issue of the control of land and development. Fourthly, plans such as Abercrombie's 1945 Greater London plan and the crucially important Circular 42/55 published in 1955 by Duncan Sandys, then Minister of Housing and Local Government, clearly indicated central government's determination to introduce a series of green belts around all of the major cities. And fifthly, beginning with the 1945 Distribution of Industry Act, controls were introduced allowing central government to intervene in the national distribution of industry, largely to encourage its relocation from the apparently prosperous areas of the South and Midlands to the older depressed regions. In this book, where the focus of attention lies with cities rather than regions, regional policy will not be addressed directly, although clearly the cities and the regions within which they are located are mutually interdependent. It may suffice to say here that for much of the post-1945 period industrial development certificates normally needed to be obtained from central government before industrial plants could be constructed. In fact many I.D.C.'s were approved, nonindustrial employment was often not controlled and various exemptions allowed many industrial firms to expand *in situ*. For those unable to obtain I.D.C.'s or willing to relocate to the Assisted Areas to the North and West of the United Kingdom various grants and loans were available. It is often estimated that more than half a million jobs were created in the Assisted Areas as a result of regional policy. Nevertheless, the cities tended to benefit less from regional policy than did smaller settlements. London and Birmingham lost some industry to the Assisted Areas; parts of the car industry, for example, were forced to relocate from the Midlands to Merseyside and Scotland. And when firms moved to the regions few located in the cities, preferring instead greenfield locations. In any event by the early 1980s Conservative administrations had substantially reduced the scale and scope of regional assistance (HMSO, 1984) and the whole policy area appeared increasingly marginal. The great debate about regionalism and the efficacy of regional policy, which had proved so important in the 1960s and 1970s in political and academic circles (see for example, Glasson, 1974; Hayward and Watson (eds), 1975), seemed a distant mirage by 1985.

Post-1945 planning: a framework for analysis

This chapter has been concerned with the evolution and development of the planning system in the 1940s. In the remaining chapters in this section of the book an attempt will be made to evaluate urban planning in the postwar era. Problems of classification inevitably emerge here. How in effect can the principles, outcomes and activities of planning and planners be categorized for critical assessment? Planning can, for example, be seen as a local government activity dealing with land-use activities, as an aspect of social reform, or as a profession revolving around the Royal Town Planning Institute. Here a different classification has been adopted. In Chapter 9 the emphasis will be placed on the system of planning and land-use intervention developed in the post-1945 era. In the following chapter the impact of town planning on, and within, the cities will form the central focus of debate. Finally, in Chapter 11 social aspects of planning such as the search for community and citizen involvement will be examined. However, before embarking on any detailed critiques of town planning it is important to locate urban intervention within postwar social, political and economic change. Planning is not an independent force: its dynamism reflected and, at the margins, caused the evolution of British society after 1945.

References

Cullingworth, J.B. (1975) *Peacetime History, Environmental Planning*, Vol. 1, *Reconstruction and Land Use planning 1939-1947*, HMSO, London

Glasson, J. (1974) *An Introduction to Regional Planning*, Hutchinson Educational, London

Hall, P. *et al.* (1973) *The Containment of Urban England*, George Allen and Unwin, London

Hall, P. (1976) *Urban and Regional Planning* (2nd edn), Pelican, Harmondsworth

Hayward, J. and Watson, M. (eds) (1975) *Planning Politics and Public Policy, The British, French and Italian Experience*, Cambridge University Press, London

HMSO (1940) Report of the Royal Commission on the Distribution of the Industrial Population, Cmnd 6153, HMSO, London

HMSO (1942) Social insurance and allied services, Cmnd 6404, HMSO, London

HMSO (1984) Regional industrial development, Cmnd 9111, HMSO, London

Further reading

That conflagration of reports and plans emerging in the 1940s which was to prove so important to the evolution of the cities in the postwar era has received considerable attention. Hall *et al.* (1973) and Hall (1976) are good on this. Cullingworth, J.B. (1982) *Town and Country Planning in Britain* (8th edn) George Allen and Unwin, London, and Cherry, G.E. (1974) *The Evolution of British Town Planning*, Leonard Hill, London, also cover the area. For those interested in the details of the history of planning in the postwar period, however, J.B. Cullingworth's *Peacetime Histories of*

*Environmental Planning 1939-1969,*HMSO, London is essential. Volume 4, for example, on *Land Values, Compensation and Betterment* will satisfy the most ardent researcher interested in this area.

The previous chapter provided an outline of the planning system which, as succeeding sections will confirm, was to have a formidable impact on the evolution of the British city in the post-1945 era. But urban Britain crystallized out of more than the prevailing system of land-use planning. Cities reflect, and in turn mould, society as a whole. Historically the urban way of life has often been perceived as the highest form of civilization. It says much for the evolution of British society and the dynamism of urban change within it that many would now argue that cities reflect not the apogee of contemporary civilization but rather its nadir.

Many changes that have occurred in British society since 1945 contain implications for the fate of the cities in the later 1980s. But five issues seem especially important: National economic performance; the evolving political context; social change; financial and administrative parameters; and technological advance. Each merits separate consideration.

National economic performance

It is hard to avoid the conclusion that British economic performance in recent decades has been little short of disastrous. It is true that in certain periods, notably the 1960s, there was a steady rise in output and productivity of about 3 per cent per annum. But, even in this period of expansion, United Kingdom productivity and investment levels fell by comparison with those of major competitors. At other periods, notably after the massive increase in oil prices in 1973-74 and after the election of the Conservative administration in 1979, there were truly horrendous declines in output and investment. Manufacturing output actually fell between 1970 and 1980 for example, and industrial investment declined by a quarter in the three years prior to 1982.

The reasons for this steady deterioration in Britain's economic performance have to be beyond the scope of this book. Some would point to an enlarged public sector apparently squeezing out private investment; some to a lack of entrepreneurial spirit; others to the unwillingness on the part of central governments to implement policies with regard to import controls or reflating the economy.

Although broader debates concerning the state of the national economy cannot be considered here, it is important to tease out some of the implications of this decline for the cities. A relatively, and sometimes absolutely, deteriorating economy has, for instance, inevitably culminated in rising urban unemployment. By the mid-1980s unemployment was still increasing nationally, despite the creation of several hundred thousand jobs annually. The cities have tended to suffer from this contraction in employment more than most other parts of the spatial economy. Some have been over-dependent on manufacturing, which has declined more than any other major employment sector. Between 1971 and 1981 alone employment in virtually all manu-facturing sectors declined by more than 20 per cent. Between 1979 and 1984, moreover, fully one-third of those employed in steel or vehicle production lost their jobs. It is apparent that there was an element of de-industrialization in all of this. Some established British manufacturers in the cities proved unable to compete with interna-tional competitors at a time when new indigenous investment sought out more profitable nonurban locations in the south of England and abroad. It should, however, be remembered that even when enhanced output was achieved by city-based companies this was often associated with fewer jobs as capital replaced labour. In practice, as a number of commentators have shown (Goddard, 1983; Massey and Meegan, 1982), a whole range of corporate strategies — rationalization, restructuring and expansion — can all lead to fewer jobs. In addition, those that have examined future employment prospects indicate that regions dominated by smaller plants and towns, populated by better-educated workforces and specializing in new products and processes are likely to perform markedly better than other areas characterized by larger, older cities and factories (Fothergill and Gudgin, 1982).

Unfortunately too from the point of view of the cities the growth in service employ-ment that occurred in the 1960s and 1970s is unlikely to be repeated. By 1981 the Census revealed that a higher proportion of employed urban residents worked in the service sector than equivalent national figures would suggest (HMSO, 1984). However, the expansion in areas such as health, education and public utilities, a feature of much of the post-1960 era, is likely to be replaced by a steady decline in employment opportunities in these areas. In addition, technological change (of which more below), the loss of port-related activities from many cities, decentralization and rationalization of office employment and a probable decline in jobs within local government all suggest at best a stability in terms of urban service-sector employment. In London especially there will be an expansion of financial and professional services. But here and in the provincial cities job opportunities for the semiskilled and unskilled, ethnic minorities, and those made redundant from declining manufacturing sectors seem poor.

The extent of urban economic malaise had become clearly apparent by the 1981 Census. In 16 urban parliamentary constituencies unemployment rates stood at more than 25 per cent. In two Liverpool seats and one Glasgow seat the rate was in excess of 30 per cent. In pockets within constituencies the real figure must have been in excess of 50 per cent with much higher figures for the young. After 1981, moreover, unemploy-ment continued to increase. In Sheffield it rose by more than 40 per cent in three years. Unemployment at this sort of level has an impact across the board. It reduces local purchasing power for public and private goods; it aggravates deprivation as individual households and entire communities encounter increasing problems in meeting bills, obtaining food and paying for accommodation; and it nurtures discontent, not all of which is going to be channelled into orthodox political organizations. Unemployment will also increase demands on local social services, themselves operating on ever tighter nationally regulated budgets. Medical and health care needs will rise. In many respects the cities will find themselves in that most vicious of dilemmas: increasing needs and diminishing resources.

This problem will be felt acutely by ethnic communities in cities. Labour from the New Commonwealth and Pakistan was recruited in the 1950s and 1960s for certain industrial and service sectors which could simply not otherwise have operated. It was the expanding economies of London and some Midland towns and cities in particular that demanded additional manpower. Hence by 1981, although only 4.2 per cent of the British population lived in households, the head of which was born in the New Commonwealth or Pakistan, in about 50 urban parliamentary seats the figure stood at more than 15 per cent. In some respects the assimilation within the labour market of groups such as ethnic minorities could once have been seen as one of the successes of the British economy in the post-1945 period. Once severe recession replaced relative expansion, however, inevitably the economic, social, and political status of immigrants declined. There is little doubt that many urban administrations perceive a particular moral responsibility towards the immigrant community. It is not at all clear, however, as the 1981 riots showed (HMSO, 1981, Rex, 1982), that the rhetoric of support has given rise in practice to any improvement in the position of immigrants within society as a whole. Economic decline will breed general social and political strife in the cities. Unless the material circumstances of immigrants at least equates with that prevailing within the community as a whole, there seems every reason to imagine that an additional and especially acute level of conflict will come to dominate certain inner cities: that between blacks and some agencies of urban government.

The urban political context

The fate of the British city is becoming an ever more political question. In some respects, say in the debate over public housing, differences between the major parties have been apparent for many years. But the increasing polarization of political opinion, combined with pressures engendered by acute economic failure, have brought the urban question to the centre of political controversy. It is true that few specifically urban policies have been proposed either by governments or opposition parties. On the other hand many proposals emanating from political quarters contain implications for the cities. These warrant examination.

The election of a Labour government would usually appear to be the best option for the cities for reasons which will be explored below. However, recent elections indicate both a general decline in votes for the Labour party and a steady retreat in its influence towards its largely urban heartland. In terms of its national appeal, the party obtained only 28 per cent of the popular vote in 1983 — its poorest performance since 1931. In that election the Labour party obtained just over 200 seats. It needs more than 100 additional constituencies to attain power. Moreover, as Kellner (1982) points out, by the early 1980s all of the 17 unemployment bright spots with male unemployment below 5 per cent in 1981 were Tory seats in the Home Counties, and all but one of the constituencies with male unemployment in excess of 25 per cent were Labour controlled. Labour is increasingly finding its support from the older, industrialized regions with the most complex of economic and social problems. Although this is understandable, it is also unfortunate for a party seeking power nationally. Too many people have left the cities, which after the 1983 reallocation of seats anyway lost constituencies, and too few ex-urbanites retain an allegiance to the Labour party for it easily, if at all, to regain power. The voting strength of the nation increasingly resides south of the Humber-to-Bristol line where, outside London, Labour's impact proved negligible in the 1983 election. In this part of the country it was the Alliance rather than Labour that came second to the Conservatives in dozens of seats. Hence, writing in 1985, it would appear that Labour's chance of regaining power without a pact with the Alliance is slim, although an agreement between the parties seems equally improbable.

This division in the anti-Conservative vote, and hence the possible perpetuation of Tory administrations in the short to medium term, is not good news for the cities. It is true that some of them have not always returned an especially large contingent of Labour MPs to Westminster and some, such as Birmingham and Liverpool, have recently had non-Labour local authorities. But nevertheless most would normally expect to nail their colours to Labour. With its relative decline in the early 1980s and the concomitant success of the Conservative Party in national elections in 1979 and 1983, a series of measures were implemented which were to prove unfortunate for many within the older urban cores.

As Cobham (1984) establishes, substantially different national economic strategies were expounded by parties standing in the 1983 election. The Tories won that contest on a platform of diminishing public-sector intervention and expenditure, tight monetary control and a market-orientated approach towards industrial intervention. A clear alternative was propounded by Labour. Its Alternative Economic Strategy argued for increased public-sector expenditure, a substantial reflation of the economy, enhanced industrial intervention and import and capital controls. It is not hard to see that this Strategy would have benefited the cities. Policies of reflation would have boosted the renewal and construction of housing in the cities. There would have been an amelioration in the welfare support system so vital for large urban groups such as the old and single-parent families. Import controls would have protected, say, steel production in Sheffield or vehicle manufacture in the West Midlands. Capital controls would have encouraged the major institutional investors to direct their resources to British industry. Of course criticisms can be levelled at policies developed within the A.E.S. In particular it is unclear whether such a programme could be effected without fuelling inflation, inefficiency and international retaliation over tariffs. In the event these issues are of academic interest. The Labour party was decisively defeated in 1983 and would be unlikely again to present so radical a programme at a national election.

The return of Conservative administrations in 1979 and 1983 proved unfortunate in other ways for the major cities. Economic strategy has revolved around objectives such as reduced public-sector intervention and expenditure. This has obvious implications for the cities. There is less to spend on housing, social services, industrial support or education. The raising of controls on capital expenditure has allowed up to £10 billion per annum of British industrial investment to be spent abroad, with grave consequences for the older industrial regions of the UK. It is true that no major political figure in the Conservative party has followed the logic of the market position and simply argued for the cities to be written off. The urban cores are still ostensibly perceived as sources of wealth and economic vitality. However, as extensive sections of this book will indicate, Tory policy since 1979 has severely undermined the status of the contemporary British city. To some extent declining public support for the urban cores might be justified. It can be argued that national economic decline merits reductions in public expenditure which should fall on the cities because their populations have declined so rapidly. Whatever the merits of this position the reality is that, in line with the declining impact of the Labour party, the cities have endured a substantial erosion in their political influence. Anti-Conservative forces have proved simply unable to moderate the acuity of market-orientated policies introduced since 1979.

In the mid-1980s it is hard to discern the probable implementation of any policies likely to bring relief to the conurbations. The Chancellor might, for example, be exhorted to introduce an enhanced programme of public works by a range of academics (Cowie et al, 1984), the Confederation of British Industry (1981) and pressure groups such as The Royal Town Planning Institute (Byrne, 1985), but is unlikely to do so. Although infrastructural improvements will have to be undertaken eventually which fortunately will utilize British goods and labour, the Conservative government in the mid-1980s remains wedded to the totally unproved assumption that tax cuts, benefiting the better-off in particular, will generate jobs. Proposals therefore for specifically urban-orientated subsidies are simply not on the Conservative's political agenda. For example, Gudgin et al's (1982) suggestion that additional resources should be allocated to the cities for retraining and employment subsidies will not be implemented. The radicalization of the Conservative government in the post-1979 period puts suggestions of this sort which in the past might have received a degree of consensual political support, beyond the pale. This in itself must be depressing for the cities. Their real worry should be that if an effective anti-Conservative alliance cannot be formed a permanent Tory parliamentary majority will eventually embrace objectives of a far more explicitly anti-urban nature than had proved to be the case by 1985.

The urban social framework

Economic and political determinants affecting the cities impinge upon and in turn are influenced by social change. In particular, economic decline and diminishing political status have tended to be closely associated with declining urban populations of a markedly different social composition than prevailed for much of the post-1945 period. This sociodemographic change can be seen as both a cause and a symptom of economic and political weakness.

The major demographic characteristic of the British city after 1961 and especially in the post-1971 period has been decentralization. This trend does not always dominate statistical evidence, partly because of the problem of defining 'urban'. If, for example, definition is based on the extent of physical development, about 90 per cent of the population of Britain were living in urban areas in 1981. On this basis too, fully one-quarter of the population lived in the four largest urban areas of Greater London, the West Midlands, Greater Manchester and West Yorkshire (Denham, 1984). However, as a whole range of commentators have pointed out (Champion *et al.*, 1983; Hamnett and Randolph, 1983; Redfern, 1982), in real terms the cities have lost population from the central cores in a quite dramatic fashion. The largest losses occurred from the principal cities of the metropolitan counties. Glasgow lost more than 22 per cent of its population between 1971 and 1981, and Manchester and Liverpool lost more than 16 per cent each. Some inner London boroughs had lost more than a quarter of their 1971 populations by 1981. Even relatively free-standing towns such as Hull, Nottingham and Stoke lost 5 per cent or more. In effect there has been a steady rippling out of populations within the city regions from the largest of the cities to the suburban rings and to the communities beyond. In addition, superimposed on this intraregional change, certain interregional migrational trends can be identified. In the 1960s Greater London was the only region in England and Wales to lose population. In the following decade four other regions, the North, Yorkshire and Humberside, the North-West and the South-East, all declined in size. Growth of more than 5 per cent was, however, recorded for the remainder of the South-East, beyond the immediate influence of London, and for the South-West and growth of more than 10 per cent was recorded for East Anglia. In essence there has been a steady movement outwards of the population away from the older cities and regions to areas more divorced from the largest of the urban cores.

The reasons for this outward migration are complex (Kennett and Hall, 1981). Slum clearance and policies of planned decentralization (discussed in Chapter 11) clearly encouraged some to move to peripheral developments and to the new and expanded towns. The desire for owner-occupied accommodation in environmentally more attractive areas influenced many to move from the older towns to new housing schemes which sprouted up in many smaller towns and villages within thirty or forty miles of major conurbations. A virtual doubling in car ownership rates between 1961 and 1981 allowed more households to commute to the cities from peripheral housing schemes. The steady movement out of population encouraged and reflected economic decentralization. The movement out of jobs from the cities has not been as marked as the decentralization of people and tended to occur a good decade after the initial dispersal of population. Relatively few manufacturing jobs have literally moved from the urban cores to new locations beyond the cities. Nevertheless, over a period of decades industrial investment has been reconstituted away from the older cities and regions to the expanding regions of the South of England in particular. In addition, some service employment has moved out of London, seeking out more environmentally attractive locations where rents and rates may be much lower. Many service jobs in any case serve local populations. As the latter rise so more teachers, administrators, health workers and so on will be required. The combined impact of these impulses has been to encourage relatively rapid job growth in areas such as the M4 belt, East Anglia, the South-West, and parts of the East Midlands (Owen *et al.*, 1984). In turn this very expansion has encouraged additional out migration from the depressed regions of the country. This is not to suggest that the regions of relative growth suffer little unemployment. By 1985 Milton Keynes, often perceived as an area of affluence and growth, was subject to unemployment rates in excess of 18 per cent. Nevertheless, in general in the post-1971 period it has been the free-standing communities of the South

of England that have tended to enjoy both relative economic and absolute demographic growth.

The mere decline in population from the major cities need not of itself prove
undesirable. It might, for example, be possible to redevelop cities at lower densities.
What has tended to worry the cities has been the selective nature of decentralization. In
general it would appear to be the younger, the more skilled and the more affluent who
have left the older urban areas. In part this reflects higher car ownership rates enjoyed
by the better-off. In addition it is clear that virtually the only way for many households
to decentralize is through the owner-occupied sector, since in practice this tenure
dominates housing beyond the cities. For those in rented accommodation in the cities
prevailing prices for suburban and ex-urban housing may simply be too high even for
those in employment. The proportion of the urban populace living in rented accommodation should not be underestimated in this context. Over 15 per cent of the households
of London, Newcastle, Liverpool and Manchester lived in the private rented sector in
1981, and virtually all of the cities had a much higher proportion of households in the
public rented sector than the national figure of 31 per cent would suggest. For many of
these households opportunities to decentralize remain slim indeed; little rented accommodation exists beyond the cities and prevailing house prices are too great. In essence
they are trapped in the older urban areas.

Because the housing trap tends to retain less advantaged groups in the cities, it is
not surprising to find that the urban cores reveal much higher indicators of deprivation
than do either the outer parts of the cities (Redfern, 1982) or the country as a whole
(HMSO, 1984). For example, inner Birmingham has six times as many households
with a New Commonwealth or Pakistani head of household as outer Birmingham, 50
per cent higher rates of unemployment, and 250 per cent more rented accommodation
and overcrowded dwellings. Compared with the nation as a whole, moreover, the cities
tend to contain far more households without the exclusive use of a car. Only 30 per cent
of Glasgow's households had a car in 1981 compared with a national figure of 60 per
cent. Similarly, with the exception of London, the cities reveal much lower proportions
of households with heads in the higher socio-economic groups I and II. Over 23 per cent
of the country's households fell into these categories in 1981, but only 13 per cent of
Liverpool's. Educational standards and qualifications were consistently lower in the
cities than elsewhere, and housing standards worse. Also many cities accommodated
higher proportions of lone pensioners than national figures would suggest.

Of course it is important to place these figures in context. There are many affluent
people in the cities. Most still continue to be employed. The position of the inner cities
has not always deteriorated by comparison with the conurbations as a whole in the
postwar period. In some respects, housing standards for instance, conditions
apparently improved in the 1960s and early 1970s (Department of the Environment,
1975), although recent dramatic reductions in expenditure available to local authorities for housing improvement and repair may well change this in the 1980s. Interestingly enough, it is by no means clear that many in the cities are multiply deprived (Hall
and Laurence, 1981). It might be imagined that those suffering from particularly acute
manifestations of, say, housing deprivation would similarly endure high rates of
unemployment. In fact it has often proved the case that the poorest housing has been

found in the private rented sector where unemployment rates are usually not as high as those in public housing schemes, especially those constructed on the edges of cities where casual jobs, which may be available within the older cores, simply do not exist. On the other hand some indicators of deprivation are closely correlated: for example, unemployment and low car ownership rates (Hamnett, 1983). In any case much empirical material on the deprivation issue was collected in the 1970s and appears dated by 1985. It seems probable that dramatically higher unemployment rates combined with diminishing levels of public investment must have thrown more into some state of multiple deprivation, particularly those in the cities of the North.

Social disadvantage in Britain is often indeed seen to reflect the growing realization of a two-nation state. Although this is an idealized simplification, it is nevertheless relevant to an understanding of the British city in the 1980s. Usually the two nations are perceived in regional terms (The Royal Town Planning Institute, 1984). That area to the south of the Humber-to-Bristol line seems to contain an increasing proportion of the population, has a better-educated workforce and a higher rate of job generation than the area to the north. In addition wages are higher and unemployment rates lower. And from the point of view of an urban perspective this region contains few major towns and cities, except for the specialized case of London.

This regional analysis is important to an understanding of the British city in the 1980s. Too many cities are located in the wrong regions and produce the wrong goods in the wrong kinds of factories with the wrong kinds of labour forces. This problem of two nations, moreover, can be identified not simply at the interregional scale but within the intraregional dimension as well. Within the generally more depressed regions of the North of England there are, for example, small industrial communities with much higher rates of unemployment and more obvious manifestations of disadvantage than prevail within many of the large cities. There are also towns within the more impoverished regions that are clearly more prosperous than those elsewhere. Donnison and Soto (1980) call these 'the Good Cities'. They apparently offer a wide range of job opportunities, better educational facilities, more part-time jobs for women, good and varied housing, and are administered by councils determined to boost local economic development. Such communities may not always appeal to higher socio-economic groups since many of them are based on engineering. Most of them are located in the South, but a few, such as Teesside and Ormskirk, are to be found in the North. Perhaps more imaginative and innovative local government can help create others. But surely for many communities in the depressed regions the scale of market retreat and the severity of centrally inspired restraint suggests that a more or less semipermanent state of social and economic deprivation is likely to be perpetuated.

The financial and administrative context

Urban governance has to operate within administrative and financial parameters laid down by central government. For much of the postwar period these remained relatively uncontentious. By the mid-1980s, however, it can be argued that the central-local issue has become one of the most bitter of contemporary political debates. There is indeed a case that the severity of constraint imposed by central government after 1979 has brought into question the very existence of an independent system of local government. This assault has occurred as a result of proposed changes to both the system of local government itself and to the financing of that system. Each of these themes merits separate consideration.

The system of local government largely established in 1888 was to last until 1973. As Goldsmith (1980) indicates, it was apparent by the 1960s that this Victorian approach towards urban government was inadequate to meet the needs of the cities. There were too many authorities, and the delegation of powers was confusing. The Redcliffe-Maud Commission established in 1966 suggested instead that new boundaries should be created which took into account the growing interdependence between town and country and which would help create efficient and viable units of administration. In essence the Commission went for eight provincial councils which would provide the strategic framework for 58 large unitary authorities, with three higher-tier authorities for Birmingham, Manchester and Liverpool alone, under which there would be 20 metropolitan authorities. London had already been reformed in 1963 with the creation of a higher-tier Greater London Council and 32 lower-tier boroughs.

There was considerable opposition to the system proposed by the Commission. Derek Senior, a member of the Committee, for example recommended in a minority report the creation of a threefold administrative structure: provincial councils, city regional authorities, and district councils. In the event the election of Heath's Conservative administration in 1970 heralded a marked reorientation in central government attitudes towards the entire question of local government reform. Whereas the 1964-70 Labour government had largely endorsed the findings of the Commission, since unitary authorities would have boosted the influence of the cities and towns to the detriment of the shire authorities, the incoming Tory administration took a different view. The 1972 Local Government Act reprieved the traditionally Conservative-dominated counties by establishing a two-tier system for England and Wales. In the main there would be counties and beneath these district councils. In six conurbations, however — West and South Yorkshire, Greater Manchester, the West Midlands, Tyne and Wear, and Merseyside — there were to be relatively weak metropolitan counties, below which districts would operate. In Scotland there were to be large regional councils with districts as a lower tier of administration. The concept of large, unitary, city-regional authorities, which many considered the most appropriate vehicle through which to administer the conurbations, was not accepted.

In the 1970s a number of trends came to dominate local government, more especially urban local government. The numbers employed in local authorities rose dramatically. Planning departments, for instance, were often initiated as separate entities within the decade and were subsequently expanded. Following the Bains Report (HMSO, 1972), many authorities also adopted corporate planning objectives. Typically, an overarching policy and resources committee would be created to co-ordinate authority goals, policies and expenditure within structured annual programmes. Councillors sitting on such committees gained power at the expense of other local representatives. In an attempt to overcome this, many councils also introduced various forms of area management whereby some services, such as housing and personal social services, were decentralized to mini town halls. But perhaps the most crucial change which characterized some urban authorities was the steady politicization of local administration.

It is true that neither the politicization nor the radicalization of local government should be exaggerated. In many authorities political control rarely changes. A large number remain in Conservative or Independent hands more or less permanently. Even some of the cities return non-Labour administrations. Nevertheless, from the late 1970s onwards a more radical spirit came to dominate ruling Labour groups in authorities such as Liverpool, Sheffield and the Greater London Council. Some of the activities of these administrations, for example in pursuing independent local economic strategies, are discussed later in the book. Whatever the merits of radical local strategies — and these administrations were after all elected on such a platform — the ruling Conservative government decided by the early 1980s that the independence of some councils was to be restricted. In particular, as will be examined below, rate-capping was to be introduced, and the metropolitan counties and the Greater London Council were to be disbanded.

In the White Paper, 'Streamlining the Cities' (HMSO, 1983), the government argued on a number of grounds for the removal of the higher tier of urban administration. Apparently the functions of these higher-tier authorities overlapped with those undertaken by the districts. They had never satisfactorily established a strategic role. Doubts were indeed expressed as to whether a strategic level of city-regional government was anyway needed. In fact, writing in 1985, it is still not certain that all seven of the authorities concerned will in the event disappear. There is perhaps an argument that some of the metropolitan counties are not essential. But the case for the retention of the Greater London Council, Merseyside, West Midlands and Greater Manchester seems overwhelming (Breheny and Hall, 1984; Leach and Stewart, 1984; Bradshaw, 1985). The demise of the counties will save little and may in the event actually involve additional expenditure. Functions undertaken by the counties are to be devolved to a whole host of undemocratic boards and conferences. But, most crucially, the higher-tier authorities are absolutely essential because of their strategic role. It may well be argued that these authorities have not proved effective at ordering the strategic development of their administrations (Davis, 1985). This is largely because the councils concerned were never given sufficient powers so to do. For example, the planning of London's transport system has been subject to decisions taken by up to nine separate organizations. Yet the major conurbations need a genuinely strategic authority; and to assume that *ad hoc* boards can fulfil this role is absurd. Strategic authorities are needed to coordinate major development and transport proposals, to organize mobility in the public housing sector, to undertake programmes of economic regeneration and infrastructural improvement and to provide refuse and environmental improvement services. There is in fact a valid case that not simply should the G.L.C. and some counties be retained but also that their boundaries should be enlarged. Who, for example, is to administer and to co-ordinate the enormous development pressures which will emerge as a result of the construction of the M25? The need for broadly based strategic authorities to govern the evolution of the conurbations is incontrovertible. Their demise will prove a disaster.

Although the planned abolition of the higher-tier authorities has attracted a great deal of interest in the mid-1980s, in many respects the proposals to deal with local authority expenditure represent a more insidious threat to local government. Even with the planned removal of the metropolitan counties the cities will still have some form of government. With the marked decline in central government funding for local authorities, however, and the imposition of rate-capping, it is clear that many administrations will be unable to implement the programmes for which they were elected.

The system for financing local government has proved inordinately complex and in detail is beyond the scope of this book. Briefly, however, capital expenditure, running at several billion pounds in the mid-1980s, is controlled through central government allocation and approval. In some years local authorities have not spent their total allocations, often because capital expenditure cannot be undertaken unless there is a commensurate increase in current expenditure. For instance, new housing for the elderly will require adequate staff funded out of current expenditure. But the position with regard to current expenditure has proved unfortunate for many cities. A proportion of local authority current spending is provided annually by central government through the rate support grant. The remainder is funded by rate and fee revenue and other sources available to local councils. However, the proportion of local authority expenditure funded by central government fell from over 60 per cent of council spending in the mid-1970s to under 50 per cent a decade later. The system of support was, moreover, changed in 1981-82 by the introduction of the block grant. This was designed to equalize between authorities in terms of both needs and rateable value per head. From this date too central government in effect imposed two disincentives to discourage local authority spending. A centrally assessed measure of need was devised on top of which was superimposed an expenditure target. Spending over either of these targets resulted in financial penalties. By 1983-84 both urban and shire authorities were being penalized to the tune of more than £240 million. Virtually all of this 'overspend' was, however, incurred by Labour councils (Boddy, 1984). These controls remained indirect and some authorities elected to ignore them, thus receiving appropriate penalties. The 1984 Rates Act changed all that. It allowed the Secretary of State for the Environment to impose either general schemes of rate-capping on all local authorities or, as appears to be the case for 18 largely Labour controlled authorities in 1985-86, selective rate limitations. In effect some authorities will not be able to set their own rate.

The rationale behind the Conservative government's actions is held to be the conviction that public expenditure has to be controlled in some of the more profligate Labour authorities where high rate calls are apparently undermining business confidence. As Midwinter (1985) points out, however, much of this is simply untrue. Local authority capital and current expenditure combined declined in real terms between 1979 and 1983. Much of the increase in public expenditure occurred as a result of the much enlarged social security budget and increased spending in areas such as defence. Local rates increase not because of the decisions of local authorities but largely because of inflationary pressures on wages and other costs. High rates have little impact on economic output. 'Overspending' in any case is a feature of a wide range of authorities, not simply a handful of apparently radical councils. The latter might find themselves in the immediate firing line in the mid-1980s. However, there can be little doubt that the vast proportion of local councils will find themselves operating on increasingly stringent budgets. And no constraint on the independence of local activity will prove as acute as will tightening financial control.

The impact of changing technologies

Technological innovation will impose considerable changes on the economic structure and physical patterning of cities. In some respects it is difficult to identify the exact consequences for the conurbations because the full outcome of innovation is uncertain. Some cities may reap benefits from technological change. London's Docklands, for example, appears likely to accommodate a wide range of companies in the communications, electronics and publishing fields. Whether such a relatively optimistic picture could be painted for, say, Sheffield or Newcastle is another matter. Indeed most commentators examining the spatial implications of technological change (Breheny *et al* 1983; Goddard and Thwaites, 1980) tend to assume that in general the cities are unlikely to benefit a great deal, if at all, from innovation.

It is important to point out that 'new technologies' can embrace a catholic range of goods and services. The term incorporates the production of silicon chips and allied products, new consumer goods such as home computers, information technology, advances in communications, biotechnology, food processing, drugs and so on. The production of these goods is unlikely to be located in the older cities and regions. In the UK a large proportion of the investment in the production of new technologies has occurred along the M4 belt, in the Cambridge area and in the so-called Silicon Glen between Glasgow and Edinburgh. The first of these zones is undeniably the most innovative and is usually seen to have occurred because of the fortunate juxtaposition of a number of relevant factors. These include proximity to a major airport and government research establishments, the existence of a relatively well-educated labour force, and a pleasant residential environment. As the vexed case of Inmos indicates all too clearly, moreover, even when a government is prepared to invest substantial sums into a high-tech firm, technological entrepreneurs will retain control over the location of corporate headquarters. In effect central governments do not have the power nor innovators the inclination to guide the production of high-tech goods to the older regions of the country.

These regions will suffer on another account too. A great deal of technological advance will occur as a result not of the production of new goods but rather through the introduction of new processes. The same sorts of goods will be produced, but capital-intensive processes will involve the shedding of labour. This has occurred especially in manufacturing industry where dramatic reductions in employment can be associated with stable or even enhanced output (Massey and Meegan, 1982). This has proved to be the case in vehicle production and the steel industry for example. The cities in the older regions will certainly find this process continuing to affect manpower levels in industrial establishments. In similar vein, some cities, notably London, will see intensive investment in process innovation in the service sector. Many routine administrative, clerical, retail and secretarial jobs will disappear, and although other employment sectors will grow — word processing for instance — the net result may be a loss of jobs overall.

This combination of forces — product development in the South of England and the extensive introduction of process innovation in both service and manufacturing sectors — seems certain to lead to formidable urban job losses. The likely scale of this decline has indeed encouraged some observers (Pahl, 1978) to suggest that a more informally based household economy will need to be fostered in the older cities. Others would point to a probable, even desirable, expansion in the black economy. Even then it will have to be accepted that unemployment rates in many older cities will remain at unprecedentedly high levels. Talk of a leisured society should, however, be dismissed as simplistic nonsense when so many of the urban disadvantaged exist at or below official poverty lines.

A concluding comment

In this chapter we have attempted to present some of the major constraints and processes that have influenced — and will continue to mould — the evolution of British urban society. In virtually every respect the cities must be seen to have undergone a dramatic decline. Economic bases have been devastated; political support and influence have diminished; demographic vitality has weakened. If anything, the future appears bleaker. National economic decline will raise questions about all forms of public subsidy. If the cities are perceived as a net drain on national resources, their status will be subject to increasingly unsympathetic scrutiny. Technological change will not operate to their advantage. Their fate may indeed ultimately lie with society's fear of outright urban strife. The 1981 disturbances apparently came as something of a shock to central government, although predicted for many years by independent observers. And yet if the cities are anything they are the focus of racial and class conflict in Britain. They accommodate so many of those marginalized by economic processes and prevailing sociopolitical trends that perhaps this very weakness becomes their strength. No government will wish to preside over a semi-permanent state of urban conflict. It is hardly an encouraging prospect for the cities, however, that one of their few remaining trump cards may be the ambivalent advantages emanating out of outright urban violence.

References

Boddy, M. (1984) *Local councils and the financial squeeze.*In M. Boddy and C. Fudge (1984) Local Socialism? Macmillan, London

Bradshaw, M. (1985) Abolition of the mets — no case to answer, The Royal Town Planning Institute, Summer School, *The Planner*, Vol. 71, No. 2, pp 21-25

Breheny, M., Cheshire, P. and Langridge, R. (1983) The anatomy of job creation? Industrial change in Britain's M4 corridor, *Built Environment*, Vol. 9, No. 1, pp. 61-71

Breheny, M. and Hall, P. (1984) The strange death of strategic planning and the victory of the know-nothing school, *Built Environment*, Vol. 10, No. 2, pp 95-99

Byrne, S. (1985) Economic regeneration and the battle for the environment. 1985 Presidential Address, *The Planner*, Vol. 71, No. 1, pp 20-24

Champion, T., Coombes, M. and Openshaw, S. (1983). A new definition of cities, *Town and Country Planning*, Vol. 52, No. 11, pp 305-307

Cobham, D. (1984) Popular political strategies for the UK economy, *The Three Banks Review*, No. 143, pp 17-36

Confederation of British Industry (1981) The fabric of the nation, C.B.I., London

Cowie, H., Harlow, C. and Emerson, R. (1984) Rebuilding the infrastructure. The needs of English cities and towns, No 633, Policy Studies Institute, London

Davis, C.J. (1985) Will strategic planning disappear with the GLC and the metropolitan counties? The Royal Town Planning Institute, Summer School, *The Planner*, Vol. 71, No. 2, pp 17-20

Denham, C. (1984) Urban Britain, *Population Trends*, No. 36, pp 10-17

Department of the Environment (1975) Study of the inner areas of conurbations. D.O.E., London

Donnison, D. and Soto, P. (1980) *The Good City. A study of urban development and policy in Britain*, Heinemann, London

Fothergill, S. and Gudgin, G. (1982) *Unequal Growth. Urban and regional change in the UK*, Heineman, London

Goddard, J.B. (1983) *Structural change in the British spatial economy*. In J.B. Goddard and A.G. Champion (1983) The Urban and Regional Transformation of Britain, Methuen, London

Goddard, J.B. and Thwaites, A.T. (1980) Technological change and the inner city. The inner city in context, Paper 4, Social Science Research Council, London

Goldsmith, M. (1980) *Politics, Planning and the City*, Hutchinson, London

Gudgin, G. Moore, B. and Rhodes, J. (1982) Employment problems in the cities and regions of the UK: prospects for the 1980s *Cambridge Economic Policy Review*, Vol. 8, No. 2, pp 19-64

Hall, P. and Laurence, S. (1981) *Deprivation in the inner city*. In P. Hall (1981) The Inner City in Context, Social Science Research Council and Heinemann, London

Hamnett, C. (1983) The conditions in England's inner cities on the eve of the 1981 riots, *Area*, Vol. 15, No. 1, pp 7-13

Hamnett, C. and Randolph, W. (1983) The changing population distribution of England and Wales, 1961-1981: clean break or consistent progression? *Built Environment*, Vol. 8, No. 4, pp 272-280

HMSO (1972) The new local authorities: management and structure (the Bains Report), HMSO, London

HMSO (1981) The Brixton disorders, 10-12 April 1981 (the Scarman Report) Cmnd 8427, HMSO, London

HMSO (1983) Streamlining the cities, Cmnd 9063, HMSO, London

HMSO (1984) Key statistics for urban areas; Great Britain, cities and towns, Office of Population Censuses and Surveys, London

Kellner, P. (1982) For richer, for poorer. *New Statesman*, Vol. 104, No. 2692, pp 7-8

Kennett, S. and Hall, P. (1981) *The inner city in spatial perspective*. In P. Hall (1981) The Inner City in Context, Social Science Research Council and Heinemann, London

Leach, S. and Stewart, J.D. (1985) Strategy and the case for metropolitan government, *Built Environment*, Vol. 10, No. 2, pp 113-123

Massey, D.B. and Meegan, R.A. (1982) *The Anatomy of Job Loss*, Methuen, London

Midwinter, A. (1985) Five myths about local government spending, The Royal Town Planning Institute, Summer School, *The Planner*, Vol. 71, No. 2. pp 69-71

Owen, D.W., Gillespie, A.E. and Coombes, M.G. (1984) 'Job shortfalls' in British local labour market areas: A classification of labour supply and demand trends, 1971-1981, *Regional Studies*, Vol. 18, No. 6, pp 469-488

Pahl, R. (1978) Will the inner city problem ever go away? *New Society*, Vol. 45, No. 834, pp 678-681

Redfern, P. (1982) Profile of our cities, *Population Trends*, No. 30, pp 21-32

Rex, J. (1982) The 1981 urban riots in Britain, *International Journal of Urban and Regional Research*, Vol. 6, No. 1, pp 99-113

The Royal Town Planning Institute (1984) The planning response to social and economic change, R.T.P.I., London

Further reading

This chapter has covered an enormous area. Only a hint of the available literature can be provided here. For a radical view of national economic policy and performance, Glyn, A. and Harrison, J. (1980) *The British Economic Disaster*, Pluto Press, London, is very readable. Demographic and economic change in the city regions is considered in Goddard, J.B. and Champion, A.G. (eds) *The Urban and Regional Transformation of Britain*, Methuen, London. This is an excellent if somewhat dated work. More recent statistical data on the cities are available in HMSO (1984) and in *Population Trends*. Local government financial issues are considered in Boddy (1984) and in a succinct article by Travers, T. (1985), A forest guide, *New Society*, Vol. 71, No. 1152, pp 147-149. The politics of urban policy making are explored in McKay, D.H. and Cox, A.W. (1979) *The Politics of Urban Change*, Croom Helm, London. Employment trends and job loss are analysed by Fothergill and Gudgin (1982) and Massey and Meegan (1982). Both books are required reading for anyone interested in the fate of the city in the UK.

9　Intervention in land and town planning in the post-1945 period: the system and its defects

In this chapter two major issues will be considered: the structure of the planning system which was to emerge in the postwar period, and the land question. In the succeeding chapter the impact of these interventions on, and within, the cities will be explored.

The legal and administrative basis for town planning

The 1947 Town and Country Planning Act laid a requirement upon county councils and county borough councils to produce a development plan within three years of the 1 July 1948. The plan was to consist of a map and a statement illustrating the planning authority's view of how land should be developed in the area. In particular the plan was to indicate sites for proposed developments, comprehensive development areas where extensive redevelopment was to be undertaken and areas for agricultural, residential, industrial or any other use. The plans were supposed to last five years and had to be approved by the relevant central government minister. Individuals had the right to object to a development plan, and this could lead to a public inquiry.

The system, while undoubtedly a distinct improvement on interwar planning legislation, had run into considerable criticism by the early 1960s. Bor (1974) has suggested that four pressures for reform were building up at that time which eventually led to substantial revisions: too many plans were being forwarded to the Ministry of Housing and Local Government, which was inevitably taking too long to deal with them; the rapidly growing planning profession was eager for a more flexible and continuous form of planning; social and economic issues needed to be integrated more clearly into the physical framework of development plans; and the public needed to be much more involved in the planning process. In addition it might well be argued that the development plans produced under the 1947 Town and Country Planning Act (later to be consolidated under the 1962 Act) were often little more than zoning maps indicating existing land uses. This was seen as an increasingly naive form of planning. It did little to incorporate change and intimate relationships between land use and transport remained unexplored.

In an attempt to overcome some of these deficiencies the Planning Advisory Group was established which reported on the future of development plans in 1965. As Goldsmith (1984) points out, the planning profession itself dominated the Group, and it is not therefore surprising to see that it suggested a considerable intensification of the system. In effect PAG argued that there should be a twofold hierarchy in plan production. At the higher level there should be broad strategic planning statements: structure plans, and below these, but intimately connected with structure plans, would be local plans. The rest of this section of the chapter deals with the objectives and drawbacks of the new development plan system which was to form the basis of the 1968 Town and Country Planning Act, later consolidated as the 1971 Act.

The structure planning system

Those interested in a comprehensive review of the format and objectives of the structure planning system are recommended to read the 1970 development plan manual (HMSO, 1970). Briefly, however, structure plans were to consist of a written statement and supporting diagrams, including a key diagram, which were to outline the broad development trends and policies in the county. Structure plans were to coordinate the land use activities and programmes of relevant local government departments and other public bodies and were to incorporate likely economic and demographic changes into possible strategies for the area. Such potential strategies were themselves to be subject to appropriate financial, administrative and political evaluation before a realistic, argued strategy for the area was to be decided upon. The selected plan was to indicate the interrelationships between key elements such as employment, settlement, transport, retailing, conservation, recreation and so on and

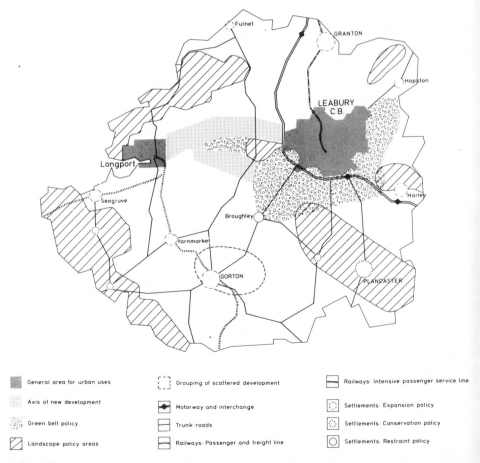

Figure 3   The structure planning system (*Source:* adapted from 'Development Plans: a manual on form and content' HMSO, 1970)

was to be placed under permanent review. The plan, once approved by the Secretary of State for the Environment, was to be monitored and amended where appropriate, although projected population trends were to be undertaken for ten-year periods. Structure plans were also to take into account relevant information in regional plans and to lay down a framework for a programme of local plan preparation.

Although there was to be considerable variety of practice, most authorities tended towards a comprehensive, if complex, approach to plan preparation (Ratcliffe, 1981). This included an extensive survey, detailed subject reports on likely trends in major policy areas such as employment, liaison with adjoining planning authorities on issues of mutual interest, the preparation of a draft plan, its examination in public and finally central government's decision, which became part of the final approved plan. At times in fact central government introduced substantial modifications to structure plans. In the case of South Yorkshire for instance, the Department of the Environment decided that one of the main policy initiatives devised by the County, that of job priority areas in more disadvantaged localities, should be abandoned and economic development encouraged to go to areas of regional strength, notably Sheffield. Ultimately, however, as Figure 3 indicates, the end product of the structure planning process often appears relatively bland. Typically the key diagram indicates areas of restraint, settlements that might accommodate additional development, major new proposals and the framework for local plans. However, for many of those producing structure plans, implementing their proposals, or attempting to pursue development within their guidelines it has become clear that there are real drawbacks. Indeed throughout the 1970s the structure planning system, originally hailed as one of the most sophisticated in the world, fell into some disrepute. Some of the main criticisms are developed below.

(1) It had always been anticipated in the 1960s that structure plans would be produced by unitary authorities emerging from the impending reorganization of local government. In the event, however, the 1972 Local Government Act created a two-tiered planning system consisting of counties and districts. It was the former that were to produce structure plans. Inevitably conflicts arose between the counties and the districts below on policies such as areas of restraint, sites for new development and so on.

In the early 1970s, under the 1972 Local Government Act, counties were given powers to determine themselves which planning applications might prove inconsistent with policies reflected in the structure plan. By the 1980 Local Government, Planning and Land Act, however, the scope of matters to be decided by counties had been drastically reduced, a development which, as Bracken (1982) points out, appears to be stretching to the limit the at times unsatisfactory relationship between counties and districts. In addition the Department of the Environment Circular 22/84 on structure and local plans made clear that local plans would prevail over structure plans in any conflicts, except where counties specifically indicated that a local plan was no longer in general conformity with an approved, altered or replaced structure plan receiving central government approval. The developments described above, combined with the steady retreat throughout the 1970s of the assumption that local plans could not be adopted before the appropriate structure plan was approved, have clearly shifted planning powers away from the counties to the districts. For those who believe some sort of strategic framework is needed to govern physical and economic development this cannot be seen as an entirely favourable trend.

(2) For a period in the 1960s and early 1970s the process of plan preparation clearly came to dominate the strategic planning debate. The actual mechanism through which the plan was to be devised ludicrously became more of an issue than did policies contained within plans or the success with which plans were implemented. This in fact was the period when the systems approach to planning came to dominate the profession, with unfortunate consequences. It is unnecessary in the 1980s to revisit this terrain. An idea of the approach and its complexity can be gleaned through an examination of texts seen as critically important at the time (McGloughlin, 1969; Chadwick, 1971). In brief, however, it might be mentioned that the approach assumed that after an exhaustive survey a series of independent strategies could be devised, each capable of implementation. The lengths to which some plans went in attempting to devise and evaluate independent options seems extraordinarily optimistic in the 1980s when most would argue that planning can play only a marginal role in altering future development patterns.

(3) The new development plan system was supposed to be more flexible than the old approach and much speedier in its operation. However, by 1978, out of 89 expected structure plan submissions for England and Wales only 23 had actually been approved. There were a number of reasons for this unexpected delay. Examinations in public lengthened proceedings, and some structure plans were too concerned with detail that should have been considered in local plans. In an attempt to ensure that counties concentrated on key issues, the Department of the Environment in Circular 98/74 (Department of the Environment, 1974) tried to persuade authorities to deal primarily with the central issues of the location and scale of employment and housing and with the transportation system. Later advice, such as that contained in Circular 22/84 from the Department of the Environment, reiterated this in broad terms and indicated that structure plans were in essence about the control, scale and location of development within national and regional parameters. Structure plans were thus usually not concerned with social and economic considerations, which had originally been seen as intimately bound up with physical development patterns. Whatever the merits or otherwise of limiting the content of structure plans it is clear that delays in plan preparation and approval created difficulties for many authorities. Some structure plans appeared out of date before they were finalized. Although policies relating to, say, housing or industrial development were supposed to last ten years or so, basic premises governing the allocation and location of land could alter enormously in a decade. In particular, whereas the Planning Advisory Group reported in an era of apparently permanent demographic and economic growth, very different assumptions govern the production or modification of structure plans in the 1980s. No growth will not mean no change, but it will require new approaches to deal with rising unemployment, lower spending and less public investment. Not surprisingly, by 1984 (Department of the Environment Circular 22/84) it was made clear by central government that neither structure plans nor local plans should designate areas such as Housing Action Areas or Industrial Improvement Areas (discussed later in the book), presumably exactly because the centre wished to retain control over policy instruments such as these with their inbuilt expenditure mechanisms. Financial resources, perhaps more than any other input into

structure plans, are likely to become both more unpredictable and subject to greater central control. Exactly because of this unpredictability of budgeting some authorities, of which East Sussex is perhaps the best known, prefer intimately to link the production of the structure plan to annual expenditure targets and over all authority objectives.

(4) Structure plans were originally intended to provide a basis for development control through which new development could be guided in the broader context. It is doubtful if this aim has been achieved. Policies tended at times to be stated in structure plans without any clear indication of how public- and private-sector organizations were to implement them. To some extent that might not have been the fault of the planning authorities concerned. Structure planning involved the coordination of the activities of a wide range of bodies over which planning authorities had little or no control. Ambiguity in terms of implementation was perhaps not therefore particularly surprising. Nor, although equally unacceptable, was the apparent determination on the part of some counties to limit monitoring activities. Despite assumptions that the new development plan system would avoid the tendency inherent within the older approach of creating an end-state plan, it is clear that not all structure planning authorities are undertaking the sorts of reviews that changing economic political and demographic circumstances merit (Bracken, 1982).

(5) One main group that was supposed to have benefited from the new system was the public at large. In Chapter 11 the vexed question of public involvement in planning issues will be examined. But in the context of structure planning it is clear that public involvement has been unsatisfactory for all concerned. As Bruton (1980) points out, the assumptions held by the Planning Advisory Group that public participation would increase cooperation and understanding appears naive in retrospect. Necessary changes in decision-making procedures to accommodate public sentiment were not undertaken; there was no apparent realization that participation would conflict with representative democracy; and the approach assumed that consultation would enhance consensus when the real outcome of extensive public involvement was likely to be conflict. In any event, public participation in structure planning has generally been muted in the extreme. Relevant organizations such as motoring societies or local chambers of trade and commerce may well make predictable representations. But for the public at large the strategic, nonspecific nature of this tier of planning has proved largely incomprehensible. Indeed after some extraordinarily long-winded examinations in public, notably that for the Greater London Development Plan in the early 1970s, a retreat from mandatory public examinations was apparent. Alterations, repeals or replacements of structure plans might eventually be subject to examinations in public, but this was not necessary.

(6) The final and most complex issue to be considered here relates to the overall function and content of structure plans. As a number of commentators have pointed out (Centre for Environmental Studies, 1975; Fisher, 1980; Bruton, 1984), structure planning has been consistently undermined because of its uncertain purpose and its ambiguous relationship with other policy documents or organizations. For example, it is clear that for a structure plan to succeed its proposals must relate satisfactorily to central government's programmes and to other local government policies. This can

prove difficult to achieve. Central government spending may vary enormously from year to year, thus affecting infrastructural proposals for example. Change of power at central government will alter the framework within which structure plans must proceed. Labour governments might for instance be more inclined to boost expenditure on public housing and other aspects of consumption. Structure plans are also supposed to take into account regional planning proposals. However, the regional plans were themselves never binding and the Regional Economic Planning Councils were disbanded in 1979. For many counties broad regional physical and economic strategies essential for the evolution of their own structure plan simply do not exist. What does exist, however, is a sort of regional government consisting of regional offices of central government departments, regional water and health authorities and so on. Attempting to establish the policies of such organizations can be far from easy; coordinating them is clearly beyond the scope of any county. The legendary rational Martian might well conclude that one way forward in the strategic planning debate would be to create elected regional authorities and disband the counties. This hardly appears on many political agendas in the 1980s.

In addition to the problems of coordinating national and regional agencies, structure planners have also to consider a whole range of local policy developments and programmes which have clear implications for strategic planning. These will be considered later, but they include policy innovations such as area housing policies, enterprise zones, conservation areas and new approaches towards coordinating policy in housing and transport — housing investment programmes and transport policies and programmes. The last two developments are in essence plans produced by housing and transport authorities submitted to central government as a basis for central funding. Whereas it may be that the essential alignments of structure plans can be retained irrespective of housing investment programmes and transport policies and programmes, it must normally be the case that the expenditure allowed by central government under these devices must, over a decade, contain substantial implications for relevant structure plans.

Structure plans: a concluding comment

A somewhat critical stance has been developed here towards structure plans. But an important point should be made: whereas there are grounds for criticizing the operation of the system initiated in 1968, there can be no doubt of the principle that strategic planning is needed. Broader plans are required to govern development, concentrate resources where they are needed, guide infrastructural investment, assist the inner cities and so on. It also seems clear that such a system can be developed. In England trends towards corporate planning whereby an authority attempts to define overall objectives, implements these within appropriate financial parameters and closely monitors outcomes should be welcomed. There is no reason why structure planning could not be integrated into this process by providing the essential land-use element, guided and in turn articulated by broader corporate objectives (Luithlen, 1976a). But probably the most interesting development in the United Kingdom has been the emergence of Regional Plans in Scotland. There local government reorganization in the 1970s produced regions, each of which was to produce an initial plan outlining corporate objectives towards social and economic development, the environment and so on. Structure plans were then to articulate these corporate objectives in land-use terms. A modified approach to this scheme whereby the land-use element was incorporated into an overall annual corporate document, the whole being subject to pertinent political, financial and administrative evaluation, offers the best possibility for an improvement to strategic planning. The political realities of the 1980s make this highly improbable in the short to medium term.

Local planning

It was originally intended in the 1968 and 1971 Town and Country Planning Acts that there should be three kinds of local plans. District plans would deal with the comprehensive planning of large areas such as parts of cities or small towns with less than roughly 75 000 people. Such plans were intended to describe specific proposals, guide the control of development and in general to set out the planning policies for such areas in conformity with the structure plan. Action area plans (an example of one is provided in Figure 4 aimed to deal with the short-term intensive change likely to occur over a ten-year period. Action area plans had to be identified in the relevant structure plan, and it was considered an essential characteristic of such local plans that they should provide detailed physical and financial proposals governing developments such as new district or city centres and redeveloped or improved residential areas. The third type of local plan was a subject plan. These were to relate to issues such as recreation or minerals development and would cover relatively large areas concentrating on issues that could realistically be isolated from other planning policies.

In all three cases local plans were to differ in certain obvious ways from structure plans. They were to consist of a map, not a diagram, and an associated written statement. They were not originally statutorily enforceable before the structure plan had been approved. In general they were to apply the strategy of the structure plan to local areas. In particular they were to provide a detailed basis for development control and for coordinating development undertaken by both the public and private sectors. Local plans were also to be more certain yet more adaptable to changing circumstances than were the structure plans which guided their evolution. The public was to be involved at various stages. Initially authorities were to ensure adequate publicity of the matters that were to be proposed in the plan, and individuals were given the right to make representations about these. Similarly, once the plan had been prepared objections to it could be made to the authority, which might decide in the light of these to hold a public inquiry. It did not have to do so, although the Secretary of State for the Environment was given ultimate powers to call in plans if he was dissatisfied with matters such as public involvement.

In general it is probably true to say that the concept of local planning has not received the same degree of hostility as has the structure planning system. Most independent observers would probably agree that there is an undeniable need for local planning. Development needs to be guided, public and private sector proposals coordinated and overall development control principles established. Nevertheless, serious reservations have been expressed about local planning. Some brief indication of these issues ought to be made.

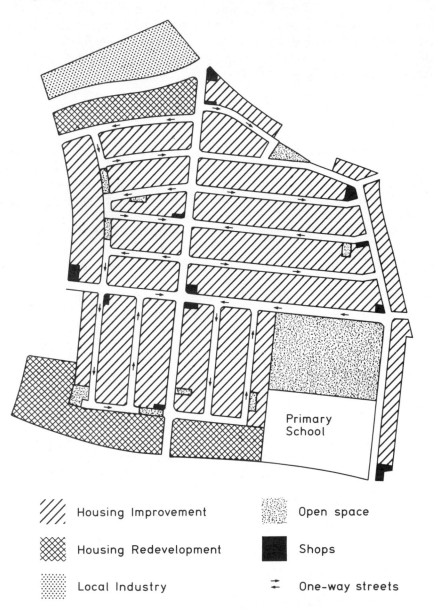

Primary
School

//// Housing Improvement   Open space

XXXX Housing Redevelopment   ■ Shops

::::: Local Industry   ⇌ One-way streets

Figure 4 A local plan (*Source:* adapted from 'Development Plans: a manual on form and content', HMSO, 1970)

(1) As with structure plans, it is by no means easy to specify exactly what ought to be the contents of a local plan. Some, like Solesbury (1974), have seen district plans as structure plans writ small in that broad social and physical considerations may be developed within local plans which may well cover considerable parts of cities or even entire towns. In this context it may be difficult to establish the extent of social as opposed to physical issues that should be incorporated into the appropriate policy vehicle. Independent observers (Bor, 1974) may argue for the incorporation of social matters into local plans, but the development plans manual (HMSO, 1970) makes clear that officialdom tends to perceive local plans as documents guiding the physical development of smaller areas.

(2) The relationship between local plans and the structure plan and between different types of local plans has not always been satisfactory. As others have pointed out (Luithlen, 1976b), policies contained within a structure plan might prove of only limited relevance to planners in the district preparing local plans. Forecasts and altern-atives produced by structure planners often proved bizarrely improbable, not simply for the public but often for those working at the lower tier of planning. In effect it was often difficult for those working on local plans to be certain of the anticipated growth, or perhaps decline, assumed by structure planners for the area of a proposed local plan, or indeed the exact boundaries of any such plan indicated within a structure plan. As has been discussed above, there was anyway throughout the 1970s a steady movement away from the assumption that local plans could only be adopted after the approval of the appropriate strategic plan. Many neutral observers might argue, however, that this reorientation of the system essentially reflects the failures of structure plans rather than the emergence of a more sensible planning system. Logically, the strategic level should lay down the framework for local plans. However, in the 1980 Local Govern-ment, Planning and Land Act it was decreed that local plans would no longer be identified in structure plans. Instead the emphasis was placed on the development plan scheme to be prepared by the counties which were to review the need for local plans, their nature and scope, the effect of any new local plans on existing plans, the scale of appropriate resources within the districts and so on. This appears a long way divorced from the original assumption that an overarching structure plan would lay the found-ations for the subsequent development of local plans.

It was also clear by the early 1980s that there was some degree of conflict between different types of local plan. Circular 22/84 (Department of the Environment, 1984) suggests that formal plans may not be suitable for all areas and that in some circum-stances informal approaches may suffice. In any event central government advice was clearly aimed at encouraging local authorities to produce general local plans — the term 'district plan' having been abandoned — on the basis that such plans would prove cheaper and more flexible than would the proliferation of action area plans. Local authorities might concur with these comments on the basis that action area plans logically needed to identify public and private resources for the implementation of the types of intensive development assumed within such plans. Clearly local adminis-trations would often not be in a position to ensure adequate resources from either sector. In the case of the public sector also, it might prove especially difficult to co-ordinate the necessary agencies and services that intensive redevelopment involves.

This can often prove a thankless task. When combined with the bargaining with private developers over local redevelopment proposals that is so frequently required it can also prove a long-winded one. In effect, entrepreneurial and coordinating skills that intensive redevelopment necessitates may impose inordinate strains on the abilities of local planners.

(3) It was always hoped that public involvement in local plan preparation and approval would be considerable. However, it is by no means clear that this objective has generally been achieved. There are problems here, as a number of commentators have established (Ratcliffe, 1981; Raine, 1982) Issues raised locally by residents often relate to services such as education or public health which may be beyond the remit of local plans; participation rates in the production of broader plans may prove disappointing; participation may raise hopes with little chance of these being satisfied; participation implies an active involvement of the public, but in practice many authorities may simply inform, or consult with, residents; plans may simply be approved, irrespective of comments received during the exercise; crucially too there is the perennial difficulty of reconciling the need for speed in plan production with the inevitable delays engendered by public involvement.

A concluding comment on the planning system

The last few pages have presented a largely critical overview of the development plan system. In no sense should this be taken to assume that planning is irrelevant or unnecessary. It is crucial. It can provide the framework for development undertaken by public and private sectors; it can reconcile land-use conflict; it can help to prevent destructive developments and assist in boosting those economies which can accrue from the agglomeration of activities in certain places. No civilized society can exist without it. Facile assumptions that it restricts freedom should be rejected for the nonsense that they undoubtedly are. Those invoking a planning-free nirvana are normally extremely eager to seek out the protection that planning legislation can provide when intrusive developments are proposed. While accepting entirely the need for a planning system, there are nevertheless valid grounds for questioning the applicability of the system that emerged in 1968. It appears now very much a creature of its day. Economic growth, mildly reformist government, rationality in decision making, and a conflict-free society appear now as improbable premises upon which to build a planning system. It should be changed. We need a more flexible and robust system and one which can relate planning to resources, public policy to private-sector aspiration, and land-use planning to other forms of intervention. The link between central government economic intervention and structure and local planning needs to be made explicit. In effect the spatial implications of national economic policy should be spelled out to form a primary input into strategic and hence local planning. In this way necessary links between economic intervention and physical planning can be articulated. Ultimately it is of little purpose blaming the planners when the system itself is at fault.

The land question and development control

The most contentious issue in planning since 1945 has been the land question. How should compensation apply to those whose land has been acquired or to those who were prevented from undertaking the development they wished? Ought betterment to be levied on those increases in land values occurring as a result of public development or private projects granted planning approval?

The Uthwatt Committee, reporting in 1942, opted for a radical approach to the land problem. It proposed, among other recommendations, that development rights in undeveloped land should be vested in the state; that land required for development should be purchased at existing values by the state and leased out at market value in order to recoup betterment; that developed land should only be acquired when needed for planning schemes; that the level of compensation should be fixed at some historic date to discourage speculation; and that a levy of perhaps 75 per cent on increases in the value of land should be imposed. Because of the assumption in the Uthwatt Report that the state would purchase rural land for urban uses, it was severely attacked and in the event even the Labour government elected in 1945 felt unable to implement the full recommendations of the Committee. Instead, the 1947 Act nationalized the right to develop all land through the creation of a £300m global fund which was to compensate persons losing existing development value. In effect this meant that those refused planning permission by the 145 newly created planning authorities in England and Wales would not be eligible for any compensation. Although this assumption was to be undermined to some extent in the following decades, in general this premise has remained valid since 1947. Compensation may well be payable in certain circumstances, for example where planning permissions are revoked or uses discontinued. But in general planning authorities can refuse planning permissions for a wide range of developments, including advertisements, caravans, changes of use and so on. This is an important consideration. What it means is that planning authorities have been able to employ negative controls on development. Within the context set by the strategic and local plans discussed earlier, planning authorities are normally able to prevent or modify proposals they do not want. It is important here to point out that this does not imply that all developments an authority might wish to occur will be implemented. Many schemes will require the support of the market. Authorities themselves have only limited powers to plan in a positive fashion. Nevertheless, development control, negative though it may be, is important in structuring land-use patterns. Some mention ought to be made of the control system before returning to the issue of betterment and positive planning.

The development control system

Eversley (1973) has argued that one central strand in the post-1947 period has been the consistent determination on the part of the planning profession to impose regulation and control on the physical environment, a tendency that can be traced to Utilitarianism and its dread of inefficiency, chaos and disease. Many working in a planning authority would concur with this. A great deal of the activity of local government planning departments is concerned with regulating, modifying and preventing development. To be fair, there is a widespread political consensus that if planning is about anything then it is certainly about preventing unacceptable development. In practice this may not be as easy as it sounds. Some developments are permitted anyway, and other proposals on agricultural or forestry land or by statutory undertakers do not require permission. Many proposed developments do, however, require permission, and approval involves a formal application to a planning authority to be adjudged by the planning committee or possibly, under delegated authority, by a planning official. Developments can range from small-scale residential infill projects to major edge-of-city retail or industrial schemes, although in the case of the latter the Secretary of State for the Environment may take the final decision. Most applications are approved, but others can be refused because the proposal contradicts existing plans for a wide range of other reasons relating to density, zoning, access, appearance and so on. Applicants have the right of appeal to the Secretary of State for the Environment.

The system has come in for considerable criticism on a number of grounds. These include delay in decision making, an inadequate planning framework within which to consider applications, the poor standard of many planning committees, the anti-development nature of some authorities, the search for perfection where any development would improve some sites and the amorphous nature of some reasons for refusal (Ratcliffe, 1981). There is some truth in these allegations. However, when the system has been subject to close scrutiny, as with the Dobry Report's review of the development control system, published in 1975, there has been a general endorsement of it. Changes in terms of the speed with which applications are considered, wider use of planning briefs to deal with particular sites, and more productive use of techniques uniting planners and developers have been recommended. But the system as a whole has survived in principle. Even with the election of an anti-interventionist Tory administration in 1979 the basic system was retained.

Betterment and positive planning

Having dealt with the question of compensation and control, the discussion must now return to the issue of betterment and positive planning. The postwar history of these is largely a political one. Without entering into the details of the proposals, which are well covered elswhere (Hall *et al.*, 1973; McKay and Cox, 1979; Ratcliffe, 1981), on three separate occasions Labour governments introduced interventionist policies towards land, only for these to be revoked by incoming Conservative administrations. Briefly, in the 1947 Town and Country Planning Act the government sought to recoup, through a development charge, all betterment created as a result of the granting of planning permission. That is, all of the difference between the existing value of the land and its new value would return to the State. A Central Land Board was given powers of compulsory acquisition to ensure a free flow of land, but its activities proved minimal and the 100 per cent charge stultified the market. In the following decade the development charge was abandoned and eventually the market came to dominate all land transactions undertaken either by the public or private sectors.

A second attempt to intervene in the land market was made by the 1964-70 Labour administration. The Land Commission was charged with ensuring that the right land became available at the right price for the implementation of national, regional and local plans, and with making sure that the development value created by the community should be returned to it. In practice it acquired only 1100 hectares and collected only £47m through the imposition of a 40 per cent betterment levy. It was at the time seen as a complex piece of legislation, but compared with the third attempt at land legislation in the postwar era, the Community Land Act of 1975, it was positively simple. On return to power in 1974 the Labour government reintroduced public-sector intervention in land following the abandonment of the Land Commission by the Tory government elected in 1970. The Act was essentially a piece of planning legislation. The financial aspects governing betterment were enacted through separate legislation, the Development Land Tax Act. This latter Act is important because, although the positive planning aspects of the Labour government's approach to the land question were to be abandoned by the Conservative government that came into office in 1979, the betterment aspects contained in Development Land Tax were to survive in modified form until the 1985 Budget.

The Community Land Act, however, was essentially about positive planning. The Act assumed that eventually all major developments would at some stage go through local authorities. Ultimately authorities would identify land required for planning purposes, purchase it at existing-use prices and manage or dispose of it. Hence once the Act was fully in force — which was never in fact to happen — local authorities would have been in a position themselves to implement planning proposals. Resultant increases in value would return to central and local government, and losses on complex and expensive urban developments could be offset against gains on simpler green-field sites. In fact the scheme hardly got into its stride before being repealed. Whatever the merits of the Act it certainly represents one of the most interventionist approaches towards positive planning by the public sector ever attempted in the United Kingdom.

Exactly because of this, however, the Act proved an anathema to the Conservative government that came into power in 1979. Public intervention in terms of positive development was seen by that administration as untenable. Of course the public sector was to undertake some forms of development. It was not solely to be concerned with adjudicating applications from the market. Some public housing for instance, amounting to about 30 000 to 40 000 starts per annum, was still being constructed in the 1980s. Also, new roads, schools and hospitals will involve the public sector to some degree or other. With much tighter regulations governing local authorities' own direct-labour organizations, however, not all, nor even any, construction work will be undertaken by the public sector. In general, indeed it might be anticipated that while Conservative governments remain in power moves towards positive local authority planning will be severely curtailed by the centre.

Finally, in terms of the land market the administration elected in 1979 decided, in the Local Government, Planning and Land Act of 1980, to introduce land registers. These were, eventually, to be produced by all English district authorities and were to indicate the extent of unused publicly owned land. More than 70 000 acres were so identified in the first two years of the scheme, over half of which was suitable for development. Authorities were given clear instructions to dispose of land as quickly and as profitably as possible or to undertake land reclamation schemes, with the private sector if possible. The approach was seen as a relatively cheap way of bringing land onto the market to stimulate the regeneration of the urban cores in particular. It must be remembered, however, that local authorities were strongly encouraged in the post-1945 period to acquire urban land for aspects of consumption, notably housing, for which there may now be less demand or inadequate resources. Land purchased in previous decades may not, by the 1980s, raise anything like the same amount from the market because of centrifugal trends. Therefore many authorities will be making a loss in selling land and the market will in effect be subsidized. In addition it may well prove beyond the ability of the market alone to devise and to implement the kinds of projects needed for the larger cities but which complex land ownership patterns make impossible. There still remains a strong case for some kind of selective public intervention in land and development.

A concluding comment

Three points might usefully be made here. First, the evolution of the planning system has been a political process. Some degree of consensus has governed issues such as development control. But other matters, such as the scope of structure planning and the land question, have proved extremely contentious. Secondly, whatever the merits of the system it has been consistently undermined by an unwillingness on the part of all governments effectively to integrate economic and physical planning on national, regional and local scales. Other countries have managed to achieve this. Britain has not. Thirdly, the system itself analyzed in isolation is nevertheless a complex and sophisticated edifice. It has undoubtedly guided the development of the post-1945 city. This theme forms the focus of the succeeding chapter.

References

Bor, W. (1974) The Town and Country Planning Act 1968, *The Planner*, Vol. 60, No. 5, pp 696-702

Bracken, I. (1982) Problems and issues in structure plan review, *The Planner*, Vol. 68, No. 1, pp 12-15

Bruton, M. (1980) PAG revisited, *Town Planning Review*, Vol. 51, No. 2, April 1980, pp 134-144

Bruton, M. (1984) *Strategic planning and inter-organisational relationships.* In M. Bruton (1984) The Spirit and Purpose of Planning, Hutchinson, London

Centre for Environmental Studies (1975) Aspects of structure planning in Britain, Research Paper C.E.S. R.P.20, C.E.S., London

Chadwick, G. (1971) *A Systems View of Planning*, Pergamon Press, Oxford

Department of the Environment (1974) Structure plans, Circular 98/74, D.O.E.,

London

Department of the Environment (1980) Development control — policy and practice, Circular 22/80, D.O.E., London

Department of the Environment (1984) Memorandum on structure and local plans, Circular 22/84, D.O.E., London

Eversley, D. (1973) *The Planner in Society.* Faber and Faber, London

Fisher, E.A. (1980) PAG revisited, *Town Planning Review*, Vol. 51, No. 2, April 1980, pp 144-151

Goldsmith, M. (1984) *The politics of planning.* In M. Bruton (1984) The Spirit and Purpose of Planning, Hutchinson, London

Hall, P. *et al.* (1973) *The Containment of Urban England*, George Allen and Unwin, London

HMSO (1970) Development plans. A manual on form and content, HMSO, London

Luithlen, L. (1976a) Structure plans and corporate planning, *Built Environment Quarterly*, Vol. 2, No. 3, pp 311-315

Luithlen, L. (1976b) Structure and local plans, *Built Environment Quarterly*, Vol. 2, No. 2, pp 163-166

McLoughlin, J.B. (1969) *Urban and Regional Planning. A systems approach*, Faber and Faber, London

McKay, D.H. and Cox, A.W. (1979) *The Politics of Urban Change*, Croom Helm, London

Raine, J. (1982) *Local planning*, Unit 22, D202, Urban Change and Conflict, Open University Press, Milton Keynes

Ratcliffe, J. (1981) *An Introduction to Town and Country Planning* (2nd edn.) Hutchinson, London

Solesbury, W. (1974) *Policy in Urban Planning. Structure plans, programmes and local plans*, Pergamon Press, Oxford

Further reading

On the planning system, Cullingworth, J.B. (1982) *Town and Country Planning in Britain* (8th edn), George Allen and Unwin, London, provides a comprehensive coverage. Ratcliffe (1981) is better on development aspects. Solesbury (1974) raises pertinent questions about planning and policy making. Land policy before 1976 and the land question are discussed by Ratcliffe, J. (1976) *Land Policy: An Exploration of the Nature of Land in Society*, Hutchinson, London. McKay and Cox (1979) are good on the political aspects of intervention in land.

10   Town planning and the city in the postwar period: the physical dimensions

The previous chapter provided an overview of the town planning system and interventions in land in the post-1945 era. In this chapter the impact of these constraints both on the city regions and within the cities themselves will be explored.

Interventions in the city regions: containment and control

A strong and persistent theme in the development of planning has been the idea that the growth of the city should be curtailed. From Howard through to Barlow and beyond, independent observers and official commentators alike have argued that urban sprawl should be avoided through constraining green cordons. The apparently undesirable nature of the city should in essence be overcome by policies designed to decongest socially mixed groups of city dwellers from the constrained urban cores. Strategies designed to relieve urban problems were thus generally couched in terms of removing individuals from the cities to newer utopian communities divorced by green belts from the pervading influence of urban life. Admittedly in the post-1945 period less emphasis was placed on physical, moral or health hazards prevailing in the cities than had been the case in the late nineteenth century. Nevertheless, as late as 1955 Ruth Glass could reasonably argue that postwar planning re-experienced a distaste of cities so typical of Victorian Utopianism through its policies of urban containment and decentralization. Anti-urbanism certainly persisted in planning ideology well after the flowering of planning legislation in the late 1940s.

In fact urban containment through the operation of green belts predated the Barlow Commission by a number of years. Both Middlesex and the London County Council had bought land for the provision of regional open space in the 1930s, and from 1937 land could be so designated without the authority concerned having to buy it. Interestingly enough, Raymond Unwin, a consultant to the Greater London Regional Planning Committee in the 1920s and 1930s, argued for a flexible barrier that would retreat with urban growth, rather than for a rigid barrier which in the event came to characterize green belts throughout the country. In retrospect Unwin's suggestion would have proved a more sensible approach to the problems of urban sprawl. Certainly it would have eased some of the rigidities which occurred as a result of the policy of tight containment.

The functions of green belts, according to Circular 42/55 published by the Ministry of Housing and Local Government in 1955, were threefold: to check the further growth of large built-up areas; to prevent neighbouring towns from merging; and to preserve the special character of historically or architecturally important towns. Green belts were ideally to be several miles wide and in general it was assumed that developments of a nonagricultural or nonrecreational nature would be refused. These assumptions were reiterated by central governments after 1955. For instance in 1962 the Ministry argued strongly for the perpetuation of green-belt policy. So too did the Secretary of State for the Environment in 1983 (Jenkin, 1983). In this latter case, however, initial draft circulars hinting at a more pragmatic approach towards proposed developments within green belts were rapidly withdrawn after a barrage of criticism from conservation groups. Instead formal departmental advice was later issued, indicating both the permanent nature of sensibly drawn green belts (Department of the Environment, 1984a) and the necessity for finding adequate land for housebuilding within and around the major cities (Department of the Environment 1984b) — a subtle balancing act if ever there was one.

In practice, planning authorities have not proved entirely antagonistic towards developments within green belts. Munton (1983) indicates the scale of development pressure within London's cordon. Some new housing has been allowed within the belt, and a great deal has been permitted on its outer boundary, thus fuelling development pressures generally. Over 10 000 hectares of London's belt were lost to sand and gravel extraction between 1948 and 1976; and much farmland is inadequately managed and aesthetically displeasing. These developments cannot be perceived as surprising. As Herington (1984) establishes, pressures on agricultural land in the 1980s are enormous. The market would prefer to locate a great deal of manufacturing, service, high-tech, warehousing and retailing developments beyond the cities, preferably in green-belt areas close to motorway exchanges. This spatial repatterning obviously affects agricultural land — much of it in green belts — and has stimulated a somewhat acerbic debate between those that are convinced that planning has failed in its prime duty of preventing agricultural land loss (Coleman, 1977) and others that argue that the urban area of England and Wales is extending by only about 1 per cent per decade — a much lower rate than prevailed in the interwar period when minimal planning controls applied (Best, 1976; Best and Anderson, 1984). It might anyway be argued that planning's main objective is to ensure the most efficient use of land for society as a whole, not necessarily its retention in any particular use.

This issue might appear a little divorced from the question of urban containment, but it is pertinent in that it reveals the kinds of pressures imposed on green belts and the emotive nature of the interrelated question of agricultural land loss. In any event, as Figure 6 shows, the extent of designation was formidable by the 1980s. There can be little disagreement with the general observation: in Britain the outward growth of cities has been largely contained by the creation of encircling green belts.

At first glance this policy of containment might appear eminently sensible. It prevents city sprawl, it should allow urban residents greater access to open land, it moderates the social and economic consequences of huge urban agglomerations. But in practice, as Hall et al. (1973) so lucidly established some years ago, the policy imposed severe penalties on many of those living within the urban cores, and it contained implications across the board for the planning of the cities and the regions within which they were located. This complex situation might best be analyzed through two themes: the impact of containment on urbanites; and the consequences of the policy for those relocated beyond the green belts.

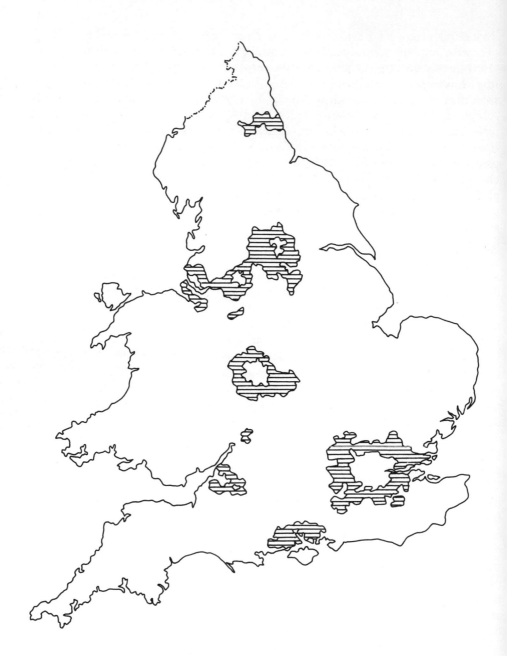

Figure 5   A location of green belts in England (*Source:* adapted from J.V. Herington *The Outer City,* Harper & Row, 1984)

Urban containment and the cities

Once the continued outward growth of cities was artificially curtailed it was inevitable that land prices in the urban cores would rise. Indeed Hall *et al.* (1973) suggest that land more than trebled as a proportion of total housing costs between 1960 and 1970 alone. As has been discussed in Chapter 9, this situation might have been avoided had the public sector been able to acquire land at prices which reflected existing land uses rather than market value. But this was not generally to occur. Instead both public and private sectors had to purchase land at much higher prices than would have been the case had green belts not been imposed. The consequences were predictable. In the private sector, dwellings were constructed at higher densities and lower internal space standards than had frequently prevailed in the interwar era. In the public sector, urban authorities, especially in the decade culminating in 1970, undertook one of the most bizarre and unfortunate housing programmes ever to be implemented in Britain. The whole issue of high-rise, high-density development will be considered in the final section of this chapter. It occurred for a variety of reasons; but clearly expensive land, due in part to urban containment, was one pertinent factor.

Of course from Howard onwards it had always been assumed that urban containment would be part of a much larger strategy intended to relocate inner urban residents to the new planned communities. This had been a central recommendation of the Barlow Commission and of Abercrombie's Greater London Plan (discussed in Chapter 7). As will be examined in the succeeding chapter, however, although a formidable new and expanded town programme was implemented from 1946 onwards, only a relatively small proportion of those leaving the cities went as a result of planned decentralization. The vast majority moved to owner-occupied housing in the commuter towns and villages surrounding all of the major conurbations and, increasingly, to the free-standing towns of the South of England. Many in rented accommodation in the older urban cores may also have wanted to move from the cities. Their opportunities to do so were, however, limited. Because of relatively low incomes many were unable to enter the owner-occupied tenure which dominated housing beyond the cities. There was little private-or public-sector rented accommodation outside the major conurbations. In addition bureaucratic regulations frequently inhibited mobility in the public sector. In essence many poorer urban dwellers were trapped within the urban cores with little opportunity to move to environmentally more attractive — and often economically more active — regions of the country. For them the planning system had clearly failed. They found themselves in poor residential accommodation, increasingly distanced from areas where jobs were more readily obtained. In reality many were consigned to a dependence upon the ability of the cities to extract central government support. By the mid-1980s this appeared a somewhat forelorn position.

The impact of containment within the city regions

As Chapter 8 indicates, many households were to leave the cities in the post-1961 period. Improvements to the general standard of living, higher car ownership rates and intensified communication systems have all allowed for the widespread decentralization of the better-off from the conurbations. Not all counties, especially those around London, have been eager to accommodate new development, preferring instead to operate policies of restraint. But, overall, many smaller country towns and villages expanded in the 1960s and 1970s. Sometimes county planning authorities attempt to direct development to specific localities. Sometimes, however, although certain sensitive zones may be protected from new development, small-scale proposals may be approved virtually anywhere. The costs of such policies in terms of infrastructural provision, the diversification of demand for public and private goods and the loss of good agricultural land may be considerable.

The total costs of commuting have proved formidable too. As the better-off have left the cities there has been an inevitable increase in commuting. Between 1966 and 1971, for instance, the proportion of the nation's economically active people working outside the local authority where they lived rose from 36 per cent to 38 per cent (Gillespie, 1983). In many cities the proportion of the working population living beyond the urban administrative boundary continued to increase after 1971. Between 1951 and 1976, for example, inward commuting into Birmingham and Newcastle increased by more than 100 per cent, and commuting into Glasgow rose by more than 350 per cent. Not surprisingly, during this same period the share of urban jobs taken by inner-city residents fell in all the conurbations — in the case of Liverpool from 88 per cent to 58 per cent (Gudgin et al., 1982).

Inward commuting continued to rise despite the decentralization of some employment from the cities (discussed in greater detail in Chapter 14). This apparent contradiction can be explained because although jobs left cities, or died within them, this was more than counterbalanced by demographic decentralization. In addition, whereas those most likely to decentralize have been better-off office workers, service-based employment has traditionally been the least likely sector to move out. The sector most inclined to decentralize has usually been manufacturing; and its movement to suburban locations and beyond has triggered off reverse commuting patterns for some blue-collar workers — a frequently expensive and difficult task. This apparent mismatch between residential locations beyond the cities sought out by higher socio-economic groups, and the continued preference on the part of service employment for inner urban sites must, however, abate. Service-sector employment is increasingly moving to nonurban locations in search of cheaper rents and rates. This trend opens up the possibility that many of the better-off living in smaller communities beyond the immediate influence of the cities will also find employment locally.

Although the numbers involved in commuting should eventually decline, it nevertheless remains true that in the postwar era travelling over the green belts to jobs in the cities has been a way of life for many. Had the green-belt policy not been implemented a substantial number of these would have lived in expanding suburban areas. They would have faced shorter and cheaper trips to work. Instead many commuters had to leapfrog the green belt in order to acquire owner-occupied housing which was often not very much cheaper than equivalent property within the cities. Many of them commute by rail into London (where this mode is used for more than half of the journeys to work) and others commute by car, train and bus into other cities. However much some commuters enjoy the environmental advantages of living beyond the green belts there can be little doubt that the steady divorcing of people from jobs has proved expensive. The process of commuting imposes individual and collective costs for instance. The cities have lost rate revenue from those that maintain an economic dependence on the urban core but live elsewhere. Most disturbing of all are the costs that society will have to pay as a result of the segregation of the better-off from the less advantaged trapped within the conurbations. And yet, as a final paradox, green belts, while undeniably accentuating social divisions, might ultimately assist in the balanced redevelopment of the urban areas. As demographic and economic decentralization occurs from the major cities, so opportunities will emerge for the sensitive redevelopment of urban areas contained within the belts. There is no reason to imagine why many provincial cities cannot eventually create environments of an altogether more attractive nature than has usually been the case. By so doing both jobs and people may be retained, although admittedly at much lower densities than before. Green belts might thus focus public intervention and private investment into the older urban areas. London will prove an exception. Here decentralization to new developments beyond the green belt is likely to persist. The best that public intervention can hope to achieve here is to try to ensure that some of the less affluent are also given opportunities to move.

Physical planning policies within the cities

In this chapter and the previous one, which is linked with it, discussion has concentrated on urban containment, the land question and the planning system. Emerging out of these considerations it is important finally to outline the kinds of physical planning policies that have been implemented in the cities in the last few decades. It is clear that shortages of land, the peculiarities of the planning system and weak positive planning powers have severely constrained the ability of planners to intervene within the urban cores. Nevertheless their activities have had a considerable impact on the cities and can, according to Hall *et al.* (1973), be perceived as attempting to achieve two objectives: a better environment and improved accessibility.

The search for environment

One of the central themes in planning in the post-1945 era has been the determination to create a better, more ordered and more rational environment. This has been attempted through a variety of policies: land-use zoning, traffic management, conservation and redevelopment. Each of these trends will be considered in turn.

Land-use zoning

Zoning has been widely employed as a mechanism through which land-use patterning might be organized. Under the old development plan system, introduced in 1947 and later to be superseded by structure planning, this typically involved the division of urban areas into acceptable land uses. Industrial, retailing, commercial and residential land was tightly defined, and applications proposing alternative uses were generally refused. Expensive compulsory acquisition procedures were also implemented to remove nonconforming users from inappropriate zones. In retrospect the approach appears hugely irrelevant. For instance, industry scarcely needed to be segregated from residential areas since not much of it was unacceptably intrusive. On the other hand, by delineating specific areas for certain uses travelling within cities had to increase. For some observers, moreover, such as Jane Jacobs (1965) writing from an American perspective, simplistic zoning policies weakened the essential diversity and heterogeneity of cities and vitiated wealth creation and community safety. It might also be argued that zoning epitomized the inability of the planning system to integrate physical images with economic reality — a problem which a number of commentators have identified (Penny, 1984). By relocating companies, by boosting commuting and by removing older industrial premises local planning authorities were imposing costs on urban development. It was true that by concentrating similar users in specific local-ities certain economies of agglomeration may well have been accentuated, but the necessary equations relating costs to benefits were not undertaken nor often even appreciated.

Traffic management

Planners pursued policies of segregation, moreover, not simply in terms of land-use zoning but also within transport planning. Following the Buchanan Report into traffic in towns (HMSO, 1963) (which is discussed in greater detail in Chapter 15), many local authorities implemented policies which tried to divorce pedestrians, and indeed entire residential areas, from heavy traffic. Efforts were also made to isolate heavier inter-urban and intra-urban traffic from local movements by designating certain areas free from intrusion by larger vehicles and by improving the status of trunk roads designed to accommodate more and heavier traffic. Such policies are often expensive to implement and, by throwing additional traffic onto major roads, operate to the obvious detriment of people living close to them. Any parking restrictions imposed on improved trunk routes will, moreover, weaken the economic viability of on-street shops and commercial establishments. It ought nevertheless to be pointed out that segregating through-traffic from residential areas can help to create a much more attractive and safer environment and is often popular locally.

Urban conservation

This concept of environmental amenity has figured prominently in postwar legislation. In a series of acts, of which the most significant was the 1967 Civic Amenities Act, local authorities were given an increasing array of powers designed to improve local environments. Advertising controls were tightened up and powers made available for the preservation of trees and listed buildings. Under this Act, moreover, conservation areas could be declared where particular attention was to be paid to planning applications that might adversely affect the character or appearance of these areas of historic or architectural interest. This important conservationist strand in planning has proved an increasingly contentious issue in recent years. It might be imagined that conservation improves the appearance of cities at relatively little cost while at the same time enhancing local confidence in the long-term future of localities that are improved. There is evidence too that minor environmental improvements, such as tree planting in industrial areas, can help to 'lever' out additional private-sector expenditure. On the other hand, some aspects of amenity planning, such as the declaration of conservation areas, should be viewed somewhat sceptically. Many localities so declared could be protected through the normal powers of development control. Resources allocated to the improvement and maintenance of conservation areas — and these can amount to quite formidable sums — might be better spent elsewhere. Conservation areas tend often to be populated by higher socio-economic groups quite able to protect their environments. Too often conservation area status is sought by residents not because they fear the consequences of new development but because they wish to enhance the value of their property. It is not at all clear that planning should assist them to achieve this end.

Urban redevelopment

Predictably, the most adventurous approach towards environmental planning implemented since 1945 did not, however, occur in areas housing the better-off. Clean-sweep redevelopment proposals initiated especially under the 1947 Town and Country Planning Act totally altered the physical structure of all major cities and many larger towns. The origins and evolution of this process, which dominated planning design between 1950 and the early 1970s, have been explored elsewhere (Ravetz, 1980). Briefly, however, it might be pointing out that a number of contributory factors initially encouraged this approach. Comprehensive development-area legislation contained in the 1947 Act provided authorities with the necessary instrumentation. The possibility of developing a new urban environment ordered by guiding principles governing density, daylighting access, height and so on, issued by the Ministry of Housing and Local Government, proved an irresistible force for authorities intent on dramatic slum clearance and new-build. Although the process was to prove more expensive than many authorities had imagined, although popular support for redevelopment was minimal and although the process proved desperately long-winded, authorities pushed on in an orgy of destruction.

The reasons for the perpetuation of high-rise, high-density development — and most new-build was of this nature — were manifold. The high urban land prices alluded to previously were clearly a factor. The determination on the part of both central and local government to construct large numbers of new units was important. So too was the widely held opinion that system-built high-rise accommodation would prove an answer to the formidable housing waiting lists held by many urban authorities. The widespread diffusion of the ideas of Le Corbusier were also influential in persuading a generation of architects that rational urban design on the grand scale would produce a more efficient and humane city (Mellor, 1982). A glance at, say, the Park Hill/Hyde Park complex in Sheffield might lay low that assumption in the 1980s; but the ideal was powerful in the 1960s nevertheless. Moreover it was an ideal that dovetailed neatly into the business activities of a relatively small group of large construction companies, which through lobbying, and through business and political contacts helped to ensure that by the late 1960s virtually all public housing would be high-rise and only a few companies would be in a position to tender for contracts.

Whatever factors stimulated a predisposition towards high-rise redevelopment, the consequences for those rehoused in such accommodation were singularly unfortunate. Internal layouts and the provision of basic amenities were often reasonable. But the overall environment within and around high-rise accommodation was frequently poor, vandalized and undermaintained. In addition a substantial proportion of new estates were located on the peripheries of cities; thus many were distanced from job opportunities. Not surprisingly, unemployment rates in the 1980s often tend to be higher in suburban public housing projects than in estates closer to, or within, the inner urban core.

Clearly improvements could be made to many high-rise, high-density schemes. Some could be converted into sheltered housing for the elderly or into student accommodation. Some have been moved into other tenures, such as owner-occupation or private rented accommodation. Some might best be maintained, or even owned, by residents through some form of cooperative arrangement. But whatever improvements are undertaken some will prove consistently unpopular and will have to be demolished. For those authorities borrowing funds over 60 years to construct such developments in the first place this must be regarded as little short of disastrous.

The principle of accessibility

A second principle dominating post-1945 urban planning has been that of accessibility. In Chapter 15, greater consideration will be given to questions relating to the nature of urban transport infrastructure and policy. It will suffice to say here that since 1945 planning authorities have often introduced policies designed to balance the competing demands of public transport with the growing requirements of the private vehicle. Cities have certainly differed in the degree to which they have been prepared to construct extensive road systems or to support public transport. But either way improving accessibility has been seen as the norm. Clearly policies such as zoning, suburbanization and city centre redevelopment have segregated and distanced different land uses and therefore boosted mobility. Reference has already been made to zoning and urban decentralization; but city centre redevelopment merits some additional comment.

After 1945, just as a series of factors coincided to encourage the redevelopment of extensive areas of older residential accommodation, a number of emerging impulses ordained the extensive reconstruction of many central business districts. Bombing of city centres during the Second World War was one obvious issue. In addition, with the rapid postwar expansion in service employment it became clear that not enough city centre retail and commercial property existed. Central and local government themselves sought new offices for their expanding functions. Commercial development, moreover, unlike manufacturing, normally did not require central government approval and was thus not subject to the redistributive tendencies apparent within regional policy which undoubtedly encouraged the decentralization of industry, particularly from London and Birmingham. Hence for considerable periods within the postwar era commercial development continued apace in London especially, but in other cities too.

Typically, city centre redevelopment depended on a partnership between local authorities, developers and institutional investors such as pension funds, which from the mid-1950s onwards were allowed to invest in property. Local authorities might be involved in a variety of ways, but their powers of acquisition were especially useful in implementing large schemes with complex landownership patterns. Resultant city centre schemes, too often designed in a brutalistic style and on an inhuman scale, typically included retail developments, cultural or recreational uses and, crucially, lucrative commercial accommodation.

In pursuing policies of city centre redevelopment, authorities were inevitably stimulating mobility within the conurbations. The concentration of shopping and commercial development in the urban cores accentuated centripetal commuting. This approach had some advantages: facilities were equally accessible for those living within cities and public transport could cater easily for inward commuting. There were costs, however. Lower-value land uses such as industry and housing proved unable to compete with the prices potential commercial schemes could offer. Industrial establishments were acquired and many moved to other, less central locations. Some manufacturing firms took the compensation and ceased activities altogether, thus reducing employment opportunities for those in the inner cities. Local authority housing was increasingly constructed away from higher-priced central zones, sometimes on the very peripheries of the cities. In the private rented sector landlords perceived material advantages in selling their accommodation, preferably to developers anticipating planning approval for the conversion of this residential land to commercial use. Because of this, and the more widespread sale of private housing to owner-occupiers, some private tenants were harassed out of their accommodation. Thus, although city centre development schemes were probably inevitable and certainly proved advantageous in some respects, such projects were not without their costs. The irony in the mid-1980s for urban authorities, which had proved so eager to embrace the market twenty years earlier, is that so much new retail and commercial investment is now seeking out locations beyond the urban areas. Not everyone can of course follow this trend.

Planning policies and the cities: a concluding comment

One persistent theme that emerges in any analysis of the impact of planning policies on the cities is the extent to which the system has clearly benefited some groups in society more than others. Frequently, however, the sociopolitical implications of policies have been ignored in the implementation of many, though as the next chapter will show not all, planning programmes. Certainly for more deprived urbanites the system has proved unfortunate. Urban containment raised land prices and helped reduce housing standards. Green belts rarely offered much in the way of easily accessible open land. Zoning and land-use segregation divorced residents from public and private services. Mobility became an increasingly expensive necessity. Things should have been done differently. As a final comment, however, it should be stressed that the system devised in the 1940s was implemented in some respects but not others. In particular, public control of, or even extensive intervention in the urban land market was muted in the extreme. And, as will be examined in the succeeding chapter, the programme of planned decentralization proved marginal to the needs of the urban populace.

References

Best, R. (1976) The changing land use structure of Britain, *Town and Country Planning*, Vol. 44, No. 3, pp 171-176

Best, R. and Anderson, M. (1984) Land use structure and change in Britain, 1971 to 1981, *The Planner*, Vol. 70, No. 11, pp 21-24

Coleman, A. (1977) Land use planning: success or failure? *The Architects Journal*, Vol. 165, No. 3, pp 94-134

Department of the Environment (1984a) Green belts, Circular 14/84, D.O.E., London

Department of the Environment (1984b) Land for housing, Circular 15/84, D.O.E., London

Gillespie, A.E. (1983) *Population and employment decentralisation and the journey to work*. In J.B. Goddard and A.G. Champion (1983) The Urban and Regional Transformation of Britain, Methuen, London

Glass, R. (1955) Anti-urbanism. Excerpt from introduction to urban sociology in Great Britain. A trend report and annotated bibliography, *Current Sociology*, Vol. 4, pp 5-19 (Reprinted in M. Stewart (1972) *The City Problems of Planning*, Penguin Books, Harmondsworth)

Gudgin, G., Moore, B. and Rhodes, J. (1982) Employment problems in the cities and regions of the UK; prospects for the 1980s, *Cambridge Economic Policy Review*, Vol. 8, No. 2, pp 19-64

Hall, P. *et al.* (1973) *The Containment of Urban England*, George Allen and Unwin. London

Herington, J. (1984) *The Outer City*, Harper and Row, London

Jacobs, J. (1965) *The Death and Life of Great American Cities*, Penguin Books, Harmondsworth

HMSO (1963) Traffic in towns (The Buchanan Report), HMSO, London

Jenkin, P. (1983) The Secretary of State's Address, The Royal Town Planning Institute, Summer School

Mellor, R. (1982) *Images of the City: their impact on British urban policy*, Unit 2, D202,

Urban Change and Conflict. Open University Press, Milton Keynes

Munton, R. (1983) *London's Green Belt: containment in practice,* George Allen and Unwin, London

Penny, J.L. (1984) The master planners, *The Planner,* Vol. 70, No. 9, pp 16-18

Ravetz, A. (1980) *Remaking Cities. Contradictions of the recent urban environment,* Croom Helm, London.

Further reading

Hall *et al.* (1973) is excellent on the impact of pre-1966 planning policies. Ravetz (1980) provides a very readable, if somewhat acerbic account of the consequences of planning for the cities. Gudgin *et al.* (1982) is good on economic and employment changes and prospects for the cities in the 1980s.

11   The Social Dimensions of Urban Planning

Foley (1960) has argued that town planning in Britain has reflected three complementary ideologies. It has been concerned with reconciling competing land uses, with
providing a better physical environment, and finally with stimulating improved
community life as part of a broader programme of social reform. In the previous
chapter aspects of the first two of these ideologies were explored. In this chapter the
third ideology, the social strand of planning, is examined.

In practice 'social planning' is not easy to define. As has been mentioned
previously, it may be far from simple effectively to delineate social planning from
economic or physical planning. But, as Lomas (1984) points out, 'social' implies that in
some way market forces are being countered or amended within policy initiatives. Of
course, many aspects of social intervention are examined throughout this book. Inner
urban policy, for example, or subsidizing public transport can be perceived as aspects
of social planning because their operations amend patterns which would occur if the
market was left to its own devices. In this chapter, however, three questions emanating
from the central core of post-1945 social planning will be examined. First, the issue of
community will be considered. The market of itself would not have indulged in the
social experimentation that has characterized both the construction of new communities as a whole, the new towns, and efforts to create locally based communities, the
neighbourhoods. Secondly, the question of public involvement in planning will be
considered. This tendency might well be seen as one of the central planks of post-1968
planning practice, and it clearly reflects a determination on the part of planners to
subject development pressures to wider political debate. And thirdly, emerging out of
reformist and indeed radical strands in planning, have come a variety of criticisms and
interpretations of the philosophy and function of planning that collectively form a
fitting climax to this section of the book.

The search for community

As Thorns (1976) has argued, there are a number of historical strands of thinking in
sociology, in turn articulated within town planning, that can help explain consistent
attempts to define and to create 'community'. These include ecological attempts to
establish territory — hence community — and the assumption that an urban life-style
could be identified as specifically inferior to the 'community' apparent within nonurbanized areas. These assumptions were readily assimilated by town planning in the
post-1945 era and culminated in two programmes designed to establish better worlds:
the new towns and the neighbourhood. In these environments the relationship between

physical structure and dominant social behaviour was perceived as a mutually inter-dependent one. There was, in effect, a strong assumption that physical environments would determine social behaviour. There was a strong retreat from this as early as the 1950s, but within planning thought the question still remains: Can planners create better societies through physical measures? As even a cursory glance at much of post-1950 urban Britain would confirm, they can certainly help create inferior worlds.

The new town programme

The new towns programme has undoubtedly been the most important achievement of the post-1945 town planning movement. In retrospect the development of new towns cannot be seen as anything other than predictable. From Howard and Osborn to the interwar Chamberlain and Marley Committees advocating satellite towns and then to Barlow, Abercrombie and Reith a clear thread of interest in new towns and a strong determination to lobby for them can be identified. Howard had assumed that the private and voluntary sectors would play a significant role in the implementation of new towns. After the 1946 Reith Report, however, and the accompanying New Towns Act, it became apparent that state-appointed new town development corporations were to be the prime agencies. They would acquire land and produce the planning framework within which both public and private enterprise would implement detailed proposals.

Although these arrangements were to differ somewhat from Howard's more ideal-istic vision, they certainly worked. By 1983 there were 32 new towns in the United Kingdom, housing two and a quarter million people. The distribution of new towns is indicated in Figure 7. Many later new towns such as Central Lancashire and Northampton were added onto existing communities, however, and hence the more significant figure here is that about one and a half million people will live in housing built during the office of a development corporation. By 1983, 12 corporations had been dissolved. The rest will largely finish in the 1980s. Nevertheless, by 1983 new town development corporations had presided over the construction of more than 700 000 dwellings, about half of them in the owner-occupied sector (Potter, 1983).

While the debates that will shortly be raised will tend to deal with new towns as a single entity, in practice there were marked variations through time in attitudes towards planned decentralization. In the immediate post-1945 era, 14 Mark I new towns were designated, eight of them around London. As Aldridge (1979) points out, these were created as part of the postwar consensual determination to eradicate ill health — in this case through the movement out of urban dwellers from the more congested parts of cities such as London, Glasgow and Newcastle. After the desig-nation of Corby in 1950, however, with one exception, no new towns were established until Skelmersdale in 1961. This was largely due to the determination of Conservative administrations in the 1950s to replace intensive state intervention, as exemplified through development corporations, by pragmatic agreements between exporting and receiving authorities. These arrangements were given legal status in the 1952 Town

Figure 6   New towns in Great Britain

Development Act.

As Hall *et al.* (1973) have established, there were some genuine differences between expanded towns designated under the 1952 Act and new towns. Many expanded town agreements were for the export of relatively small numbers of people from the major cities. Whereas many of the first generation of new towns assumed ultimate targets of around 80 000, no expanded town agreement anticipated this growth, and about three-quarters of the 60-odd arrangements were for expansions of less than 10 000 people. Moreover, many of the provincial agreements, for instance those signed by Birmingham, Liverpool and Manchester, were for the subsidized export of relatively small groups to peripheral estates rather than to independent new communities. In the case of London on the other hand most agreements were with more distant authorities such as Kings Lynn and Thetford. Indeed in general the impression of the expanded town programme remains that of a somewhat ill-coordinated, *ad hoc* policy initiative which left the cities desperately seeking often tiny overspill agreements with receiving authorities. There were successes, none more so than London's agreement with Swindon (Harloe, 1975). But there were too many ill thought out schemes involving the random scattering of urbanities around a multitude of small authorities.

In an effort to re-establish the direction of the planned overspill programme, another 17 Mark II new towns were designated in the period 1961 to 1970. These were much more varied in location, size, design and function. They were sited throughout the United Kingdom, tended broadly to be somewhat larger than the first generation of new towns and some, as Brook (1982) points out, began to play a role in the implementation of regional strategies. Washington in the North-East, for example, was clearly seen not simply as an overspill community for the local conurbation, but also as a potential growth centre for the area. Similar functions were ascribed to Newtown in Mid Wales and Irvine in Central Scotland. Regional strategies in the South-East, moreover, at various stages assumed that growth would be concentrated in certain growth zones such as around Milton Keynes.

In this book, however, our interests in the new town programme has to be centred on the position of these planned communities within the city regions. In particular, it is quite evident that after about 1973 the cities, for so long more than eager to assist in the movement out of jobs and people, began strongly to attack the operation of the new towns. The consensus of opinion which had led central and local government into the widespread acceptance of a programme of planned decentralization in conjunction with a policy of urban containment rapidly dissolved. It is important to establish why this occurred. There are, perhaps, four factors which ultimately persuaded both central and local governments that a reorientation of policy was necessary: the financial context; economic self-containment; social balance; and the degree to which the new towns assisted those in the more deprived urban areas. Each of these will be considered in a little more detail.

The financial context

It had always been assumed by Howard and his disciples that new towns would eventually make a profit. As land was being acquired at agricultural values and developed for other more profitable uses there must eventually be a profit. Howard had wanted this to return to the community after any private stakeholders had been paid off. In the event, much of the ultimate surplus achieved by the Mark I new towns designated between 1945 and 1950 was appropriated by central government, either directly or through the Commission for the New Towns, which dealt with the management of unused land and some commercial and industrial property developed by defunct development corporations. But, despite the fact that it was the Treasury rather than individual new towns which tended to benefit for much of the post-1945 era, profits nevertheless were substantial. Thomas (1980) estimates that the cumulated surplus, as a percentage of advances for the Mark I new towns around London, was almost 20 per cent some thirty years after designation. It is true that it will take time before development reaps profits in the later new towns. The Mark II new towns have to deal moreover with higher interest charges, and this may push back the date at which profitability is achieved. By 1980 it appeared that the later new towns were incurring a 14 per cent deficit as a percentage of advances ten years after designation. But in time, as more profitable industrial and commercial property comes onto the market and as more investment in community facilities is paid off, a profit can be expected.

The financial problems that began to affect the new towns from the mid-1970s onwards related not so much to the somewhat delayed date for profitability of the later towns but rather to the ease with which central governments were able to use the new towns as scapegoats in times of changing economic performance and financial attitudes. Two issues appear pertinent here. First, as Thomas (1983) indicates, the 1972 Housing Act, which imposed so-called 'fair rents', massively increased central government subsidy to new town housing. Because by definition new towns consisted largely of newer and more expensive housing which could not be cross-subsidized through rents raised from older, profitable dwellings, inevitably central support for housing revenue increased. By 1977 for instance 87 per cent of Milton Keynes's housing revenue came from central government, only 13 per cent from rents. Secondly, figures of the order indicated above made new towns prime targets for radical innovation after 1979 with the election of Conservative administrations determined to sell public assets and reduce state intervention. This issue appears profoundly important in the mid-1980s for in effect it signalled the end of the new town adventure. Between 1979 and 1982 asset sales in the English new towns raised nearly £300m for the Exchequer (Thomas, 1982). Much of this has come from purchases made by the major financial institutions such as the pension funds and insurance companies. Some of it too will be used to complete the work of the development corporations, which in essence will use revenue raised from sales to work themselves out of existence. Although the completion of the towns may be seen as a sensible move there can be little doubt that too many public assets have been sold too cheaply and that substantial returns to the community could have been assured had the new town programme continued. However, as will be established shortly, by the mid-1970s the new town programme was receiving less and less political support.

Economic self-containment Self-containment can imply a number of conditions. It can refer to social, retail and cultural facilities provided by the development corporations, which in fact were reluctant, with the Mark I new towns in particular, to sanction much expenditure on some of these areas. The debate has tended to concentrate on economic self-containment, normally taken to mean the provision of a sufficiently large and heterogeneous employment base to satisfy local demand. It is important to stress that not all new towns have assumed this objective as a primary aim. Some, such as East Kilbride near Glasgow, have always tended to operate as outlying communities housing white-collar commuters (Hebbert, 1980). Equally so, by 1981 the unemployment rates for some new towns was, by historical standards, exceptionally high (Potter, 1982). Milton Keynes, Northampton, Corby, Peterborough and Stevenage all had unemployment rates higher than Greater London as a whole. Only in Scotland did the new towns consistently reveal unemployment rates lower than those prevailing for the region within which they were located. Quite obviously, national and regional unemployment trends have affected new towns as well as everywhere else. For some new communities, in the North-West and North-East in particular, the recession has struck hard and has often involved the closure of branch plants developed by major companies in times of economic expansion up to 1974 but closed in the decade afterwards.

Despite these caveats there has nevertheless been an assumption that some new towns, especially those declared around London in the late 1940s, which were supposed to be economically self-contained, did indeed achieve this status. Hall *et al.* (1973) and Thomas (1973), for example, used a variety of statistical techniques to establish the degree to which these new towns created local jobs. The results tend to indicate an impressive early evolution of the planned communities. Whether it be a gross comparison of people with jobs, or the extent to which residents in new towns commuted back to London, the conclusion is the same: on the whole there were more than enough jobs in the Mark I new towns for local residents. Often unskilled labour had to be imported. Of course, through time, as those working in the new towns moved out and commuted back and as those resident within them sought out jobs elsewhere so economic self-containment would decline. But in principle London's Mark I new communities clearly revealed the potential for planned decentralization of both jobs and people, especially in times of economic expansion within regions best suited to benefit from growth.

Social balance Balance, as much as self-containment, can mean a number of things. It can imply a balance in terms of age structure. This has in fact always been difficult to achieve because many immigrants tend to be under 35. This meant, for example, that the proportion of pensioners in new towns in 1981 was lower than for either the counties within which the new towns were located or their parent conurbations (Potter, 1982).

Usually, however, the debate about social balance has related to social class. From the Reith Committee onwards it was assumed that new towns would not replicate the single, working-class communities typical of some interwar peripheral estates, such as Becontree, developed by the London County Council. They would instead accommodate social groups roughly in proportions approximating to national averages. However, as Aldridge (1979) establishes, according to the 1971 Census there is only one feature common to most new towns: skilled manual workers are over-represented nearly everywhere. In some cases, such as Peterlee, Washington and Corby, there were fully 10 per cent more in Class III than equivalent English figures would suggest.

In other respects, however, generalizations are far from easy. Aldridge (1979) suggests that the new communities can be divided into two broad groups. In the first, the upper social groups are overrepresented. These tend to be the early Mark I new towns around London and also those in Scotland where new town housing has often been perceived as more attractive than has been the case in England, possibly because of the relative shortage there of owner-occupied accommodation. Where there is an over-representation of Classes I and II, this tends to be at the expense of both Class IV and Class V. The second major group of new towns tends to be under-represented in Classes I and II and consists of Mark II new towns largely built in the provinces. These were often constructed to serve existing industry or were added onto working-class communities. In a very real way, however, the extent to which some later new towns were clearly not middle-class communities was frequently ignored in the consistent attack on the new towns led by the Greater London Council. For that authority in particular it became apparent that new towns were not taking a balanced group of residents but instead were creaming off the more talented and those living in less congested parts of London. In many respects this debate was to prove crucial to the ultimate fate of the new town programme.

New towns and old cities Abercrombie's Greater London Plan indicated that fully 60 per cent of the overspill population would come from the old County of London, where the poorest housing conditions were generally to be found. Some twenty years later, in a formidable piece of social science research, Heraud (1966) established the relatively poor performance of London's new towns in housing those from inner London. Although at least three-quarters of those going to the new towns were from London, normally at least half had come from outer London where housing conditions were undeniably better. Indeed the central boroughs sent about 1.6 per thousand households to the new towns compared with a figure three times that for the outer London boroughs. No statistic was to prove more fatal to the new town programme. Most of the new towns designated in England were clearly intended to act as overspill communities taking a balance of social groups from the major cities. Implicitly, therefore, the assumption was that those in greatest housing need would benefit. This was apparently not happening — at least not with the Mark I new towns. It is true that the problem was a purely quantitative one. In the 1946 to 1974 period only about 13 per cent of those leaving London for example had gone to new towns. But this discrepancy could hardly be seen as a fault of the new towns themselves: it was central government that decided the size of the programme. What could be levelled at the new towns was quite simply the charge that they were being far too selective. This issue raises the question of nomination to the new communities.

Although there were considerable variations in time and place, development corporations often operated twin controls over both jobs and housing. Once accepted by a development corporation a firm would be provided with housing for employees. Frequently companies accepted into the new towns were in light manufacturing, and many of the smaller ones tended to negotiate with the development corporations concerned since this increased the possibilities of acquiring the necessary industrial development certificate from the Board of Trade. Development corporations were thus in a strong position to select the companies they preferred. Typically such companies were often located not in inner London but in the outer boroughs where industrial estates had been constructed in the interwar years and to where an increasing proportion of light industry had migrated. Inevitably therefore many of their workers who received houses lived in outer London too. Inevitably too, this link between employment and housing ruled out the infirm, the old, the unemployed and so on, if taken to its logical conclusion.

In an attempt to overcome this discrepancy the New and Expanded Town Scheme was established. This was supposed to provide a mechanism through which those in congested housing in the old cities not working for companies moving to the planned communities would nevertheless be able to find accommodation in the new towns. In fact only a tiny proportion of those housed by the new towns came through this process. For instance, Redditch pointed out in 1970 that only 3.5 per cent came through NETS in the previous year. This occurred partly because employers preferred to recruit labour required for expansion via orthodox mechanisms. This tended to prove quicker and avoid the recruitment of urban labour which might prove more expensive and possibly more unionized than would be the case with employees recruited from elsewhere. Also, fewer inner urban residents had ever heard of the scheme. Moreover, those that were registered often lost interest if wages were lower or housing rents higher. Possibly too, some urban authorities tended to play down a mechanism that would lose them yet more residents.

Whatever the reasons for the failure of NETS it proved a crucial error. Too few of those from the congested cores were moved out. This peculiar nomination system, however, explains the degree of economic self-containment and social structure apparent in so many of the new towns. Initially economic self-containment is assured because only those with jobs are housed. Manual skilled workers might expect to be over represented since they formed the main labour input into light manufacturing industry so popular with many development corporations in the 1950s and 1960s. The unskilled might be expected to be under-represented in the older new towns, in particular because of the link between housing and employment and because so few were recruited from the congested urban cores. And perhaps most significantly, once NETS failed the new towns proved extremely vulnerable to the criticism that they were not assisting those in greatest need.

The demise of the new town programme

By the early 1970s the major cities began to attack the new towns in what was to prove a remarkably successful political campaign. Birmingham as early as 1972 decided to try to concentrate industry within the boundaries of the city; and some four years later the Great London Council announced an end to its sponsorship of town development schemes undertaken through the 1952 Town Development Act (Aldridge, 1979). In that same year too, Stonehouse, designated as an overspill community for Glasgow, was abandoned and resources allocated instead to the renewal of East Glasgow.

In retrospect it can be seen that the new towns were in many respects wide open to attack. Independent commentators such as Jameson (1976) argued that the planned communities were taking too many of the relatively prosperous from the cities and some of their jobs while at the same time swallowing an inordinate proportion of public and private resources that might be allocated to the cities. These criticisms were countered by advocates of planned decentralization (Lock, 1976; Self, 1977). Self argued that the planned communities took less than 10 per cent of jobs and people leaving cities such as London; that decentralization would continue apace, irrespective of the demise of the planned communities; that because about half of the accommodation within new towns was in the public sector a socially balanced decentralization could be implemented; and that although traditionally the planned communities had not taken enough of the socially and economically disadvantaged there had been a marked change in attitudes. Shelter for example had formed agreements with second-generation new towns by which some of those in London with acute housing problems were found accommodation in the new towns (Raynsford, 1977).

Those advocating the continuation of planned decentralization might have won the intellectual battle, but they certainly lost the political war. Crucially the ideology of the time proved consistently antagonistic to any continuation of the programme. In the immediate post-1945 period new towns reflected the dominant mood of collectivism wherein planned communities were but one aspect of intense state intervention. In the 1960s too their expansion mirrored the widely held view that continuous demographic and economic growth would need to be guided to parts of the city regions. From the mid-1970s, however, both major parties began to distance themselves from planned decentralization. For Labour the emerging inner-city dimension was to prove politically more popular than any continuation of new towns — which helps explain the dramatic reductions in planned intakes announced by Peter Shore, the then Secretary of State for the Environment, in 1977. Planned targets were substantially reduced by about 400 000, with Milton Keynes and the Central Lancs New Town severely trimmed, the latter from an originally anticipated 430 000 down to 285 000. When elected to power in 1979, moreover, the incoming Tory administration proved equally unenthusiastic, in this case because reductions in planned decentralization were seen as likely to lead ultimately to reduced state intervention and expenditure. The winding up of development corporations was brought forward and public assets were to be sold. In Scotland the five development corporations are likely to last into the 1990s, but elsewhere they will disappear before the end of the 1980s.

Does the end of planned decentralization really matter? Is not the vision generated by Howard and continued by Barlow, Abercrombie and a whole plethora of reports and plans outdated? Surely not. Without some form of planned decentralization how will so many of those trapped in public housing in the cities manage to move to areas with better job opportunities? And if decentralization is to continue without guidance and coordination, how will the stretched public purse manage to provide the necessary social infrastructure for the multitude of small-scale private-sector developments sprouting up throughout the country and particularly in the south of England? It is intriguing in 1984 to see proposals emerging for the construction of privately implemented, socially mixed new communities in the South-East (Shostak and Lock, 1984). Perhaps Ebenezer lives after all.

The neighbourhood

The development of local neighbourhoods has closely paralleled the new town programme. Indeed in the early evolution of the new town programme after 1945 the concept of the local neighbourhood was to loom large. Most of the Mark I new towns designated before 1950 adopted a design based on the local neighbourhood. This is perhaps predictable for, as Blowers (1973) established, from Howard onwards many of those advocating the planned decentralization of urban dwellers to garden cities assumed that the new communities would consist of discrete residential areas. Howard called these wards. Later developments of the concept, particularly those schemes undertaken by Stein and Perry in America, were, however, termed neighbourhoods, and this was the term adopted by the Dudley Report of 1944 which was to give official endorsement to the idea.

Forty years on it is easy to see why that Report, and indeed many planners and architects working in the cities and new communities, should want to adopt the design principles intrinsic to the neighbourhood idea. Anything seemed better than the unaesthetic sprawl so typical of the interwar period. Neighbourhoods, moreover, would help perpetuate the sort of community spirit reflective of the consensus in society that so clearly typified Britain during and immediately after the Second World War. It seemed inconceivable that the nation would recreate divisive class interests during peacetime reconstruction. The neighbourhood was thus but one aspect of the overall determination to create a better society. It would therefore, as the Dudley Report made clear, pursue both social and physical objectives.

The social objectives of neighbourhoods It is interesting to see that in the postwar development of the neighbourhood idea social objectives were rapidly to be abandoned. Two social goals were originally assumed for neighbourhoods: instilling a sense of community, and social integration. In the case of the former it was anticipated that neighbourhoods would help to create local communities. In the mid-1980s it seems surprising that it was ever considered that the attainment of such a goal was within the brief of planning. But nevertheless, through adopting the kind of physical proposals that will be developed below, it was hoped that social contacts would be engendered and a sense of belonging, of place, would emerge. These goals appear dubious. Communities may not exist in the spatial sense, or prove so complex to unravel that attempts to create them artificially inevitably fail. It is not even clear that many want to live in a locality-based community or wish to participate in local affairs. Equally so, attempts to encourage social integration appear fraught with problems. Presumably the major objective here is to foster social mix — a theme which, as Sarkissian (1976) establishes, has strong roots in planning ideology. As a policy it has been pursued for a variety of reasons. It has been perceived as useful in encouraging aesthetic diversity, cross-cultural fertilization, equality of opportunity, social cohesion and social stability. Neighbourhoods undoubtedly offered ideal opportunities for exploring these ideals. In fact in some of the early new towns constructed along neighbourhood principles efforts were made to mix social classes at the local street level by building public housing alongside private dwellings. As Heraud (1968) discovered, such efforts proved unsatisfactory and ultimately particular neighbourhoods became in effect either workingclass or middle-class residential localities. It is not within the ability of planning to create mixed class communities. Such intervention is unacceptably patronizing and doomed to failure.

This was perceived by the middle of the 1950s, and there was a marked reaction against the neighbourhood idea as a whole. Some of the second generation of new towns, such as Cumbernauld designated in 1955, totally abandoned the idea and adopted designs based on higher-density housing constructed within walking distance of a strong central area. Perhaps this reaction was too precipitous. There are undoubtedly certain advantages to be gleaned from the physical design of neighbourhoods.

The physical design of neighbourhoods The pure neighbourhoods designed according to principles laid down by the Dudley Report tended to adopt the following planning principles, some of which are outlined in Figure 7. They were to consist of between 5000 and 10 000 people, the former proving adequate for one primary school, the latter for two. Each neighbourhood was supposed to be self-contained in terms of local shops, churches, libraries, pubs, clinics and so on, although it soon became apparent that neighbourhoods would not necessarily contain all such facilities. A variety of housing styles and densities was to be used within each neighbourhood, and there was to be ample provision of open space within each area. In addition, through-traffic was to be kept on peripheral primary routes in order to keep the residential core free from vehicular movement. Often a system of modal split was to be introduced in that separate pedestrian routes, and sometimes cycle routes, were to be built. Such an approach clearly made neighbourhoods much safer than other forms of residential development. In many cases too neighbourhoods adopted Radburn layouts. Typically this involved the construction of cul-de-sacs, the provision of rear parking and the reversal of residential layouts, resulting in dwellings looking inwards onto a communal green or open area. Lack of privacy and poor parking facilities often made such designs unpopular, however.

Other aspects of the physical design of neighbourhoods proved unsatisfactory too. Narrow streets within neighbourhoods made the introduction of public transport a problem. Parking was often inadequate. The actual design of dwellings within many early neighbourhoods appears uninspired. And most crucially, many decentralized

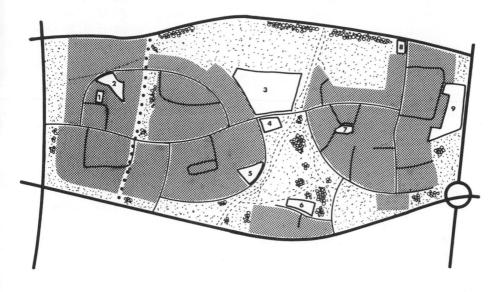

Figure 7 The neighbourhood ideal (*Source:* based on P. Merlin *New Towns*, Methuen and Co., 1971)

local services in both the public and private sectors have been severely affected by the tendency for all forms of service provision to become larger. Larger shops, schools, clinics, libraries and so on have undermined the principle of decentralized provision. Finally, too, it appears unfortunate that employment was not decentralized to the neighbourhoods. After 1945 little of it was intrusive and its local development would have reduced commuting.

Despite these undoubted shortcomings, the neighbourhood principle should not totally be dismissed. Compared with so much interwar housing or postwar high-rise developments the approach appears positively successful. Ideas, moreover, such as modal split and the removal of heavier traffic from residential areas have been widely adopted throughout urban Britain. The feeling remains that the largely valid criticism of unrealistic social objectives has undermined the more useful physical aspects of neighbourhoods. Perhaps too, the degree of physical intervention apparent in neighbourhoods seems, by the mid-1980s, to fit the age of collectivism so apparent in post-1945 Britain. We live now in a different world.

Public participation

The major boost to public participation in planning came with the publication of the Skeffington Report in 1969 (HMSO, 1969). In general the Report concluded that public involvement in planning issues was intrinsically desirable. It could help to improve the relationship between local government and the community and the making and taking of decisions. In addition it could improve the information base required by planning authorities and ward councillors. Also, wider public participation might help in educating the public with regard to environmental issues and might conceivably assist in the implementation of projects, a few of which could be undertaken in cooperation with local residents. Surveys for instance, or environmental improvements could realistically be pursued with direct local help. It was not going to be easy to achieve all of these potential advantages. However, if authorities appointed community development officers, used the media to full effect, informed residents of impending plans and told participants of the outcome of their representations, then more fruitful relationship between the community and its planning authority should emerge.

Such prognostications might appear naive in the 1980s, for reasons that will be elaborated upon below, but there is no doubt that the Report fitted the mood of the age. A whole host of official reports and independent commentators strongly promoted the concept of greater public involvement in planning issues and in decision making. For instance, some of the urban experiments undertaken in the late 1960s and early 1970s argued strongly for greater public participation. The Community Development Projects were based on the assumption that the community should be heavily involved in local issues and local self-help. One strand of thinking apparent within some of the C.D.P.'s, and explicitly developed in the Area Management Trials (Lawless, 1979), was the concept of area management. Here the improvement of services and the involvement of the public are assumed to be bettered by the creation of locally based teams dealing on the spot with many client-based services while at the same time incorporating local residents into the formal decision-making machinery within which the area teams had to operate.

This trend towards community involvement was given official recognition by The Royal Town Planning Institute in the mid-1970s (The Royal Town Planning Institute, 1976). Here the Institute argued for a much more integrative approach to planning which would involve the formulation of comprehensive local strategies and programmes based upon a variety of economic, social and political constraints, one of which would be explicit community participation. This view of the role of planning inevitably called into question the function of planners themselves and indeed of plans. Would formal plans be abandoned and would planners work as partners with the public in the teasing out of consensual community strategies? To some planners, working more in America than in Britain, there was no doubt that formal planning machineries were quite inadequate to deal with the problems of economic deprivation and political powerlessness encountered by so many communities in the cities. Advocacy planners argued instead that the true role of planners should be to counter the activities of the market by working within more deprived areas to foster political awareness and to fight for public support. Such a strategy would clearly move planners away from their traditional roles within public authorities and might indeed involve them in tactics of direct confrontation with elected local politicians and with appointed officials (Goodman, 1972).

Few planners in the event were to take this path. But planning certainly presided over a massive increase in public involvement. Formal procedures were written into plan-making activities to encourage the involvement of residents in the preparation and evaluation of structure and local plans. In addition, planning and environmental issues have stimulated a tremendous public response from individuals and from pressure groups. For instance, major road proposals for the widening of the Archway Road in London or for the building of the M40 have elicited considerable representation at public inquiries. So too have proposals for nuclear installations, major incursions into green belts, the declarations of Areas of Outstanding Natural Beauty and so on. This is not to imply that public sentiment over planning and environmental issues is centred solely on formal planning applications. Permanent pressure groups, often with an interest in environmental issues, play an increasing role in lobbying for, say, additional legislative protection for sensitive areas. Unfortunately, despite this growth of interest in planning issues, it is clear that the somewhat simplistic assumptions held by Skeffington and others simply underestimated the problems created by public participation and the inherent contradictions in its operation. Some attempt should be made to develop these issues.

Technical and methodological constraints

Some problems might be seen as of a technical nature. Structure plans for example have been widely evaluated as too broad and generalized, perhaps giving the impression of control over issues that an authority may be unable to influence in reality (Whitehead, 1976). Local plans on the other hand often attract far more comment; but frequently issues raised at public meetings relate to activities beyond the control of the planning authority. Moreover, the actual techniques involved in gleaning public response appear weak at times. Questionnaires often seem complex, exhibitions dull, and entire exercises are undertaken as one-offs rather than as part of a more permanent relationship.

There are, moreover, real doubts as to whether all authorities have been exactly enthusiastic about the entire concept of public involvement. As Arnstein (1971) has pointed out, there are many variations in public involvement. Whereas some forms of citizen participation can involve a partnership between officialdom and residents, in practice exercises in public involvement often consists of an authority merely informing residents of what is going to happen anyway. Some empirical case studies tend to support this assertion. Dennis (1970) for example, in examining housing redevelopment policies in the North-East in the late 1960s, suggested that attempts by the public to gain some say in rehousing schemes were regarded by officials as an intrusion into effective policy making. In an interesting development of this theme Davies (1972) argued that it was not so much that planners prevented public involvement but rather that they tried to imbue planning policies with an aura of technicality and professionalism which effectively prevented meaningful participation. Planning was apparently too difficult for most people to understand.

It is important, however, to point out that the case studies mentioned above are dated. It might be hard in the mid-1980s to identify authorities that actively discourage participation or to argue that planning hides behind the sort of technical veneer that so clearly characterized it in the late 1960s and early 1970s. Many planners and planning authorities would nevertheless argue that the kind of optimistic appraisal of public participation made by Skeffington is simply too easy. Several issues have clearly worried practitioners in this context. Most people do not make public representations about planning proposals. Should their views be taken into account and if so how? Sometimes technical expertise is required and it may effectively decide certain decisions (Garner, 1979). Participation certainly delays decision making at a time when authorities are being placed under increasing pressure to make decisions quickly, and in particular to speed up economically based proposals, which are often unpopular. Here of course it may be easy for an authority to accept the widespread objections that almost inevitably accompany such applications. But if the majority want increased standards of living and if growth requires physical development, how are authorities to get around the dilemma that everyone wants enhanced wealth-making infrastructures, but not in their own back garden? Proposals for new economic developments, moreover, raise the intriguing question of who should be asked to comment on applications received. Local residents certainly, but what about those likely to benefit from new jobs?

Perhaps the basic drawback which many authorities have identified in the area of public involvement is the issue of the representativeness of community response. Frequently authorities may be faced with vociferous interest groups. In this case local planning authorities have to question the true validity of the public response. Some Conservative authorities for instance have argued that radical groups, perhaps demanding improvements in housing standards, do not represent overall community views. They are not elected and ward councillors, who are, reflect popular opinion far better than self-appointed malcontents. At times there is undoubtedly some truth in this. Local areas may well be made politically active because of a relatively small number of 'radical passers-by' whose ideas may not at all coincide with those held by many local residents. Authorities anyway have to bear in mind that the most active of areas may not be the most deprived. Quiescence might hide desperation, not reflect satisfaction.

Left-wing authorities ought to prove equally sceptical about some aspects of public involvement. The idea, for example, that a community consensus would emerge from participation exercises should be seen by all radical councils as naive in the extreme. Planning issues hinge on the allocation of resources, and this essentially political action will highlight conflict not consensus. In situations of conflict it so often tends to be the case that those who are better off, better educated and better able to use the political system will be at a marked advantage compared with more deprived groups. One classic example of this is contained within Ferris's (1972) work in North London. The lessons emerging from this case study are that public participation is a far more complex and divisive concept than was ever hinted at by Skeffington.

Another damaging criticism of the entire philosophy of public involvement developed by Skeffington and followed by so many in the early 1970s was the inability of the approach to place public participation within the context of decision making in local government. For example, if public participation was to be fostered, how were its results to fit into the committee structure of local government? Were the results of public participation exercises automatically to be incorporated into decision-making machineries and, if so, how important were these inevitably unreliable findings to be? How, moreover, were local ward councillors to fit into this structure? Were their opinions to hold greater sway than those of the participants?

One final issue that needs to be mentioned here is the question of the theoretical underpinning appropriate for the development of participation. Presumably Skeffington assumed a pluralist local political environment. In effect, different groups were supposed to emerge at different times with different political bases and varying electoral support. Power would thus change quite frequently within an open, flexible and sensitive political structure. As Dunleavy (1982) indicates, this is generally not applicable to local government in the United Kingdom. Voting tends to follow national patterns, with local issues usually proving of little interest to the electorate. Many councils never change power at all. Many councillors have little power and interest; and groups proving influential often consist of the better-off and more articulate.

Other models of urban political power may hold greater relevance to the British scene. In some authorities oligarchies appear to hold power. Real decisions may lie with a small number of councillors in key committees; and outside influences may prove of little importance compared with the attitudes and values of this élite. In Conservative authorities such an élite may retain close relationships with local commercial and business groups and is likely to implement proposals of benefit to this sector of society. Many of the larger cities, on the other hand, are normally Labour controlled, and here frequently the major decisions will be made through Policy and Resources Committees, on which a relatively small number of councillors will sit. Many Labour members and members of minority parties will have limited if any influence. Under such circumstances public participation is likely to be closely controlled, with many issues not subject to public appraisal and others carefully manipulated. Perhaps in the final analysis that is what should happen. Those that have been elected should have the responsibility for making final judgement. That is not to imply secrecy. The generally secretive circumstances prevailing within both local and central government should be changed. Information should be far more widely available than is generally the case. But decisions cannot be subcontracted out to unrepresentative interest groups.

Town planning: a political comment

For an activity that has profound implications for so many, it is surprising to find relatively little debate within professional planning circles about the political objectives appropriate to planning. Reade (1982a,b) has suggested a number of reasons for this. The ideals of planning have changed considerably since 1945. In general there has been a movement within planning away from coherent social and political objectives of reform towards professionalized bureaucratic positions that have not been over-concerned with planning's ultimate role. Indeed, as a distinctly antiplanning sentiment has come to the fore within Conservative political circles, and more generally within society as a whole, it is clear that planning has tended to adopt an ever more pragmatic approach. The older dispensations which argued that planning was a device through which inequality and want might be ameliorated have faded. Instead planning has adopted a somewhat ambiguous package of policies which collectively appear to indicate that it does little to interfere with the market, has minimal redistributive effects, but is necessary in any society to ensure an efficient use of land. The political nature of planning is accepted in the sense that planning issues must ultimately be decided by politicians. But wider political questions relating, say, to the extent to which planning policies and proposals create clear gainers and losers are played down or frankly ignored, even within the planning profession itself. Indeed as Reade (1982b) points out, there has been relatively little monitoring of planning policies, partly because evaluations of public policy clearly depend upon assessing outcomes in relation to objectives. But so often in planning it has proved difficult if not impossible to establish the nature of objectives in the first place. If planning itself has proved slow to consider its impact, this has not always been true of independent observers (Kirk, 1980; Dear and Scott, 1981). Synthesizing these and similar approaches, it appears as if at least four independent interpretations of planning can be developed: pluralist, institutional, reformist and radical. A brief mention should be made of each.

Pluralist approaches, which have been mentioned above, argue that planning reflects the contrasting views of local and national political interest groups. At times planning adopts more radical stances because of the influence of left-wing reformist groups perceiving planning as a mechanism for mild social change. On other occasions conservative influences operating locally and nationally, and within the Planning Institute, dominate and more pragmatic, land-use orientated objectives return to the fore. There are problems with this interpretation, however. Some pressure groups are far more influential than others. Major corporate organizations for instance might prove consistently more effective than community-based organizations. Ultimately the function of planning surely largely reflects the prevailing political ideology of the party in power. Local or national pressure groups frequently retain little independent power or influence.

Institutional views argue that planning decisions emerge out of powerful local and central bureaucracies, which operate with a considerable degree of freedom. Clearly in some authorities the power of the chief planner can indeed prove formidable in structuring the land-use system of the area. On the other hand, detailed explorations of how planning operates within authorities will increasingly run into two obvious problems. First, planning has little if any power over many aspects of the urban system, most notably over aspects of production that are still largely undertaken by the market in isolation from, and at times in opposition to, the desires of local authorities. And secondly, the independence of local authorities has been severely curtailed by central government intervention.

The third, reformist, perspective of planning is perhaps that most reflective of the views of planners themselves. The inequalities of the economic system are seen as real, and planning is perceived as a mechanism that might potentially be able to alleviate these. Policies such as a fairer distribution of public services, better public transport, or higher standards of public housing might help redistribute wealth towards the less well-off. The problems with this approach are readily apparent, however. The ability of planners to implement policies of reform independently might be limited if not non-existent. There is also a discrepancy in appproach, according to more radical observers, in that reformist positions in effect argue for the perpetuation of an economic system which itself creates economic inequalities in the first place.

Radical critiques of planning would avoid this contradiction. In this perspective, planning is seen as directly supporting the structuring of the economic system. Planning has ensured that the most profitable sites have been made available for industrial, commercial and retail markets. Manufacturing and retail developments have been allowed to move to their perceived optimal locations beyond the cities, frequently assisted by public subsidy and without any consideration for the fates of those left behind in the cities. Commercial development similarly has been allowed to expand at high densities and in preferred locations, despite clear indications that the cities contain a surplus of office accommodation and a shortage of cheaper housing and open space. In addition, planning has ensured the reproduction of an educated labour force adequately provided with housing and transport. Capital is thus able to withdraw from the provision of these less profitable activities and at the same time offer lower wages than would otherwise prevail because of a higher social wage. Planning has thus done little more than ensure the perpetuation of the prevailing economic systems. The latter will be changed, not through well-meaning planning policies but through the development of social movements emerging as a result of conflicts generated by contractions in aspects of collective consumption such as the provision of public transport, housing or educational investment.

Many criticisms can be made of a radical perspective on planning. There is little empirical evidence in Britain for the emergence of urban social movements, for instance. The more widespread provision of public facilities can be perceived, moreover, as a distinct improvement for many of the deprived, not merely as a technique to ensure the continued reproduction of an urban labour force. Control of the market is politically unacceptable; and it raises the question of what would happen to investment finance if the United Kingdom were ever unilaterally to impose sweeping regulation. Market efficiency may be essential if profits are to be achieved and hence taxation raised to fund public expenditure.

But whatever the shortcomings of the radical approach, it is true to say that, more than any other interpretation, it has directly addressed the question of the role of planning. Whether one accepts its prognosis or not, it is nevertheless vital that the overall function of planning should be examined. It is clear from material contained within Part Two of this book that planning has helped achieve some unexpected results since 1945. The better-off have tended to benefit more than the deprived; the cities have not been assisted as much as they should have been; the relationship between planning and the market has remained uncertain. It must of course be accepted that planning has a limited ability to introduce change. Ultimately it must reflect the ideology and policies of central governments and the concomitant controls, or freedoms, that are placed upon it. But nevertheless it has had a long tradition of reform and of social inquiry. The planning movement should therefore be more certain of its function in this area. Is it just about easing the way for the market or is it about trying to help create a society based on premises other than purely that of profit?

References

Aldridge, M. (1979) *The British New Towns. A programme without a policy*, Routledge and Kegan Paul, London

Arnstein, S.R. (1971) A ladder of citizen participation in the USA, *The Planner*, Vol. 57, No. 4, pp 176-182

Blowers, A. (1973) *Planning residential areas*, Unit 29, DT201, Urban Development, Open University Press, Milton Keynes

Brook, C. (1982). *Regional planning*, Unit 21, D202, Urban Change and Conflict, Open University Press, Milton Keynes

Davies, J.G. (1972) *The Evangelistic Bureaucrat*, Tavistock Publications, London

Dear, M. and Scott, A.J. (eds) (1981) *Urbanisation and Urban Planning in Capitalist Society*, Methuen, London

Dennis, N. (1970) *People and Planning*, Faber and Faber, London

Dunleavy, P. (1982) *Political issues and urban policy-making*, Unit 18, D202, Urban Change and Conflict. Open University Press, Milton Keynes

Ferris, J. (1972) Participation in urban planning. The Barnsbury Case. Occasional Papers on Social Administration, No. 48. Bell, London

Foley, D.L. (1960) *British town planning: one ideology or three*. Reprinted in A. Faludi (1973) A Reader in Planning Theory, Pergamon, Oxford

Garner, J.F. (1979) Skeffington revisited, *Town Planning Review*, Vol. 50, No. 4, pp 412-420

Goodman, R. (1972) *After the Planners*, Penguin Books, Harmondsworth

Hall, P. *et al.* (1973) *The Containment of Urban England*, George Allen and Unwin, London

Harloe, M. (1975) *Swindon. A town in transition*, Heinemann, London

Hebbert, M. (1980) The British new towns, *Town Planning Review*, Vol. 51, No. 4, pp 414-420

Heraud, B.J. (1966) The new towns and London's housing problem, *Urban Studies*, Vol. 3, No. 1, pp 8-21

Heraud, B.J. (1968) Social class and the new towns, *Urban Studies*, Vol. 5, No. 1, pp 33-58

HMSO (1969) Report of the Committee on Public Participation in Planning: people and planning (the Skeffington Report), HMSO, London

Jameson, C. (1976) The double case against Milton Keynes, *Built Environment*, Vol. 2, No. 3, pp 251-253

Kirk, G. (1980) *Urban Planning in a Capitalist Society*, Croom Helm, London

Lawless, P. (1979). *Urban Deprivation and Government Initiative*, Faber and Faber, London

Lock, D. (1976). Planned dispersal and the decline of London. *The Planner*, Vol. 62, pp 201-204

Lomas, G.M. (1984). *Social planning*. In M.J. Bruton (1984) The Spirit and Purpose of Planning, Hutchinson, London

Potter, S. (1982). Britain's new towns: what the Census shows, *Town and Country Planning*, Vol. 51, No. 10, pp 281-288

Potter, S. (1983). The condition of Britain's new towns, *Town and Country Planning*, Vol. 52, No. 11, pp 294-299

Raynsford, N. (1977) New towns and London's housing problem, *Housing Review*, Vol. 26, No. 2, pp 35-37

Reade, E. (1982a). *The British planning system*, Unit 19, D202, Urban Change and Conflict, Open University Press, Milton Keynes.

Reade, E. (1982b). *The effects of town and country planning in Britain*, Unit 23, D202, Urban Change and Conflict, Open University Press, Milton Keynes

Sarkissian, W. (1976). The idea of social mix in town planning. An historical review, *Urban Studies*, Vol. 13, No. 3, pp 231-246

Self, P. (1977). This time listen, *Town and Country Planning*, Vol. 44, No. 9, pp 244-247

Shostak, L. and Lock, D. (1984). The need for new settlements in the South East, *The Planner*, Vol. 70, No. 11, pp 9-13

The Royal Town Planning Institute (1976). Planning and the future, R.T.P.I., London

Thomas, R. (1973). *The new town idea*. Unit 26, DT201, Urban Development, Open University Press, Milton Keynes

Thomas, R. (1980). Financial performance of the development corporations, *Town and Country Planning*, Vol. 49, No. 10, pp 341-344

Thomas, R. (1983). Caught in the tender trap, *Town and Country Planning*, Vol. 52, No. 11, pp 288-289

Thomas, W. (1982). Completing the new towns, *Town and Country Planning*, Vol. 51, No. 10, pp 265-266

Thorns, D.C. (1976). *The Quest for Community*, George Allen and Unwin, London

Whitehead, P.T. (1976). Public participation in structure planning, *Town Planning Review*, Vol. 47, No. 4, pp 374-383

Further reading

A lot of descriptive material is available on new towns; see, for example, Osborn, F.J. and Whittick, A. (1969) *The New Towns*, Leonard Hill, London. There is a useful issue of *Built Environment* (Vol. 9, No. 3, 1983) which examines the evolution of some new towns. But Aldridge (1979) is far the best text. Blowers (1973) is excellent on neighbourhoods. Cullingworth, J.B. (1982) *Town and Country Planning in Britain* (8th edn), Allen and Unwin, London, gives a reasonable overview of public participation. Simmie, J.M. (1974) *Citizens in Conflict*, Hutchinson, London, provides a more theoretical overview. Broader critiques of planning are well developed by Kirk (1980) and Reade (1982a,b).

Part Three The dynamics of the contemporary British city: Some issues

In this chapter, housing policies are taken to mean the involvement of the state or central government, in housing, though such policy is in part implemented by local authority housing departments. The focus is on changing housing policies since 1919; though the emphasis is on recent policy changes. The current housing scene and some of the issues and debates surrounding housing policy in the 1980s are also examined. Finally, attention is drawn to the imminence of a new crisis in housing, and some possible policy alternatives. In an introductory text whose main purpose is to examine the theme of change and its impact on our cities, it is not possible to provide even a cursory glance at the various components that make up the housing system. The section on further reading at the end of the chapter points the reader to some of the more recent of a wide and rapidly growing literature on housing.

It is appropriate here to provide a few general remarks on some of the factors that have influenced housing policy in Britain, as a preface to the brief historical overview provided below. As we have noted in some of the earlier chapters, housing, or rather the shortage of it, was a problem of growing political importance as the nineteenth century advanced. Since 1919, housing has been an issue at the centre of the political stage; and state intervention in, and control of, housing has grown steadily throughout the last seventy years. The ideologies of the two major political parties have clearly influenced housing policies, though the latter have been surprisingly 'reactive' to previous events and current issues, as we shall see. Arguably, though, the differences between the Labour and Conservative parties, in government, have not been as wide as some commentators suggest. The second major factor which has drastically affected housing policy and provision has been the uneven and often faltering performance of our broader national economy. Economic crises have time and again been met by public-sector expenditure cuts; and the bulk of these have fallen on housing expenditure. Thus the medium-term switches in housing strategy which have accompanied ideological changes of government have been further punctuated by rapid shifts and reversals in policy and housing investment brought about by the changing fortunes of our economy. These factors have prevented the evolution of a long-term national housing policy and, as suggested in the final section of this chapter, have led to a movement away from debate of some of the more fundamental questions involving housing provision in Britain.

The development of housing policy

The interwar period

The year 1919 is usually seen as the starting point for discussions of state involvement in the provision of housing in Britain, though, as discussed in Chapter 3, the 1890 Act allowed for the building of dwellings by local authorities, and some 24 000 dwellings had been built by local authorities by 1914 (Merrett, 1979, p. 26). Of these nearly 10 000 were built by the London County Council, though in total they constituted less than 5 per cent of the national housing stock in 1914. In July 1919 the Housing and Town Planning Act was passed, piloted through Parliament by the then Minister of Health, Christopher Addison. It was thus known as the 'Addison' Act. The Act appeared to be the fulfilment of the government's promise to provide 'homes fit for heroes'. Local authorities would have to provide dwellings for rent, not merely to replace slums but also to cover 'general needs' for housing of the local population; the Exchequer, or central government, would provide a subsidy which would allow local authorities to build dwellings to a high standard; unlike nineteenth-century legislation, the Act was 'mandatory' in nature, not 'enabling'. After the failure and disappointments of housing reform in the Victorian era, government had at last accepted its role as the provider of decent housing for the working classes — or had it?

The reality behind the passing of the 'Addison' Act suggested rather different motives. The rate of new housing construction for private renting was already falling before the advent of the First World War, and there were growing calls for the introduction of state-owned, subsidized housing. The war itself, and the diversion of resources away from housebuilding, led to a 'log-jam' of households requiring new housing, amounting to perhaps 700 000 by 1919 (Merrett, 1979, p. 31). Construction costs increased rapidly between 1900 and 1919, whereas real wages for the working classes had stagnated or fallen both before and during the war; thus landlords were clearly unlikely to buy new dwellings when the rents they would need to charge would be far above what most working-class households could afford. Even the rents for the new 'Addison' houses proved too high for poorer households. A further, very potent factor strongly influenced central government in finally providing subsidized housing — the rise of the political power of the working classes. The First World War had a catalytic effect on the politicization of the working classes. Trade union membership more than doubled between 1913 and 1919; and in 1915, in response to an attempt by private landlords to raise rents and take advantage of a local housing shortage in Glasgow, a rent strike took place. Thousands of workers also threatened strike action, and the government, in a state of panic, passed an act to control rents — the beginnings of rent controls in the private rented sector.

In 1917 the Local Government Board set up a Committee under the chairmanship of Sir John Tudor Walters to examine the standards of design and construction of new dwellings for the working classes to be built after the war. This Committee was influenced by the ideas of some of the disciples of Ebenezer Howard, such as Unwin and Parker, in terms of both housing densities and design, and it produced a report in 1918 that laid the foundations for housing standards in Britain for the next 40 years. The report recommended low housing densities of 12 to 15 houses per acre, generous internal space provisions, and the adoption of a two-storey 'cottage' style of housing. This report, along with the other factors listed above, meant the death-knell for the further large-scale construction of new housing for the private rented sector. The 1919 Act represented less a triumph for the forces of housing reform or philanthropy than a government bowing to the political realities of the day: new housing would have to be provided on a large scale by direct state subsidy. Even so, it was assumed by many politicians that the provision of council housing would prove to be a short-term measure to cover the current shortfall in housing for the working classes until economic conditions stabilized again and housing could be returned to its rightful location — the marketplace (Daunton, 1984).

The aim of the 'Addison' Act was to provide 500 000 new homes by 1923 — an ambitious target, which was never achieved. Some 214 000 had been approved by 1921, when the building programme was halted. In 1922 the new Minister of Health (Addison had resigned in protest) was already pronouncing that further state intervention in housing would be unnecessary, that the building industry should revert to its prewar (i.e. private) economic basis and that young married couples would have to live, as before, in one room, if they could not find suitable accommodation (Burnett, 1978, p. 222). So much for long-term state intervention. The plans of the 'Addison' Act collapsed for a number of reasons: there was a shortage of skilled labour in the building trade; the larger local authorities had to raise the necessary finance for new housing on the open market and often failed to gain adequate funds: Stanley, requiring £250 000, only managed to raise some £600, while Bristol raised less than half the £800 000 it needed (Daunton, 1984, p. 10). These factors delayed the 'Addison' programme. Its sudden demise, however, was caused partly by the high cost of these good-quality dwellings (still much sought after today), but principally it came to an end because of the first of the national economic crises alluded to above which have had such a strong impact on housing policy. Central government had to pay most of the cost of the new houses — about £1000 each, compared with 1914 costs of about £250 per house. Much more central to the halting of the 'Addison' building programme, though, was the unexpected arrival in 1921 of the worst economic crisis Britain has ever known. In six months unemployment rose from 2 per cent to 18 per cent, while company profits halved. This very severe economic crisis had its roots in the failure of Britains's export industries to re-establish their markets after the war. The crisis continued throughout the 1920s and was accentuated by the Wall Street Crash in 1929 and the worldwide recession that followed. The impact on housing policy in Britain was profound. There was to be no return to the prewar normality and stability craved by many Conservatives; and the state could not now abandon its commitment to intervention in the housing market. Equally, however, the state could not afford to carry the burden of the high cost of continuing to build public-sector dwellings to the standards laid down in the 'Addison' programme — subsidies, and standards, would have to be reduced. As Short has written: 'The Addison Act represents both the starting point and the peak of post-war housing legislation [after the First World War.]' (Short, 1982, p. 33).

In 1923, with the Conservatives in office, a further housing act was passed — the 'Chamberlain' Act — which drastically reduced central government subsidies and encouraged the private building sector by providing subsidies for both private and public housing. This in effect put a very sharp brake on local authority housebuilding, which fell from 81 000 new units in 1921-22 to only 14 000 dwellings in 1923-24 (Bowley, 1945, p. 271). In 1924 a minority Labour government was briefly in power and passed the 'Wheatley' Act, which increased the subsidies to local authorities. John

Wheatley was from Cyldeside, where housing conditions were particularly bad, and he began to put into operation a bold programme for council housing which was designed eventually to produce a replacement of the private rented sector by a public rented sector (see Merrett, 1979, pp 45-46). However, electoral politics intervened again and the Conservatives returned to power before the end of 1924. Both the 'Chamberlain' Act and the 'Wheatley' Act survived until 1933, when the Conservatives finally abolished central government subsidies. Local authority building programmes remained modest over this period with only some 300 000 new dwellings completed in the public sector between 1923 and 1933. The long-term economic crisis is partly to blame for this low level of public investment in housing; though the attitude of the Conservatives, who were in control for most of this decade, and their view of public-sector housing as a short-term, residual form of housing for the poor is also responsible.

One further housing act is worthy of mention in the interwar period — the 'Greenwood' Act, passed in 1930. By the late 1920s the housing conditions in the 'slums' and their unacceptable nature, were back on the political agenda. A minority Labour government was returned to power in 1929, with a pledge to demolish the slums — from 1919 to 1930 only 11 000 slums had been demolished, using provisions under the 1890 Act (Merrett, 1979, p. 49). The 'Greenwood' Act essentially concerned itself with the first concerted attack on slum dwellings and the rehousing of the displaced, low-income households in new municipal dwellings. It was also hoped to continue to provide 'general needs' public-sector housing, though the prevailing economic conditions, together with Conservative rule from the early 1930s onwards, led to still modest completion rates. However, a start on slum clearance was made in the 1930s and some 245 000 dwellings were demolished or closed by 1939, while nearly 290 000 new dwellings were built. Under the 'Greenwood' Act the subsidies, and therefore the standards for new dwellings, were particularly low, reflecting the overall economic position of the country. Also an increasing number of the new dwellings were in the form of 'walk-up' four- and five- storey blocks of flats which were provided with particularly poor facilities and formed a bleak, utilitarian addition to the housing stock. They did, however, allow the building of new dwellings in the inner-city districts where the slum dwellers lived. This was in contrast to the displaced households being relocated in 'cottage' estates on green-field sites on the edge of the built-up area, usually a long way from their 'home' neighbourhood.

In all, some 1.1 million council dwellings were built in the 20 years between the two World Wars — an impressive total, given the minute number of dwellings built under the 1890 Act prior to the First World War. However, some four million new dwellings were built altogether in the interwar period, so the local authorities contributed only a quarter of the new housing stock. The great majority of the rest were built for sale — for the rapidly expanding owner-occupied sector. But what had happened to the classic tenure of Victorian and Edwardian times, the private rented sector? In 1900 nine out of ten households rented from a private landlord. By the mid-1980s this position had completely reversed itself with the private rented sector housing barely one in ten households. The reasons for the inexorable contraction of this sector are numerous, and some have already been mentioned. The main initial reason for the demise of new construction for the private rented sector lay in increasing housing standards, and costs, from 1900 to 1920, which were not reflected in rising wages for the working classes. Thus the mid-Victorian pattern threatened to reassert itself, with households renting, and sharing, rooms rather than whole houses. The rise of the political power of the working classes, however, made such a 'market solution' unacceptable, and hence subsidized state-owned housing became an inevitable part of the housing scene after 1919. Also, rent controls, though legislation varied their extent from time to time, were to remain a permanent policy from 1915 onwards, restricting the freedom and profit margins of many landlords. In more recent years legislation protecting the rights of tenants has further eroded the position of private landlords. The twentieth century has also seen a massive increase in alternative forms of investment for the small bourgeois investor, who in the Victorian period traditionally invested in a few houses. Thus investment has switched from housing to the Stock Exchange, for example, and even indirectly back into housing through the building societies. In the postwar period the private rented sector has further shrunk through demolition of many older properties — still in the hands of private landlords — and the sale of many properties, encouraged by the greater availability of improvement grants in recent years.

The great majority of dwellings built in the interwar period were for the owner-occupied sector. This tenure formed roughly 10 per cent of the housing stock in 1914, but by 1938 this had risen to 32 per cent, compared with only 10 per cent in the public sector and 58 per cent in the now declining, but still dominant, private rented sector. Owner-occupation had been increasing during the Edwardian period and was encouraged, and even subsidized, under the Chamberlain Act (1923), in the interwar period. The massive increase in the quantity of dwellings built, and sold, in the interwar period was the result of a number of factors. The crucial element was an easing of credit availability, since few households could afford to buy a new house outright. The building societies expanded their activities enormously in the interwar period, principally by reducing the deposit required on a house, and extending the repayment period considerably, thereby reducing monthly repayments and bringing owner-occupation within the grasp of a significant number of middle-class households. Deposits were often as low as £25 in provincial towns, where in the 1920s bungalows could cost as little as £250. Even in London reasonable houses were available for between £400 and £600 in the late 1930s. After 1931 interest rates fell from 6 per cent to as low as 4.5 per cent in 1935. Housing costs also fell during the 1930s, though real wages, for those in work, rose during the interwar period as commodity prices fell in response to the world market recession. The building societies eagerly sought to expand their activities and the amount advanced by them rose from £9.3m in 1910 to £137m in 1938 (Burnett, 1978, p. 247), while the balance owed on mortgages expanded from £120m in 1924 to £636m in 1937 (Merrett and Gray, 1982, p. 8).

Most of the new owner-occupier estates were built by speculative house builders in semi-rural locations, taking advantage of the increased efficiency of the public transport system. In London this meant a belt from 5 to 15 miles from the centre, and in the larger provincial cities perhaps some 4-6 miles from the centre. The builders pandered to the rustic rural image sought by the new middle classes seeking status in the suburbs and segregation from the older, increasingly working-class, Victorian residential districts. Such uniform, often monotonous middle-class suburbs became the objects of much derisive comment both from the working classes and the upper classes. They were even unofficially classified into groupings such as 'Wimbledon transitional', 'Bypass variegated' by their critics (Burnett, 1978, p. 250). The 'boom' in private housebuilding reached its peak in the mid-1930s when over 250 000 new dwellings were built each year for owner-occupation. Indeed by 1939 the supply had outstripped demand with many new houses unsold (this was to influence early postwar planning forecasts of housing demand between the two growing tenures).

By 1938 the astonishing growth in output of new dwellings since 1919, over a third of the nation's total housing stock built in a period of unparalleled recession, had led to a crude balance between the number of households and the number of dwellings. This misleading figure led some commentators to observe that the housing problem was at long last 'solved'. Similar sentiments have been repeated in recent years. In fact an increasing percentage of the population were well housed, and overcrowding had been reduced. Many, many households still lived in Victorian dwellings which were clearly unfit by twentieth-century standards: dwelling numbers took no account of quality. The interwar period saw both the beginnings of the long-term demise of the private rented sector and the rise of owner-occupation and public renting.

The changing balance of tenures had also developed strong ideological overtones between municipal housing as a residual form of dwelling for the poor, accentuated by the poor quality of such housing built in the 1930s, and owner-occupied housing, associated with affluence and social status. The infamous example of the Cutteslowe Wall, built across a road to separate a private housing scheme from a public one, thus demonstrating the exclusive nature of the former, serves to emphasize the point (Collison, 1963). One unforeseen result of the massive boom in private housebuilding in the 1930s was the rapid physical expansion of urban areas through the growth of low-density, unplanned and unchecked suburbs or, even worse, 'ribbon' development along main roads. This gave rise to growing resentment against the speculative house builder, and this hostility led to some 14 years of cessation in the uncontrolled growth of owner-occupation from 1939 to 1953. It also heavily influenced the deliberations of the Barlow Commission and its conclusions, particularly since so much unplanned sprawl occurred around London, whose growth particularly concerned the Commission.

The postwar period

The Second World War inevitably brought about a severe slump in new housing completions, as labour and investment were again channelled into the war economy. The war had two other negative effects on housing. The population grew by over a million between 1939 and 1945, and the virtual cessation of housebuilding over this period led to a 'log-jam' of demand similar to that experienced as a result of the First World War. By 1945 the overall balance between dwellings and households achieved by 1938 had turned into a net shortage of some 700 000 homes. German bombing had reduced the existing housing stock: some 200 000 dwellings had been destroyed and 3.5 million damaged.

For the incoming Labour government in 1945 the major need was for a rapid new housebuilding programme to offset the war losses and reduce the overall housing shortage. Since it was broadly accepted that the owner-occupied market had been virtually saturated by 1939, and because a government-regulated programme would allow for a faster, more controlled rate of building, most of the new housebuilding was envisaged as being within the public sector. Private housebuilding was deterred by a licensing system, and in 1947 speculative private building was set at one-fifth of the total housing programme. The speculative builder was seen as the principal villain of the unplanned sprawl of the interwar period, and as such he was the antithesis of planned and controlled urban growth.

Much has been made of the ideological differences between the basic housing policy positions of the Labour and Conservative parties who, between them, have been responsible for housing policy since 1945. Labour is seen as favouring the public sector, the Tories the private one. This perception is not merely misleading in focusing attention on tenure, it is also wrong. The early postwar Labour administration did aim at a principally public-sector building programme (in 1948 over 190 000 dwellings were completed in the public sector compared with less than 33 000 private sector dwellings). However, Labour was not wedded to a socialist, state-owned housing policy and saw a large public-sector building programme as the most practical means of providing new housing quickly. Indeed there is evidence that Labour did not see council housing as a long-term 'solution' to the housing problem. Equally the Conservatives, though strongly encouraging the growth of the private sector through owner-occupation, nonetheless were responsible for the highest number of local authority housing completions in the postwar period (nearly 230 000 in 1953). There have been clear differences in emphasis and priorities between the parties, but also surprising elements of continuity between changes of government, notably in slum clearance and rehabilitation, which are given separate treatment below.

Returning to postwar policies, the early promise of the 1945-51 Labour administration soon fell foul of an economic crisis in 1947, which led to the usual retrenchment in housing expenditure. In 1951 the Conservatives were returned to power, partly because of a promise to build 300 000 new dwellings a year (the beginning of a 'bidding' process between the political parties in promised completions which culminated in Labour's victory in 1964). Initially this target was achieved through a rapid expansion of council housing, though the licensing system for private housebuilding was abolished in 1954 and the private housebuilding industry and owner-occupation strongly encouraged. Council housing was reduced to a relatively minor role, with the subsidy for 'general needs' council housing being abolished in 1956. This proved in the long term to be a political handicap for the Conservatives, and the Labour party under Harold Wilson was able to take advantage of Tory failures in the 1964 election. By the early 1960s there was a growing housing shortage and a public impatience with the large number of households still condemned to live in slum housing, despite the growing rate of slum clearance. Labour promised to build no less than 500 000 dwellings a year by increasing public-sector housing, but also continued to encourage owner-occupation. In 1967 housing completions reached over 380 000 dwellings, of which 181 000 were in the public sector. However, in the same year the failing economy led to a devaluation of sterling and the all-too-familiar public-sector cutbacks, which inevitably included housing. In 1965 the government had put forward a national housing plan embodied in a White Paper, 'The Housing Programme 1965 to 1970', but the last years of the Labour government were years of economic crisis and austerity. By 1970, when Labour was defeated in the general election, the national housing plan was no less than 28 per cent short of its target for new housing.

The 1970s saw Conservatives (1970-74), Labour (1974-79) and then the Tories again (1979-   ) in power. Throughout this period the economy continued to falter, entering a major recession towards the end of the decade. The usual pattern of Conservative cutbacks and Labour encouragement of the public sector occurred through this decade, though public housing investment began to decline in 1977, again as a result of broader economic difficulties. But until the election of the Conservatives under the leadership of Mrs Thatcher in 1979 it was still possible to point clearly to continuity of some policies between the parties and this has proved to be particularly true of redevelopment and rehabilitation.

Slum clearance

Despite an awareness that the clearance programme of the 1930s under the 'Greenwood' Act had no more than begun the process, the first postwar Labour administration concerned itself with the repair of war-damaged dwellings and a programme of new housing. In a period of such dire shortage, demolition would have to wait. By the early 1950s, however, the new Conservative government was able to turn its attention to the problem of the old, now decaying Victorian slums. Since 1945 nearly 1.5 million new dwellings had been built and the slum problem could no longer be ignored. Harold Macmillan, the new Housing Minister, set the scene for the new policy change in a government White Paper published in 1953 — 'Houses — the Next Step'. For the Conservatives, local authority housing was to be increasingly confined to rehousing those displaced by the slum clearance programme which they saw as 'the remaining finite task necessitating state intervention' (Gibson and Langstaff, 1982, p. 27).

The problem was to find out how many unfit dwellings there were, and their location. The last estimate of slum housing had been made prior to the Second World War, when there were 472 000 dwellings officially classified as 'unfit'. Local authorities were required in 1955 to send in returns of the number of slums in their area, and a collated figure of some 850 000 dwellings was arrived at for England and Wales. This figure became a benchmark, and governments lulled themselves into a sense of false security on the basis that the figure itself was accurate, and that it was static. Thus, given a planned annual clearance rate (set at about 75 000 dwellings per year), it was possible to forecast a date when all the slums would be demolished and the housing problem solved. By the late 1950s a number of academic critics began to cast serious doubt on this wisdom. Cullingworth (1960) in particular, through a detailed analysis of the 1955 returns, was able to show their widespread inaccuracy. Some local authorities had failed to submit any returns at all, while others had either grossly underestimated the number of slum properties in their area, or had sent in the figure for those dwellings for which they actually had a programme for demolition. Cullingworth was also scathing about government complacency concerning the fixed and finite nature of the figures. The government seemed oblivious to the fact that the figure had nearly doubled from the 1939 survey to 1955. Cullingworth pointed out that there was continuing obsolescence in housing, that much of our older Victorian housing was fast approaching the end of its economic life. He suggested that some 141 000 dwellings would need replacing every year because of obsolescence, giving an overall replacement rate of over 200 000 dwellings per year if the already known slums were added in.

The Conservative government effectively ignored the warning, and the annual clearance rate remained at about 60 000 dwellings per year from the late 1950s into the early 1960s. It was this Tory complacency over housing that helped Labour to win the 1964 election.

The new Labour government responded to the increase and to the criticism of the accuracy of the 1955 'slum' figures, but some 255 000 dwellings still awaited demolition ten years later. A further set of local authority returns of unfit dwellings, asked for in 1965, suggested a figure not of 255 000 dwellings but 824 000. Clearance rates accelerated to a new peak of 70 000 dwellings in 1967 and 90 000 in 1971-72. However, in 1967 a national Housing Condition Survey was conducted using teams of government public health inspectors. The results of this more accurate survey suggested that the real figure of unfit dwellings was not 250 000, or even 800 000, but 1.8 million. The impact of this new horrendously high figure, amply confirming the views of Cullingworth and others, coincided roughly with the devaluation crisis of 1967 and immediate cutbacks in public housing investment. Economic misfortune, the expense of demolition and rehousing and the sheer size of the problem of older housing led to a radical rethink of policy by the government. From the late 1960s onwards, clearance programmes were to be slowly reduced, and by 1979 the figure had fallen to 33 000 dwellings demolished. (see Table 12.1).

Table 12.1   Clearance 1945-79 (England and Wales)

Years	Total dwellings demol-ished or closed ('000)	Persons moved ('000)
1945-54	90	309
1955-59	213	669
1960-64	304	834
1965-69	339	896
1970-74	309	704
1975-79	213	378
TOTALS	1,468	3,790

Source: adapted from Gibson and Langstaff (1982)

The time lag between moving people out of slum clearance areas and the availability of large sites for redevelopment inevitably meant the breakup of existing communities and the dispersal of households. Some, mainly young, households took the opportunity to move to new towns, but most displaced households in the late 1950s and 1960s were rehoused in new peripheral council estates. Most cities developed these overspill estates, which were often remote from the city centre, poorly served by public transport and lacking in amenities such as shops, libraries, pubs, community centres and churches. Good examples of such overspill estates, and many of their resulting problems, are to be found on the outskirts of Liverpool (e.g. Kirkby, Cantril Farm) and Glasgow (Easterhouse and Drumchapel). Flats had made an appearance as part of local authority housing in the interwar period, and they made their presence felt again in the 1950s and 1960s, with a movement to medium- and high-rise developments, served by lifts. The high-rise 'boom' is graphically discussed by Dunleavy (1981), who points to the interplay of architectural fashions, government subsidies (which were much higher for flats until 1966, in theory to reflect their greater cost), changing construction methods, and increasing local authority concentration on inner-city redevelopment where flatted accommodation allowed greater dwelling densities than conventional 'cottage' housing. In brief, much of the public-sector housing built in the 1960s has left a legacy of social and structural problems for the 1980s. Many four-storey, low-rise, concrete, deck-access flat or maisonette complexes built in the late 1960s and early 1970s, employing prefabricated techniques, have had to be demolished in the early 1980s, while others have become priority estates with unenviable reputations and high vacancy rates.

Rehabilitation

Improvement grants to help rehabilitate older properties were first introduced in 1949. In essence these were to provide improvements for older housing that was in otherwise reasonable condition. The main aim was to provide better sanitary conditions in these older houses. Grants were at the discretion of local authorities — up to 50 per cent of the improvement costs, though with various strict conditions attached. Improvement grants remained a low-key, minor element in housing policy until the enormity of the task facing government with regard to older unfit housing came to be realized in 1967. By the late 1960s slum clearance was becoming subject to increasing criticism by the public because of the breakup of old communities, the bleak aspect of many new overspill developments and the huge areas of derelict open space left in inner-city areas after the bulldozer had done its work. These criticisms, coupled with the expense of redevelopment and the new financial stringency facing the government, combined to bring about a radical change of policy direction by central government. In 1968 a new White Paper, 'Old Houses into New Homes', was published. It formed the basis of the 1969 Housing Act.

The 1967 House Condition Survey, in addition to showing that 1.8 million dwellings were unfit out of a total stock of 15.7 million in England and Wales, showed that a further 2.3 million lacked one or more basic amenity (judged as an inside toilet, a fixed bath, and running hot and cold water), while another 3.7 million required sub-stantial repairs. There was clearly a case for placing greater emphasis on the rehabilit-ation of older dwellings. The economics of rehabilitation, as opposed to redevelop-ment, also naturally appealed to a government in economic straits and facing a slum problem which seemed to be growing rapidly, despite attempts to whittle it away. Under the 1969 Housing Act, improvement grant ceilings were to be improved (to £1000 in most cases) to cover up to 50 per cent of the total cost. The Act also aimed to encourage improvement by landlords and owner-occupiers in areas with older houses by declaring General Improvement Areas (G.I.A.'s). These would be areas normally covering from 300 to 800 houses. The essential aim was to encourage the take-up of improvement grants for internal house modernization in each G.I.A. by the local authority undertaking a variety of external environmental improvements. Initially, local authorities could claim from central government half the cost of environmental works up to a ceiling of £50 per dwelling. Such external improvements included tree planting, closing of ends of roads, provision of car parking, landscaping of derelict plots, provision of children's play areas etc.

Between 1969 and 1973 the number of improvement grants increased by 230 per cent from 109 000 to over 360 000 (Balchin, 1985, p. 65). Discretionary grant expenditure increased over the same period from £40m to over £300m per annum. By the end of 1973 some 733 G.I.A.'s had been declared in England and Wales, but already the results of the Act were coming under fire. Local surveys showed that it was the better-off owner-occupiers who were taking up grants, while many landlords were using the grants to improve properties and turn them into high-rent luxury flats. This meant displacing the 'sitting' low-rent tenants. In many instances, particularly in London, a process of 'winkling' tenants out, either by offering them money to quit or by harassing them, was found to be occurring. A further criticism of the workings of the Act involved speculative builders buying unimproved properties cheaply, using grants to help cover modernization costs and making large windfall profits in selling the properties. Some previously working-class, largely privately rented housing districts became subject to the process of 'gentrification' whereby young middle-class profes-sional households gradually displaced working-class households, the new owners taking advantage of grants to improve the properties (e.g. see Ferris, 1972). A final, damning criticism of G.I.A.'s was the low take-up of grants within them — most grants were taken up for properties located outside G.I.A.'s. Surveys of the demographic and socio-economic make-up of the households living in G.I.A.'s showed large proportions of heads of households as unemployed, on low incomes, or retired. For such households it was a major problem to find the money for their 50 per cent of improvement costs. Many older households displayed hostility towards the idea of improvement. Where the property owners were absentee landlords, the latter were often very reluctant to improve, since they could not recoup their capital outlay in the foreseeable future in higher rents if the tenants remained because of rent controls.

Much of the early work under the 1969 Act took place with a Conservative govern-ment in office; and in 1973 a further White Paper, 'Better Homes — the Next Priority', was published, which suggested ways of preventing landlords from removing tenants, or speculative builders profiting from the availability of improvement grants. The new

White Paper also suggested a stronger, more discriminating approach to area improvement — Housing Action Areas (H.A.A.'s). Most of the ideas in the White Paper were incorporated into the incoming Labour government's new Housing Act in 1974. The continuity of policy with regard to clearance and rehabilitation between the two major political parties is worthy of comment.

Housing Action Areas were to be declared in areas where severe physical and, for the first time, *social* problems were to be found. The criteria were to include overcrowding, shared accommodation, furnished tenancies, dwellings lacking basic amenities and concentrations of older households and large families. In response to criticisms of the 1969 Act grant ceilings were raised: grants were to be 60 per cent, though they could be as high as 90 per cent of the total cost of improvement in hardship cases. Local authorities were given powers of compulsory purchase where owners of properties refused to improve. Each H.A.A. was to be completely improved within five years of being declared — a response to the very slow piecemeal improvement in G.I.A.'s.

In fact H.A.A.'s have proved as unsuccessful as G.I.A.'s. It had been hoped that 1 million dwellings would have been covered by H.A.A.'s by 1980; in reality only some 150 000 dwellings were accommodated. The rate of declarations was very slow, reflecting in part the strain such area improvement schemes placed on local authority housing departments. Improvement itself was also very slow — the five-year framework proved hopelessly optimistic. The social dislocation that improvement has produced has led to many households leaving H.A.A.'s, suggesting that 'improvement' is little less disruptive than 'redevelopment' for many households. Improvement grant take-up collapsed after 1973, partly reflecting the more stringent controls brought in under the 1974 Act, but increasingly reflecting the inadequacy of grant levels, spiralling building costs in the later 1970s and the low incomes of most of the affected households. Most critiques of area improvement have been damning, with criticism being levelled particularly at the slowness of improvement, its scattered nature and the low level of grant aid available. It has proved to be a policy with few friends, and most authorities are now agreed that it has failed in terms of its own goals. Improvement is still seen as a cheaper alternative to redevelopment; but the key question of whether most 'improved' dwellings will last a further thirty years remains unanswered. There is also a view that improved dwellings still remain 'second-class' dwellings, lacking gardens, and with small room sizes etc. As Gibson and Langstaff suggest, 'decisions to declare areas without a commitment of adequate resources is tantamount to a policy of benign neglect [. . .]' (Gibson and Langstaff, 1982, p. 132).

Housing policy since 1977

In July 1977 Peter Shore, the then Secretary of State for the Environment of the Labour government of 1975-79, published a government consultative document, or Green Paper, entitled 'Housing Policy: A Consultative Document'. This represented the results of two years' research and provided an excellent statement on the achievement of postwar housing policy, while hinting at serious remaining problems amongst its mass of statistical material. The overall housing stock in the United Kingdom had increased from 14 million in 1951 to over 20 million in 1977, despite the demolition of nearly 1.5 million slums. Overcrowding levels had been severely reduced, and the number of unfit dwellings had similarly declined. Most comforting of all from the government's point of view was the overall national 'surplus' of dwellings over house-holds (over 1.6 million dwellings in surplus by 1981). Glossing over the failures of rehabilitation, the 1977 Green Paper pronounced the back of the housing problem broken and set the scene for a scaling down of state intervention and public investment in housing. Faced with yet new problems in the economy by 1976, the Labour govern-ment felt able, with some equanimity, to reduce public housing investment from £2580m in 1975-76 to £1934 in 1977-78 (Short, 1982). The complacency shown in the 1977 Green Paper sowed the seeds for a major change in housing policy once a radical, right-wing Conservative government was elected in 1979.

The 1977 Green Paper can, however, be read very differently. The crude national surplus of dwellings over households ignores that over 200 000 dwellings were offi-cially second homes, and that over 100 000 council dwellings were empty, either because they were difficult-to-let, had structural problems or suffered from damp. Also, vacancy is a factor in the residential mobility process: it has been estimated that 4 per cent of owner-occupied dwellings need to be vacant at any one time if there is to be movement in the market. The national figure is also irrelevant at the local scale: in many inner city areas, even in 1977 there were clearly severe housing shortages. Thus the reality is still one of a national shortage of dwellings — not a surplus. While the number of dwellings in serious disrepair was officially decreasing, it should have been clear by 1977 that housing repair is a continuous process — not a policy area where expenditure can be reduced.

In May 1979 the Conservatives were returned to power. The new government had a clear housing policy. Council housing was to revert once and for all to a residual, welfare housing tenure and new building in this sector was to be dramatically cut. It plummeted from 79 000 completions in 1979 to 36 000 in 1982 — the lowest annual rate of new building in the public sector since 1923. Unfortunately, in the grip of a rapidly worsening recession, private sector housing completions, far from increasing at the expense of the public sector, also fell, from 155 000 in 1976 to a nadir of 116 000 in 1981. Even the complacent optimism of the 1977 Green Paper had envisaged an annual addition to the housing stock well above the actual level achieved in the early 1980s.

Apart from a clear antipathy towards the public sector in general, the Conser-vatives campaigned in 1979 on a promise to sell council dwellings to sitting tenants. Some observers suggested at the time that this election pledge, above all other consid-erations, won the election for the Conservatives. It was certainly a popular policy among many local authority tenants and, while Labour were pledged to repeal the relevant legislation in their election manifesto of 1983, writing in early 1985 it appears likely that Labour has now accepted the principle of council house sales.

The 'right to buy' for council tenants was enshrined in the 1980 Housing Act. The sale of council housing was not in itself a new idea — Conservative-controlled local authorities had sold some dwellings to tenants occasionally since the 1920s. However, it had always been left to the discretion of the local council whether it encouraged, or even sanctioned, such sales. Under the 1980 Act it is mandatory for local authorities to sell dwellings if sitting tenants wish to buy and also for local authorities to provide mortgage finance. Tenants receive a discount on their property on a sliding scale which varies with the length of time the prospective buyer has been a tenant, from a 33 per cent discount for tenants of three years' standing up to a maximum of 50 per cent for those of 20 years' standing or more. There are arguments both for and against the sale of council houses, and they are neatly summed up by Balchin (1985, pp 184-197).

In brief, the arguments in favour include the right of tenants to purchase property at a discount on which they may have paid rent for 20 or more years, and thus housing as a source of accumulating wealth might be spread amongst the less affluent of the population. The discount system clearly allows many poorer households the opportunity to move into home-ownership. Sales clearly benefit tenants. Financial arguments in favour of sales — that local authorities will gain capital from sales, will not be responsible for repairs, or be in receipt of rents well below the real cost of the housing — have proved rather more difficult to sustain. Arguments against sales include the obvious point that sales mean a diminution of stock, a point particularly difficult to justify in inner-city areas where low-income households find themselves on long waiting lists for already scarce public-sector housing. The reduction in new building in this sector clearly endorses this argument. Sales mean not only a physical loss of dwellings from the public sector but also a severe financial loss through the discount system and low valuation of council properties. Perhaps the strongest argument against sales is the fact that it is the high-income tenants who can afford the new mortgages and that it is the better-quality 'cottage' estates which are experiencing the highest rates of sales. Evidence suggests that well under 5 per cent of sales have been of flats, even though they constitute nearly 30 per cent of the public sector stock.

Table 12.2   Housing tenure changes in the United Kingdom, 1965-83, percentage changes

Year	Owner occupiers	Public sector	Private rented and other tenures
1965	46.5	28.2	25.3
1970	49.8	30.6	19.6
1975	52.9	31.4	15.7
1979	54.5	32.2	13.3
1980	55.3	31.7	13.0
1981	56.3	31.5	12.2
1982	59.0	30.1	11.9
1983	61.0	27.8	11.2

Source: Housing and construction statistics. Social Trends (HMSO) Reproduced with the permission of the Controller of HMSO

On the other hand, the policy has proved popular with tenants — in 1980 some 90 000 dwellings were sold and by 1982 the figure had reached over 217 000 (compared with the fact that only some 52 000 new dwellings were completed in the public sector). For the first time the public sector has begun to shrink as a percentage of the overall dwelling stock (see Table 12.2), though this is largely due to the slump in new building. Sales have slowed down now that the initial pent-up demand has been met. Whatever the merits of the policy, it now appears it will form a permanent feature of the broader housing scene.

Although the Conservatives slashed public housing expenditure and raised council house rents substantially as part of their antipathy towards the public sector, they rather curiously increased the amount of money available for rehabilitation, thus causing a revival of the take-up of improvement grants, mainly by owner-occupiers from a low point of 184 000 in 1981 to 463 000 in 1983. The government seems to see rehabilitation as an alternative to new housebuilding, but the creeping tide of growing disrepair continues to rise.

Some concluding comments

Writing early in 1985, after some six years of Conservative government, the triumph of owner-occupation as the most desirable tenure is all too clear, with over 60 per cent of all dwellings now in this sector (see Table 12.2). Building society managers are beginning to talk of 80 per cent as an achievable figure for owner-occupation by the end of the century, though some academic commentators have been less sanguine about the likelihood of this being achieved. The private rented sector has continued to decline, despite some efforts by the Tories to bolster this sector by easing restrictions on landlords. In truth this tenure has been neglected increasingly by both major political parties. The public sector is now clearly contracting: dwellings are being sold at a faster rate than they are being built, while council tenants are paying much higher rents, so much so that nearly all local authorities are now in surplus on their housing revenue account. The subsidized housing sector is now that of the owner-occupiers, through tax subsidies.

The last paragraph, and indeed much of this chapter, has been couched in terms of tenure and the varying fortunes of the now two largest tenures — public and owner-occupied. This is understandable, and perhaps inevitable, as a means of simplifying the complexity of the housing system, and because it is possible to point to very real differences between tenures, e.g. in access to and mobility within tenures, and in housing finance. The collation of statistical data also lends itself to reinforcing the tenurial approach, as do many ideological debates about housing. The acceptance by both Labour and Conservatives of owner occupation as the natural, desired and most rewarding tenure has sharpened the nation's perception of council housing as a second-class tenure — a view reinforced by the adverse publicity accorded difficult-to-let estates, and which is likely to receive even greater credibility given the pattern of council house sales which can only further reduce the choice of housing for low-income households dependent on the public sector. Viewing housing through a tenure framework is increasingly being looked upon as a sterile approach, clouding discussion of some of the fundamental issues; yet housing policy in recent years has become increasingly tenure orientated. Current policy is little more than a 'tenure' policy

(Donnison and MacLennan, 1985).

Housing finance is one area that is in desperate need of a radical rethink. The government is currently subsidizing the average owner-occupier to the tune of £277 per year, compared with only £88 for the average council tenant. Apart from being in surplus on their current account, local authorities now hold an estimated £5 billion in capital receipts from the sale of dwellings and land, yet government restrictions will not allow local authorities to utilize this money. Instead, starved of funds, local authorities have increasingly turned to other methods of improvement or disposal of properties — particularly with regard to difficult-to-let estates. Many local authorities have sold such estates to private developers since they no longer have the money to improve them (e.g. in Salford, Oldham and Burnley). In other cases, different remedies have been applied which have at least widened the range of ownership of housing. In Glasgow the notorious Easterhouse overspill estate is now the scene of urban homesteading where vacant, often vandalized homes have been sold off cheaply to first-time buyers, while elsewhere cooperatives have been formed to try to ameliorate conditions in both the public and private sectors. In Merseyside the Cantril Farm overspill estate has recently been sold to a new trust — the Stockbridge Village Trust — with private- and public-sector funding and management to try to revitalize the estate. Such initiatives, though intrinsically interesting, are, like housing associations, likely to involve only a tiny minority of households.

The complacent view put forward in the 1977 Green Paper and the current government's massive cutbacks on public housing expenditure are precipitating a new housing crisis. Despite the upturn in the take-up of improvement grants in 1983, this has now fallen back again. The government, like its predecessors, has chosen to ignore the fact that obsolescence and the need for substantial repair in housing requires a substantial, continuing commitment. The position with regard to older housing is worsening rapidly and, as Gibson and Langstaff (1984) point out, the bulldozer will return as of a necessity in the early 1990s unless policy changes are rapidly implemented — the legacy of older housing cannot simply be ignored.

By reducing expenditure on public-sector housing so savagely the Conservative government has also ignored the needs of the most vulnerable groups in our society, the old, the unemployed, one-parent families — in one word, the deprived (see Murie, 1983, for a detailed discussion of inequality and deprivation in housing). Current policy can only exacerbate inequalities in housing by the massive transfer of subsidies from the public to the owner-occupied sector.

What of the future? Forrest and Murie (1984) posit some of the alternatives for the public sector, while Karn (1981) has pointed out that the attack by the government on the public rented sector is likely to lead to acute stress and instability in the housing markets. Certainly the attempt by the government to give housing a lower political profile by out-and-out encouragement of owner-occupation is likely to fail. A new housing crisis is looming rapidly and the expenditure cutbacks since 1977 and the regressive policies since 1979 will need to be paid for sooner rather than later.

References

Balchin, P.N. (1985) *Housing Policy — an introduction*, Croom Helm, Beckenham

Bowley, M. (1945) *Housing and the State*, George Allen and Unwin, London

Burnett, J. (1978) *A Social History of Housing 1815-1970*, Methuen, London

Collison, P. (1963) *The Cutteslowe Walls: a study in social class*, Faber and Faber, London

Cullingworth, J.B. (1960) *Housing Needs and Planning Policy*, Allen and Unwin, London

Daunton, M.J. (ed.) (1984) *Councillors and Tenants: local authority housing in English cities 1919-39*, Leicester University Press, Leicester

Donnison, D. and MacLennan, D. (1985) What should we do about Housing? *New Society*, 11 April 1985

Dunleavy, P. (1981) *The Politics of Mass Housing in Britain 1945-1975*, Clarendon Press, Oxford

Ferris, J. (1972) *Participation in Planning: the Barnsbury case. A study of environmental improvement in London*, Bell, London

Forrest, R. and Murie, A. (1984) Beyond the right to buy, *Roof*, July/August 1984

Gibson, M.S. and Langstaff, M.J. (1982) *An Introduction to Urban Renewal*, Hutchinson, London

Gibson, M.S. and Langstaff, M.J. (1984) Housing renewal: emerging crisis and prospects for the 1990s, *Housing Review*, Vol. 33, No. 5, pp 175-179

Karn, V. (1981) Public sector demolition can seriously damage your health, *Roof*, January/February 1981

Merrett, S. (1979) *State Housing in Britain*, Routledge and Kegan Paul, London

Merrett, S. and Gray, F. (1982) *Owner Occupation in Britain*, Routledge and Kegan Paul, London

Murie, A. (1983) *Housing Inequality and Deprivation*, Heinemann, London

Short, J.R. (1982) *Housing in Britain: the post-war experience*, Methuen, London

Further reading

The field covering housing policy is now very wide indeed. The most readable text of changing housing policies is undoubtedly that by Short (1982), while Balchin (1985) provides a comprehensive and up-to-date account of the current housing situation. Merrett (1979) is the seminal work on the development of the public sector, while Merrett and Gray (1982) and Ball, M. (1983) *Housing Policy and Economic Power*, Methuen, London, provide detailed analyses of the owner-occupied sector. Redevelopment and rehabilitation are discussed in depth by Gibson and Langstaff (1982) and rather more briefly by Kirby, D.A. (1979) *Slum Housing and Residential Renewal: the case in urban Britain*, Longman, London

13   The decentralization of retailing

In strict areal terms retailing forms an unimportant urban land use for it rarely accounts for more than 5 per cent of the total built-up area of British towns and cities. On the other hand, retailing exerts an enormous influence on the pattern of urban land values and is a land use that generates ever-increasing flows of road traffic. In many smaller settlements retailing provides the largest source of employment, while retailing nationally, along with allied services and wholesaling, forms the 'distributive trades', which employ more than one in ten of the insured population. Retailing also accounts for over half the total consumer expenditure in Britain (Dawson and Kirby, 1980). Given its importance, and its influence on urban land values and land-use patterns, it is scarcely surprising that retailing has long formed an important focus of study in urban geography. In this book we are more specifically concerned with change within the urban system. Retailing is an excellent example of a very dynamic land-use and employment sector which has changed, and largely increased, its activities both spatially and quantitatively in recent years. Like most other service industries, retailing has tended to mirror population changes. In the urban context this has meant suburbanization and decentralization, processes examined in Chapter 14. The pace of change in retailing, both spatial and organizational, and the increasing pressure from developers have led retailing, as an almost totally private sector activity, into greater and greater conflict with planners, who have sought to regulate and control such changes. This has placed retail planning policies in the position of being categorized as over-restrictive. Such policies, the rationale behind them, and their effects, are examined in this chapter.

Explanations of traditional patterns of retail location

Although this chapter is primarily concerned with the changing pattern of retailing, a better understanding of such change and of postwar planning policies regarding retail location will be aided by a brief overview of the traditional pattern of retail location. This is examined through a review of the basic approaches and models that have been put forward to explain retailing patterns. For discussion of these approaches in more depth readers should refer to one of the following sources: Scott (1970), National Economic Development Office (N.E.D.O.) (1970), Davies (1976) or Dawson et al. (1980). The N.E.D.O. study suggests a threefold grouping of approaches: central place theory, spatial interaction models and rent models. This is adopted here. In addition, the growing literature on behavioural models is considered, and a final section is provided on the problems of data collection and model reliability in retailing.

Central place theory

Central place theory was originally advanced in 1933 as a theory of the location of service centres, by a German geographer, Walter Christaller. Most of the empirical work involved in testing this theory has either been confined to, or has heavily relied on, the use of retailing data. This is understandable since retailing provides a reasonably coherent set of central functions or services, located within settlements or central places and serving a wider trade area or hinterland. The detailed mechanics of the theory do not concern us here, though the concept of a hierarchy of centres offering different orders of goods and services, with complementary sized market or trade areas, has undergone extensive empirical testing, particularly in the United States (see, for example, Berry and Garrison, 1958; Berry and Pred, 1965; Berry 1967). The deterministic, static nature of central place theory, its assumption of idealized conditions (the 'isotropic land surface') and the fact that the basic theory ignores settlement development for mining or other industrial purposes have all led to criticism of its usefulness in the real world. It has, however, acted as a stimulus to much research into retailing activity and location, while the concept of the hierarchy has passed into other fields of urban planning policy both in Britain and elsewhere.

Spatial interaction models

Spatial interaction or 'gravity' models are based on an analogy with the physical laws of gravitation. A whole series of models has been put forward on the basis of this simple analogy, not merely for the purpose of studying retailing but also for studying journeys to work and population migration. Although unlike central place theory, spatial interaction models lack a strong theoretical base they have nonetheless grown in both complexity and popularity as planning tools, since they allow the researcher to test possible proposals or policy alternatives. The basic model was put forward by Reilly in the 1930s, suggesting that differently sized urban settlements would exert an influence (or gravitational 'pull') on the intervening population or trade area, in direct proportion to their own population size. More sophisticated models, utilizing more variables such as sales levels in individual shopping centres, variations in expenditure potential of different socio-economic groups etc. have been utilized in a number of empirical studies (see National Economic Development Office (N.E.D.O.) 1970, for some examples), and such models have found considerable popularity with retail planners.

Rent models

Urban rent models are broadly based on the ideas of Von Thunen, which were concerned with rural rents and the systematic distribution of agricultural land use (see Hall, 1966). Within the urban context it is assumed that landowners will wish to maximize rents for sites they own, while different locations in the urban area will vary in the amount of accessibility they can offer (accessibility being measured as the distance from the city centre). The outcome of competition between land users for individual sites will tend to allocate sites to the users who can pay the highest rents. This 'bidding' process theoretically ensures within the land market that each site will be occupied by the highest bidder. This simple 'bid-rent' theory does have some empirical validity in that land value patterns within urban areas do clearly show that higher values are attached to more accessible locations, with particularly high values being associated with city centre sites — the most accessible in the city are the most sought after.

This approach has been modified and extended by Alonso (1964), who produced a model based on a mathematical statement of the interrelationship between accessibility, land use and land values. The approach has also been modified by other urban economists. Such rent models are 'useful as general descriptions of the way land use is determined by way of the land market' (National Economic Development Office (N.E.D.O.) 1970, p.66). They do point to the influence of accessibility on land values and the traditional attraction of accessible sites for retailers. However, the rather abstract nature of such models has rendered them only marginally useful in the detailed examination of individual urban areas.

Behavioural approaches

In recent years there has been a switch of emphasis in research into urban retailing. The normative spatial models of central place theory and the theory of spatial interaction both tend to assume rational decision making by consumers. Attention is increasingly being focused on consumer behaviour and the factors that influence such behaviour. This shift to a more behavioural perspective has been mirrored elsewhere in human geography. Shephard and Thomas (1980) suggest that behavioural studies may be broadly classified into an empirical and a cognitive approach. The empirical approach subsumes within it a variety of studies that have concerned themselves with surveys of consumers and questionnaires in order to determine shopping centre trade areas, shopping habits of consumers in terms of frequency, numbers of trips etc. Questionnaires suffer from the inevitable bias of noninformation from consumers not interviewed, or consumers living near the shopping centre who choose not to shop there. The degree of market penetration by individual shopping centres cannnot therefore be accurately assessed. The collation of 'shopping diaries' by a random sample of consumers in an urban area is an alternative approach (see, for example, Davies, 1973, 1976). Such studies provide useful, detailed information on shopping trips and the varying patronage of individual shopping centres. A more ecologically orientated approach has attempted to assess the importance of socio-economic, demographic and cultural factors in determining consumer behaviour, and results suggest that these factors do indeed affect patterns of shopping behaviour (e.g. see Thomas, 1974; Potter, 1977).

The cognitive approach is more concerned with the perception of the individual consumer with regard to retailing. Much research under this heading has concerned itself with the range of shopping centres known to consumers. Spatial information fields of known, used or familiar shopping centres can be calculated, and a number of studies have suggested that these tend to be sectoral in shape, with the apex being the city centre or C.B.D. Social class has again been found to be an important factor influencing knowledge of a greater or smaller number of centres (Smith, 1976). Other research has focused on the individual's perception of the internal characteristics and attributes of shopping centres (Downs, 1970) or the attractiveness of specific shops (Bruce, 1970). The range of behavioural studies and the lack of a comprehensive theory reflect the recent origin of such research, while the results of such studies clearly show both the variety of consumer behavioural patterns with regard to retailing and the importance that must be attached to socio-economic factors.

Retailing and the 'data problem'

A common thread that bedevils all research into retailing is the dearth of official statistics on retailing in Britain and the consequent difficulty in obtaining retailing data to test hypotheses and models. The resulting paucity of information, unreliability of samples and occasionally the inappropriate nature of available data have all plagued retail research for academics, developers and planners alike. Between 1950 and 1971 there were five censuses of Distribution conducted by central government. They were normally linked with Population Censuses. These Censuses of Distribution collected information on business location, type, turnover, number of employees and floorspace, as well as stocks, purchases and capital turnover. Such information proved invaluable to researchers since the data could be tabulated at regional, urban and even individual shopping centre scales. However, since 1971 there has been no new Census of Distribution. Government statisticians attempted to simplify matters by conducting two separate inquiries — one concerned with establishment and location of retail outlets, the other concerned more with organization and business information. The latter inquiry got off the ground in 1976 and is named the 'Annual Retailing Enquiry'; the second exercise, originally entitled the '1981 Shops Enquiry' and planned to cover type, location and floorspace, was cancelled by the incoming Conservative government in 1979 (Jenkinson, 1982). Private registers and surveys in some ways do make up for these deficiencies, but the lack of a complete, up-to-date survey of retail information is a serious hindrance to research.

Many data are inevitably therefore only available on a localized, often sample-based scale. The problems inherent in questionnaires have been alluded to, and much retail survey work is very time consuming. More seriously, many potentially valuable sources of data remain unavailable, and some of the more sophisticated interaction models that have been used by planners to assess the probable impact of new retail developments have suffered from inadequacies in data inputs, either because the latter are unavailable or, arguably, because they are unsatisfactory. For example, most 'gravity' models use either sales data or floorspace as a measure of a shopping centre's attractiveness for potential customers. However, as Davies (1976) points out, neither of these indices is particularly satisfactory. Criticisms stemming from data inadequacies are common in the literature on retailing, and this is doubly unfortunate in a field where the pace of change has been so rapid and where forecasting future trends is particularly important.

The retailing revolution

It has already been noted that the pace of change in retailing has been particularly dramatic; but it is only part of a broader set of changes in marketing which are having very considerable effects on urban land use both in Britain and in the rest of Western Europe, North America and Australia. This marketing 'revolution' has been likened in its impact to the Industrial Revolution: 'the hypermarket is as different from the corner grocer as the woollen mill was from the weaver's cottage.' (Dawson and Kirby, 1980, p.107.) The business organization of retailing, the techniques of merchandizing and the scale of operation, and in addition the location and type of retail centres are all part of this revolution.

The organization and ownership of retail units can be subdivided into a number of basic categories. In Britain the growth in the market share of the multiple (or corporate) chain stores has been a significant trend over the last twenty-five years. In food retailing the four largest multiples account for nearly 25 per cent of annual grocery store sales. Although some multiple chains have continued to concentrate largely on one specific type of merchandize (e.g. food), others have deliberately widened their range of goods by adopting a 'scrambled' merchandizing policy, i.e. selling a number of unrelated types of goods. Where the latter approach has been adopted, these retail groups tend to seek prime high street sites for their stores where pedestrian flows are particularly heavy. Examples of such stores would be Boots, W. H. Smith and Marks and Spencer.

Department stores originally developed to serve the upper classes in the later decades of the nineteenth century. Although their exclusive nature has often changed, they have not significantly increased their market share in Britain in recent years and have largely remained on prime sites within the city centres. Traditionally, independent traders have played a very large part in retail provision; but this has changed radically. Many independent retailers succumbed in the 1950s and 1960s to the increasing competition from the multiple chains. Lack of capital, slowness in changing selling techniques (e.g. moving to self-service) and higher wholesale prices have all been blamed for this decline in the number of independent traders. In some cases they have survived by joining voluntary (or contractual) chains themselves (e.g. SPAR); in others by being willing to sell a wide range of goods and opening for very long periods, thus providing an important local convenience goods service. The impact of general Sunday trading on such independent traders will be worthy of investigation.

Another important grouping of retail stores in Britain has traditionally been the co-operative movement. Starting in Rochdale in 1844, it spread rapidly through the North of England and Scotland, though rather more sporadically through the rest of Britain. Traditionally geared towards urban working-class areas, the Co-op has been rather slow to adopt innovations in marketing, and investment has also been neglected. As a result it has seen its market share eroded, mainly by the multiple chains.

Apart from changing patterns of ownership there have been other major advances in retailing. Some of the larger organizations have developed a vertical structure, often moving backwards from actual retailing of goods to developing their own wholesaling and transport, and even manufacturing (or processing in food retailing) and labelling of goods. This has enabled large firms to have much greater control over quality and reliability of goods (an important factor when dealing with a fickle consumer market which often has many alternative outlets available). This has both helped and, occasionally, hindered the spatial diffusion of some firms seeking to increase the number of their stores. For example, the Sainsbury supermarket chain had to await the building of new warehouses before expanding from the South-East into the Midlands and South-West England because of distribution problems (Dawson and Kirby, 1980). Technological innovation through the adoption of self-service and cumputerization of stock control has led to significant increases in employee productivity (and thus reduced labour) in an industry which has traditionally been labour intensive. A further change has been the trend towards larger and larger stores, with the hypermarket at the top of the pyramid. This has been well documented and is discussed in more detail in the final section of this chapter. These innovations in retailing have separately, or more commonly in combination with each other and with other factors, strongly influenced the spatial pattern of retailing in British cities.

The suburbanization of retailing

In many ways spatial changes in retailing have complemented population changes, and one of the most persistent population trends over the last thirty years has been that of movement away from the 'core' areas of our large cities and conurbations: the decentralization phenomenon. Evidence of the absolute loss of population from our larger cities is not difficult to find (see, for example, Hall *et al.*, 1973), but the term 'decentralization' may not necessarily be appropriate for retailing in Britain since there is little evidence of retail decline at the centre of our cities. It is more accurate to suggest that new retail growth has been faster in noncentral locations in Britain, though in North America the 'decentralization' model does have much greater validity. In addition to population movement, the changing spatial distribution of retailing is the result of other factors at work, and these must be considered.

There is evidence that some element of decentralization of retailing was occurring in British cities before the end of the nineteenth century (Wild and Shaw, 1979); but population decentralization (i.e. loss of population) was only first recorded for inner London between 1931 and 1951, and then from 1951 onwards for the other conurbations (e.g. Glasgow's population fell from 1 089 767 in 1951 to less than 770 000 in 1981). Hall and his colleagues have shown that this phenomenon is not confined to the conurbations and that, by 1971, 49 out of the 51 numerically largest urban areas in England were undergoing population decentralization (Hall *et al.*, 1973). The evidence of the 1981 Census shows that such dramatic population losses have continued through the 1970s, with some of the larger conurbations experiencing population losses well in excess of 15 per cent of their 1971 figure (e.g. Glasgow-22 per cent, Manchester-17.5 per cent, Liverpool-16.4 per cent). Even some freestanding medium-sized cities were experiencing significant losses between 1971 and 1981 (e.g. Coventry-6.8 per cent, Nottingham-9.7 per cent, Bristol-9.1 per cent).

Actual population loss is significant in itself for retailing, but the selective nature of the population loss has magnified the problem for retailers: in essence there has been a loss of *demand* from the core areas of our larger cities. Population decentralization has seen particularly high losses of younger households and the more affluent. The 'core' areas of conurbations with over 1 million inhabitants (London, Birmingham, Glasgow, Manchester, Liverpool, Newcastle and Leeds) saw a percentage shift of the professional and managerial socio-economic groups of -18.9 per cent compared with a positive shift of +15.9 per cent in their 'outer rings' (Pinch and Williams, 1983). The spatial implications for retailing of such social class changes are obvious.

Increased personal mobility through the rise of car ownership levels is discussed in detail in Chapter 15. The influence of the car on shopping habits and patterns cannot easily be overestimated. Although access to a car is still confined to less than 70 per cent of the population, again it is generally those with higher disposable incomes who own cars; thus the significance for retailing is again particularly high. The appeal of a chain of causation which links occupation and income to consumer behaviour is appealing, but may not be very realistic (Shephard and Thomas, 1980); car ownership is now quite widely spread through the population. On the other hand, the importance that consumers attach to the availability of car-parking facilities in close proximity to shops is becoming very clear. Many medium-sized food supermarkets which located on prime sites in the middle of the traditional shopping high street in the 1960s have found themselves seriously disadvantaged in more recent years as car-borne consumers have patronized food supermarkets — often on 'free-standing' sites — which have provided large free car parks next to the store. The movement to larger selling areas which has dominated specific types of retailing (e.g. food, furniture, D.I.Y.) have normally been closely associated with the provision of mass car-parking facilities. The combination of these two land-hungry trends has heavily influenced retailers in seeking sites for new stores on low-value sites.

The city centre, with its organic pattern of narrow roads and its historic mosaic of small-sized plots, has not been well suited to take advantage of the movement to larger retail units and the need for car parking near to shops. Planners have, if anything, made life more difficult for the private car within the city centre by a plethora of 'anti-car' devices — including, significantly, much reduced parking — all aimed at reducing congestion and increasing pedestrian safety. The lack of large sites in city centres, and often site availability in general, added to the extremely high central land values, has inevitably deterred many retailers from such central locations. Obsolete buildings and the expense and difficulties involved in expansion have also encouraged multiple chains to open new branches away from the centre as a means of expanding their selling areas.

All the foregoing discussion might lead one to suppose that the traditional focus of urban retailing — the city centre — is in decline. In the United States this is indeed the case. In Los Angeles the central city share of sales turnover for the city fell from 34 per cent to 20 per cent between 1929 and 1939 (Cassady and Bowden, 1944). Numerous American studies in the postwar period have demonstrated the rapid decline of the average C.B.D. (central business district) as a retail centre, particularly in the larger cities. In Britain the percentage of retail sales occurring in the Central Areas declines as the population size increases, pointing to the importance of suburban centres.

Evidence of absolute retail decline within British city centres is, however, scanty. Most evidence suggests that the city centres have shown very healthy growth rates, aided in no small measure by the extent of city centre redevelopment schemes and pedestrianization of some streets. Schiller and Lambert (1977) have shown that between 1965 and 1977 major retail developments (exceeding 50 000 square feet) occurred in no less than 68 per cent of towns in Britain, with a Central Area retail sales level exceeding over £10 million in 1971. However, despite the widespread investment and renewal of infrastructure which has characterized our city centres in recent years, the Central Areas have clearly lost part of their one traditional advantage over other locations — accessibility. With growing levels of car ownership, and urban public transport systems struggling to retain economic viability (see Chapter 15), the city centre is in danger of losing its exclusive position at the head of the retail hierarchy for mass merchandizing. Here changing market forces and debates about the role of public transport clearly overlap with potentially serious implications for the long-term viability of Central Areas as retailing centres.

Planners and retailing

It is clear from some of the earlier chapters in this book that planning has touched on most aspects of urban life in the last forty years. In many cases planning strategies have been clearcut, e.g. population decentralization from our major cities. In the case of retailing, however, despite its recognized importance as a land use, a social service and a source of employment, and its effects on land values, road traffic etc., there has been a lack of clear policy guidelines. It is not difficult to find reasons for this. To begin with there is a dilemma between whether or not retailing should be basically seen as a social service, which should be encouraged to help provide good access to shops for all the population, or whether retailing should be viewed from a purely economic perspective as a largely privately owned service industry, often making irresponsible demands on the environment, e.g. through its role as a generator of heavy traffic flows, or through its effects on other retail outlets (Thorpe, 1975). In rural areas planners have tended to see retailing, through the survival of the village shop, as a distinctly social service, to be encouraged. In the urban context new retailing proposals have tended to be treated with suspicion.

There has been a relative lack of central government policy towards retailing, even though many government policy decisions have both direct and indirect effects on retailing. Government macro-economic policy can clearly affect consumer spending, and retailing investment decisions, while policy decisions which can lead to spatially concentrated unemployment (e.g. closure of steelworks, naval dockyards) will also drastically affect local retailers. As Dawson (1980) points out, one of the problems influencing the general lack of policy for retailing is the fact that no one department at either central or local government level is specifically and directly responsible for retailing. At central government level, departments responsible for trade and industry, the environment, and transport can, and do, put forward policies that affect retailing. At local government level it has been the local planning department that has, almost by default, been left to implement policy with regard to retailing, largely it seems through the planner's role in sanctioning or refusing changes in land use.

Because of the lack of a clear overall policy, planning policy with regard to retailing as it has emerged over the years has largely been reactive in nature. In other words policy has been developed in response to changes in retailing and the pressure from developers for new sites, largely in suburban or even 'greenfield' locations. The lack of knowledge of retail changes (the beginnings of the marketing 'revolution') and the dearth of statistical data and analysis has led planners to be initially suspicious of such developments, and suspicion has often hardened into general hostility.

Planning policy as it has evolved in the context of a lack of clear central guidelines has tended to be based on a number of criteria (Mills, 1974). The first of these has been a widespread view that existing shopping provision must not be deleteriously affected by new developments. This policy seems to have evolved from an initial wish to protect the city centre from the decline in retailing which has clearly occurred in North America. The city centre as the focus of transport routes, particularly public transport, should have its status as the major retailing centre protected or even enhanced by new retail developments or redevelopment being concentrated there. In achieving this aim planners have been very successful (see below). Concern about the effects of new developments has often been subjective, or has been based on one or other of the models discussed earlier in the chapter which have not proved very reliable indicators. As part of this policy, planners have posited a social argument in that the vulnerable retail consumers — the poor, the inner-city dwellers, the old (often lumped together as the 'transport poor') — should have their local shopping centres protected, and the city centre to which they all have access through public transport. This policy has been attacked by developers. First of all it is argued that planners are interfering in the workings of the retail market by stifling competition and, arguably, protecting 'inefficient' traders. From this, planning policies are seen as restrictive and flying in the face of the changes which are an inevitable part of the marketing 'revolution'. Equally, the argument about the importance of the city centre has been criticized, if only on the grounds that increasingly people, and employment, are gravitating to smaller free-standing settlements. The functional nature of the centres of our larger cities is changing, and planners are perhaps wrong to seek to prevent such change.

In view of criticism of this policy argument, planners have increasingly looked to the potentially deleterious environmental and road traffic effects of new schemes. Often developers have deliberately sought 'greenfield', edge-of-town sites not only for cheapness of land but also because they have often viewed location within a regional rather than local urban framework for their trading area. This has particularly been the case with applications for hypermarkets (e.g. an unsuccessful application in 1970 at Banstead Heights in the Surrey 'green belt', next to the then proposed intersection of the M25 and the A217). Developers of such large-scale developments have been very aware of the importance of good regional road networks in seeking locations — the unsuccessful application for an out-of-town shopping centre at Haydock Park in Lancashire would have had good access to both the M6 and M62 motorways and would have been midway between Merseyside and Greater Manchester.

Other arguments that have been put forward by planners have included surveys of future shopping provision in a specific area, with new developments being refused permission on the grounds of overcapacity of retail floor-space. This policy is in many ways the most dubious of all, since the lack of research into, or knowledge of, future patterns of retailing all tend to make such arguments extremely difficult to justify. Developers would again respond by suggesting that the market should be allowed to determine its own level, without planners superimposing some notional ceiling of shopping capacity for a given area.

Given the rapid pace of change in retailing in recent years, it is inevitable that planners should have found themselves in conflict with developers. That planners have slowed down the pace of change in retailing in Britain cannot be denied. Equally, there is a growing view within planning that new developments are inevitable; and there is also increasing evidence that the effects on existing shopping provision of such developments, where they have occurred, have not proved as catastrophic as some planners had feared.

New shopping developments in Britian

It is clear that the planning system in Britain, through the power of local planning authorities to either delay or successfully refuse permission for many new retail developments, has slowed down the rate of retailing change. Comparison with both North America and other West European countries is cited as evidence of Britain's lagging behind in new retailing developments. The new types of development have increasingly been of two kinds: planned shopping centres and large, single, 'free-standing' stores. In fact planners have encouraged the former type of development, in the 'right' location, but have held a very negative view of large 'free-standing' stores — particularly the giant of the species, the hypermarket.

The evolution of new purpose-built shopping centres began in the United States, where such centres have normally been built in suburban locations. Such 'planned' shopping centres have been given a variety of names (e.g. shopping malls, plaza centres, regional shopping centres, and out-of-town shopping centres), but all have the same basic attributes. They are privately owned and developed, consist of an intricate, highly coordinated complex of retail units of varying size and provide an indoor, air-conditioned environment for the shopper. Good car-parking facilities are available adjacent to the shopping centre, and the whole complex is normally, though not always, built away from existing shopping areas. The lack of strong planning controls in the United States has allowed these centres to proliferate, leading to a decline in the Central Area and what many commentators have seen as clear overcapacity of retail floor-space. It is estimated that there are over 10 000 such centres in the United States, accounting for nearly 40 per cent of retail turnover. Such centres are also quite common in mainland Europe.

In terms of their main characteristics, such planned retail developments are also familiar to most British consumers, but tend to be distinctive in Britain for two reasons. First, and most obviously, is their location within the existing Central Area in British cities. Secondly, in nearly all examples in Britian the relevant local authority has had an active role in their development, either in encouraging private developers or acquiring and assembling sites themselves, or often both. Such developments have been seen as meeting pressure from developers for more retail floor-space, and, more importantly, as emphasizing the continuing importance of the city centre as *the* major retail centre within the urban area. The extent of such city centre developments has already been mentioned. There has been marked concentration in the larger urban areas where no less than 88 per cent of towns with a Central Area retail sales level of £25m in 1971 saw a new scheme opened between 1965 and 1977 (Schiller and Lambert, 1977).

While local planning authorities have usually been willing actors in the expansion of city centre retailing, their suspicion of 'free-standing' developments has led to only one new large planned shopping centre outside an existing shopping centre — that of Brent Cross in North London. This was opened in 1976, but only after a public inquiry and strong opposition from planners on the Greater London Council. The second type of new retail development — the large 'free-standing' store — has been very slow to develop in Britain, again in contrast to North America and mainland Western Europe. Opposition to hypermarkets has been so strong and so successful among planning authorities that in 1976 one survey suggested that only four hypermarkets were open in the United Kingdom compared to over 300 in France and 538 in West Germany (Dawson and Kirby, 1980). The exact definitions of, and differences between, hypermarkets and superstores (a British nomenclature) are confusing, but basically the size of selling area and assumptions concerning the range of goods sold are implicit in such definitions. For example, one definition suggested a selling area of at least 2325 square metres for a hypermarket (M.P.C. and Associates, 1973), while a more recent survey suggested 5000 square metres as the lower limit (URPI, 1982). This later survey also suggested that 22 hypermarkets were operating in the United Kingdom in 1976, not four. This again acts as an illustration of the statistical problems involved in the analysis of retailing patterns and trends. According to the URPI survey (1982), some 41 hypermarkets were open by 1981 with a further 57 planned.

The pace of new developments of both superstores and hypermarkets clearly quickened in the 1970s, suggesting a softening of planning policies with regard to these new types of retail stores. New superstore 'openings' rose from 10 in 1974 to 29 in 1981, though the number of new hypermarkets has been far lower, though more consistent, running at between 3 and 6 per year from 1974 to 1981 (URPI, 1982). This apparent mellowing of opposition from planners, particularly towards superstores, is no doubt partially a reflection of the fact that surveys of shoppers patronizing new superstores and surveys of existing retailers within the local area have tended to show that the impact of such new developments has been rather less than disastrous. A certain folklore with regard to the impact of hypermarkets in particular has developed (Dawson and Kirby, 1980). For example, in West Germany a popularly held view is that a large hypermarket (of 10 000 metres or more of selling space) leads to the closure of 60 small shops, while another view assumes a hypermarket will take 30 per cent of sales from existing local shops. Evidence from Britain suggests a rather wider catchment area for such developments than planners have expected, leading to the 'creaming off' effect on existing shops being fairly thinly spread, with consequently less impact on other retailers. Such evidence comes from a small number of surveys (e.g. Thorpe and McGoldrick, 1974; Shepherd and Newby, 1978; Scottish Development Department, 1978), and there has been little overall analysis of the individual studies.

Retailing change: some current trends

In this chapter reference has repeatedly been made to the rate of change in retailing, and in the last section it has been suggested that retail planning in Britain is moving towards the guidance and control of new developments rather than outright resistance. Despite the success of planners in encouraging new investment in the expansion and redevelopment of our city centres, the latter are beginning to change under the impact of market forces and changing consumer preferences. In functional terms the Central Areas have experienced a loss of food retailing and are likely to lose more of their share of mass merchandizing, because of an increasing concern with the provision of specialist, high-quality shops serving the wider trade area. The city centre has clearly lost much of its traditional advantage of central accessibility in recent years and will perhaps have to rely increasingly on its captive markets of Central Area employees and inner and central area residents. Such is the strength of the continuing commitment by planners to the retention of the city centre — aided by the very considerable investment in the centre in recent years — that it is unlikely that further 'free-standing' centres on the model of Brent Cross will be built in the foreseeable future.

The pressure for new superstores and hypermarkets will no doubt continue, though there is now a debate about the possibility of saturation of the market, by superstores in particular, in some regions, e.g. the North West of England, which had 46 superstores and hypermarkets in 1981 (URPI, 1982). However, some regions are much less well catered for, while Greater London had only five such stores open in 1981. The uneven regional distribution of such developments is likely to adjust itself in the future (see Jones, 1982).

One further development that is occurring is a contemporaneous reduction in the overall number of shops in Britain, with an increasing polarization between very large retail stores and small shops. The future for the small shop, often traditionally thought of as particularly vulnerable, is now seen as quite healthy. Such evidence as there is suggests that, far from damaging small shops, the development of large stores has seen the re-emergence of a need for small, local convenience stores with long opening hours (see Dawson and Kirby, 1979).

It is clear that retailing will continue to place demands on the planning system for new developments and new sites. In some ways retailing is responding to the continual dispersal of population away from the 'core' conurbations to smaller settlements and therefore pressure for new developments will run in harness with the wider process of further urban development (see Herington, 1984, for a detailed discussion of population dispersal and development pressures). Retailing also seems to have an inbuilt momentum for change, at once both leading and being led by changing consumer preferences in a very competitive market. The losers in this process are likely to continue to be the inner-city areas with falling populations and plummeting income levels. There remains a basic need for more information on retail trends and, above all, an active, forward looking central planning policy to control retailing change.

References

Alonso, W. (1964) *Location and Land Use,* Harvard University Press, Cambridge, Massachusetts

Berry, B.J.L. and Garrison, W.L. (1958) Functional bases of the central place hierarchy, *Economic Geography,* Vol. 34, pp. 145-54

Berry, B.J.L. and Pred, A. (1965) Central place studies: a bibliography of theory and applications. Regional Science Research Institute, Philadelphia

Berry, B.J.L. (1967) *Geography of Market Centres and Retail Distribution,* Prentice-Hall, Englewood Cliffs, New Jersey

Bruce, A.J. (1970) Housewife attitudes towards shops and shopping. In Proceedings of the Architectural Psychology Conference, Kingston Polytechnic

Cassady, R. and Bowden, W.K. (1944) Shifting retail trade within the Los Angeles Metropolitan Market, *Journal of Marketing,* Vol.8. pp 398-404

Christaller, W. (1966) *Central Places in Southern Germany,* Prentice-Hall, Englewood Cliffs, New Jersey (Translated by C.S. Baskin)

Davies, R.L. (1973) Patterns and profiles of consumer behaviour, Department of Geography Research Series, No. 10, University of Newcastle-upon-Tyne

Davies, R.L. (1976) Marketing geography, Retail Planning Associates, Corbridge

Dawson J.A. (ed.) (1980) *Retail Geography,* Croom Helm, London

Dawson, J.A. and Kirby, D.A. (1979) *Small Scale Retailing in the UK,* Saxon House, Farnborough

Dawson, J.A. and Kirby, D.A. (1980) *Urban retail provision and consumer behaviour: some examples from Western society.* In D.T. Herbert and R.J. Johnston (1980) Geography and the Urban Environment, Vol. III, John Wiley, Chichester

Downs, R.M. (1970) The cognitive structure of an urban shopping centre, *Environment and Behaviour,* Vol.2, pp 13-39

Hall, P. (ed.) (1966) *Von Thunen's Isolated State,* Pergamon Press, Oxford

Hall, P. Thomas, R. Gracey, H. and Drewett, R. (1973) *The Containment of Urban England,* George Allen and Unwin, London

Herington, J. (1984) *The Outer City,* Harper and Row, London

Jenkinson, G. (1982) Retail trade statistics in the 1980's, Unit for Retail Planning Information Conference, October 1982, URPI U24, Reading

Jones, P. (1982) Hypermarkets and superstores: future trends or saturation? Unit for Retail Planning Information Conference, October 1982, URPI U24 Reading

Mills, E. (1974) Recent developments in retailing and urban planning, PRAG Technical Papers, TP3

M.P.C. and Associates (1973) The changing pattern of retailing in Western Europe, M.P.C. and Associates, Worcester

National Economic Development Office (N.E.D.O.) (1970) *Urban Models in Shopping Studies,* HMSO, London

Pinch, S. and Williams, A. (1983) *Social class change in British cities.* In J. B. Goddard and A. G. Champion (1983) The Urban and Regional Transformation of Britain, Methuen, London

Potter, R.B. (1977) Spatial patterns of consumer behaviour and perception in relation to the social class variable, *Area*, Vol.9, No.2, pp 153-6

Schiller, R. and Lambert, S. (1977) The quantity of major shopping development in Britain since 1965, *Estates Gazette*, Vol. 242, No 5839, pp 359-63

Scott, P. (1970) *Geography and Retailing*, Hutchinson, London

Scottish Development Department (1978) *The Impact of a Town Centre Superstore*, HMSO, Edinburgh

Shephard, I.D.H. and Newby, P. (1978) The Brent Cross shopping centre — characteristics and early effects, Retail Planning Associates, Corbridge

Shephard, I.D.H. and Thomas, C.J, (1980) *Urban consumer behaviour*. In J.A. Dawson (1980) Retail Geography, Croom Helm, London

Smith, G.C. (1976) The spatial information fields of urban consumers, *Transactions of the Institute of British Geographers*, *New Series*, No.1, pp 175-89

Thomas, C.J. (1974) The effects of social class and car ownership on intra-urban shopping behaviour in Greater Swansea, *Cambria*, Vol.2, pp 98-126

Thorpe, D. (1975) Retail Planning: key policy issues. In D. Thorpe (1975) Town Planning for retailing, Manchester Business School, Retail Outlets Research Unit, Research Report No. 20

Thorpe, D. and McGoldrick, P.J. (1974) Carrefour: Caerphilly: consumer reaction, Research Report No. 12, Retail Outlets Research Unit, Manchester Business School

URPI (1982) List of UK hypermarkets and superstores, Unit for Retail Planning Information, Reading

Wild, M.T. and Shaw, G. (1979) Trends in urban retailing: the British experience during the nineteenth century, *Tijdscrift voor Econ on Soc Geografie*, Vol. 70, No.1, pp 35-44

Further reading

The literature for retailing is particularly dispersed with very few comprehensive or basic texts. Scott (1970) provides a good account of traditional approaches and patterns, while Dawson (ed.) (1980) is the most comprehensive text available. A wide view of the marketing process is provided in Davies (1976).

Introduction

A huge increase in the number of people in regular, paid employment was one of the tangible results of the Industrial Revolution. The population growth of the 'great towns' in the nineteenth century was due in large measure to their expanding employment opportunities. The twentieth century has also seen major changes in population migration at two spatial scales: a reversal of the nineteenth-century flow from the rural South to the urbanizing North, as the staple industries such as iron, textiles, mining and shipbuilding have declined; and on an urban/regional scale the movement of people from our conurbation areas to surrounding suburban belts or satellite towns. In the last two decades the decline of manufacturing employment in particular has had a devastating effect on our major cities, leading some commentators to speak of 'de-industrialization' (e.g. Cairncross, 1979). Employment opportunities, or the lack of them, have therefore been a fundamental and enduring factor influencing urban and regional change in Britain and must form a key part of any analysis of such change. This chapter falls into two parts. The first looks at employment change at the regional and the urban levels in recent years, with particular emphasis on the decline of manufacturing employment within British cities. Although the service sector is examined, the main emphasis is on manufacturing, for a number of reasons (see Bull, 1983): first, the rapid decline of the manufacturing sector has had severe effects on urban areas; secondly, while spatial changes in service industries have seen rapid growth, and some decline, the pattern largely reflects changing population distributions in and around our large urban areas (Keeble, 1978); thirdly, most of the economic initiatives put forward by central government and local authorities have been geared towards halting or reversing the downward trend in manufacturing employment.

The changing pattern of manufacturing employment

The regional scale

The post-1945 period has seen considerable regional shifts in manufacturing employment. Overall there was a growth in total employment, with relatively minor reverses, until the mid-1960s. Since then it has steadily contracted, partly through increases in labour productivity, but in the last decade increasingly through contraction of capacity and decline in output. The regional impact of this period of employment growth and the accelerated decline that followed has been varied in the extreme. In essence two processes have been at work: increasing dispersion of manufacturing activity away from the traditional 'core' conurbations to smaller 'free-standing' towns and the 'rural' regions (Keeble, 1976, 1980), and a rapid decline of the manufacturing sector within many of our conurbations. The two processes are not necessarily causally linked and, despite the elegance of the decentralization model, there is comparatively little evidence to support the thesis of migration of firms from urban to rural locations.

Fothergill and Gudgin (1982) provide a critique of the reliance on 'regions' to describe or explain employment change, in that using such large areal units can mask considerable variations at the subregional level. For example, the South-East has a fairly healthy record of employment growth throughout the postwar period, though London, as we shall see, has suffered very severe employment losses. Fothergill and Gudgin suggest a sixfold division based on urban-rural contrasts for the analysis of employment changes: London, the conurbations, 'free-standing' cities, 'industrial' towns, 'county' towns and rural areas. Analysis using this classification reveals the importance and strength of the urban-rural differences in employment change, e.g. from 1959 to 1975 London and the conurbations lost 11.4 per cent and 4.7 per cent of total employment respectively. In contrast 'industrial' towns and 'county' towns gained 22 per cent and 18 per cent respectively over the same period. A further complication when looking at regional differences is reliance on percentage change, which can hide very important quantitative changes. For example, between 1965 and 1975 East Anglia gained 18.6 per cent in manufacturing employment while the North-West lost 16.8 per cent. However, in 1965 East Anglia only employed some 2 per cent of the total United Kingdom manufacturing employment force, compared to the North-West's 14.6 per cent. In terms of actual jobs, East Anglia gained some 31 000, while the North-West lost over 200 000 (Keeble, 1978).

With these caveats in mind we can now examine regional differences in manufacturing employment in recent years. As Fothergill and Gudgin note in examining regional disparities in employment growth: 'the striking feature is the diversity of experience' (Fothergill and Gudgin, 1983, p.32). The regional pattern (see Figure 8) reflects the importance of considering the effects of job losses in London and the conurbations. Thus, although the general view of a prosperous South versus an impoverished North of Britain seems confirmed by the prosperity of the South-West, the East Midlands and East Anglia, neither the South-East nor the West Midlands have done very well — a fact that reflects the massive influence of London on the one hand and the Birmingham conurbation on the other. Similarly, Wales and the northern region of England come out reasonably well in the analysis (but it is important to remember that coal mining job losses are ignored here), while the North-West, Northern Ireland and Scotland have clearly fared badly. Again, though, regional averages hide very real subregional differences: within Scotland, the Highlands and Islands region has seen substantial growth in manufacturing employment, but, even more than East Anglia, from a very small base figure. We shall return to the importance of the urban-rural shift in manufacturing activity and to Fothergill and Gudgin's preferred categorization of subregional areas in the section dealing with explanations of manufacturing change and decline.

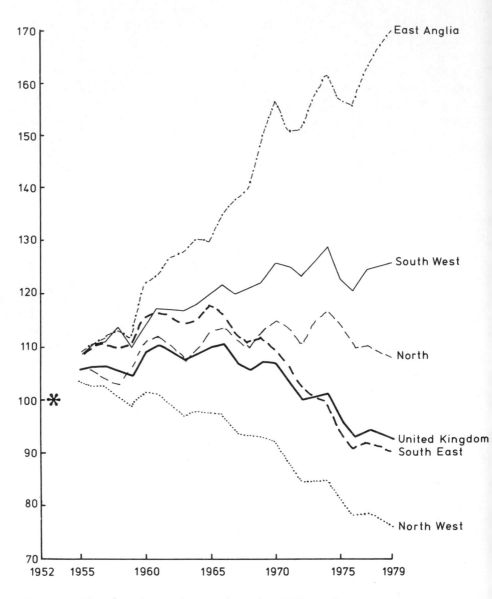

Figure 8   Manufacturing employment by region, 1952-79 (*Source:* adapted from *Unequal Growth,* Fothergill and Gudgin, Heinemann, 1982)

The urban scale

The evidence of change in manufacturing employment within urban areas has tended to concentrate on the larger conurbations, and therefore on decline. In recent years a plethora of case studies has been published, which have allowed some general analysis of the causes of decline within the 'core' conurbations to be attempted. A brief review of the evidence from three conurbations is presented here.

An approach towards the study of the changing pattern of manufacturing employment which has gained increasing acceptance in recent years involves an examination of the 'components of change'. Bull has noted the large number of British cities for which 'this kind of establishment accounting procedure' has been used (Bull, 1983, p.53). The four components of change involve: (1) plant 'births', entirely new factories or firms, or factories that are transferred into the city or study area; (2) plant 'deaths', closures resulting from complete closure or outward migration of a factory from the study area; (3) movement of factories within the study area (intra-urban moves); and (4) plant 'survivors', which remain *in situ* but which may still undergo expansion or contraction of their labour force during the time-period chosen for the study.

Despite the overall employment prosperity of the South-East of England, London has suffered a much greater decline in its manufacturing base than any other conurbation. Between 1961 and 1975 London lost no less than 560 000 manufacturing jobs — more than the *total* number of jobs in the manufacturing sector in Scotland. Between 1966 and 1974 the 'account' between 'births' and 'deaths' in London revealed a gain of 12 900 jobs and a loss of 280 300 through plant closures, or a net loss of 267 400 jobs (Dennis, 1978). The 1947 planning system was of course aiming not at job losses but at encouraging the decentralization of firms and jobs, from London in particular, to the new towns and the Assisted or Development Areas. Dennis's study shows a further loss of over 100 000 jobs between 1966 and 1974 from firms closing London plants and transferring production elsewhere. The importance of government policy in encouraging this kind of industrial movement is shown by Dennis to be a minor factor, involving comparatively few jobs, while a study of South-East London by Gripaios (1977) confirms that most job losses must be attributed to plant 'deaths'. Dennis's analysis suggests 69 per cent of the overall job losses may be attributed to this factor, while in the more detailed study by Gripaios plant 'deaths' accounted for between 70.4 per cent (Lewisham) and 90.5 per cent (Deptford) from 1970 to 1975 in South-East London.

Using the same methodology, Lloyd and Mason (1978) studied manufacturing employment change in inner Manchester from 1966 to 1972. The loss through plant 'deaths' in this instance was less than 31 000 manual jobs, but these accounted for some 33 per cent of the total in the study area in 1966. A further 6 000 jobs were lost from shrinkage in the labour forces of plant 'survivors'. One interesting point to emerge from this study was the impact of plant size (in terms of numbers employed) on job losses. During the period studied some 604 plants were lost, most of which (87 per cent) employed fewer than 50 people. However, the remaining 13 per cent accounted for 65 per cent of job losses while the largest seven plants closed accounted for no less than 17 per cent of the total employment loss. A third example of conurbation decline in manufacturing is that of Clydeside, covering the period from 1958 to 1968 (Bull, 1978). This study registered some 529 'births' of plants in the study area, alongside 711 'deaths', producing a net loss of 182 plants. Bull also notes that a further 607 plants moved within Clydeside during the time-period studied (intra-urban moves), or 52.6 per cent of the plants located in Clydeside in 1958. Other studies have confirmed the surprising magnitude of industrial movement over quite short time-periods.

The picture of considerable industrial change, but clear net decline, involving our conurbations, shows that most job losses in manufacturing have been due to complete closure or 'deaths' of plants, and that comparatively few plants have migrated to the suburbs, the satellite towns or the 'industrial' and 'county' towns of Fothergill and Gudgin's classification. However, these smaller towns have, on the whole, seen considerable growth in manufacturing employment. Quite simply this growth has been largely through the location of new firms in the smaller towns and rural areas, not through any major geographical movement of existing firms: the decentralization thesis must be rejected.

Explanations of changing manufacturing employment patterns

Manufacturing employment has been falling in the United Kingdom since the mid-1960s, with a loss of no less than 2.5 million jobs between 1966 and 1981. This contraction has in the last decade affected all regions of the country though, as we have seen, the larger urban areas have been particularly badly hit while the smaller towns and rural areas have been in many cases only marginally affected. 'Manufacturing industry' covers a very disparate group of activities, and it is erroneous to suggest that one cause, or even a small group of causes, can explain the extent and geographical pattern of job losses. In the following subsections we shall attempt to examine some of the reasons put forward to explain changing manufacturing location and the increasing decline in manufacturing activities.

(a) *Traditional geographic and economic approaches.* The traditional contribution of geography to industrial location has been largely devoted to description and as such has proved to be very limited in helping us to understand the causes of locational change. Models of industrial location at the urban scale (e.g. Hamilton, 1967) are overwhelmed by the number and complexity of factors that may affect the location of different manufacturing activities. It is significant that a seminal urban geography text such as that by Carter (1981) devotes such little space to the urban geography of industry. Industrial location theory, to which both geographers and economists have contributed (e.g. see Smith, 1971), has proved to be of little relevance in attempting to understand the changing location of manufacturing in a small country like Britain. Most theories of industrial location involve discussion of the importance of transport costs. In Britain today such costs vary little and indeed peripheral regions such as the Highlands of Scotland or the South West of England are the very areas that have seen sustained growth in manufacturing in recent decades. One much vaunted advantage of large urban areas stemmed from 'agglomeration economies' such as industrial linkages between firms, a well-developed transport infrastructure, a large labour market etc. Such empirical evidence as exists for the geography of job losses suggests that large cities appear to be clearly disadvantaged as locations for manufacturing activity. Increasingly, simple geographic description and classical economic location theory are being recognized as at best unsatisfactory and at worst irrelevant in the search for explanations of the causes and the spatial unevenness of job losses.

(b) The inner-city environment. Since it is the 'core' areas of our conurbations in particular that have tended to suffer the largest job losses in manufacturing employment — and suffered some of the highest unemployment rates as a result — it is not surprising that much attention has been focused on the inner city in seeking the causes of job losses. Again, traditional views would point to the advantages of inner-city locations, both in terms of agglomeration economies and the good accessibility provided by such locations. The inner city provided a home for many traditional industries, though since it is many of the latter that have suffered the greatest decline some explanation of inner-city job loss is immediately apparent, for example the decline in heavy engineering and iron foundries in the East End of Glasgow.

Keeble (1978) suggests a variety of reasons as to why the inner city no longer provides an attractive location for entrepreneurs, particularly for new enterprises. Keeble notes that in some cities an unfavourable industrial structure, biased towards declining industries, may be a basic explanation of plant closures and job losses, but points out that this cannot be a satisfactory explanation of the drastic decline of London as a manufacturing city since its industrial structure is biased towards expanding rather than declining sectors. Land and premises costs remain much higher in inner-city locations than elsewhere, and this must act as a disincentive to new entrepreneurs. This historic pattern of high inner urban area land values is clearly related to the accessibility of such sites and to the potential agglomeration economies to be obtained from such locations. Paradoxically, many such sites now lie derelict and unwanted by industrialists (e.g. well over 500 acres were derelict or unused in the Lower Don Valley in Sheffield by 1985), yet still retain historically high values. This is clearly not in accord with the basic tenets of supply and demand, but rather reflects a pattern of borrowing by struggling firms from the lending institutions against notionally high site and premises values. The resulting artifically high values are likely to drive new industries into seeking cheaper suburban or satellite town sites. Keeble also points to the selective nature of emigration of population from inner-city areas and to the fact that the inner city is generally typified by a negative image of a dirty, worn-out environment in which neither entrepreneurs nor their workforces are likely to want to work. Comprehensive redevelopment of many inner-city areas in the 1960s, while aimed primarily at unfit housing, nonetheless swept away numerous small industrial concerns, which often paid peppercorn rents for small, outmoded premises. In most cases the evidence suggests that these firms simply ceased to operate as a result of redevelopment, since their low profit margins made it impossible for them to move to purpose-built, but high-rent industrial premises.

The small size of many sites in inner-city locations and an obsolete infrastructure of nineteenth-century buildings and difficult, narrow access for modern lorries have also been posited as part of the unattractive nature of inner area sites for new enterprises. Fothergill and Gudgin argue strongly that it is the constrained nature of many industrial sites within the large cities that has inhibited growth. They suggest that existing firms find it impossible to expand in such locations, while the problem of small plots exacerbates 'land assembly' for potential new enterprises. A major study of Birmingham's industrial land use (J.U.R.U.E., 1979) found that 70 per cent of the factories studied had no room for further expansion, almost half the buildings were pre-1914 in age and two thirds had their production space spread over two floors or more. Such an industrial mix is clearly at odds with new manufacturing plants, which require a large amount of space, good parking and access facilities and where, increasingly all production and assembly takes place on one floor or level.

Not all views of the inner city as a location for new industry are so gloomy. Some commentators have argued that inner urban areas offer good locations as 'nurseries' or 'incubators' for new small businesses (Hoover and Vernon, 1959). It is argued that the inner city offers cheap premises as well as industrial linkages with other firms nearby for new businesses to start up, with minimal financial risks. This 'incubator' hypothesis, which argues that the inner city is an important seedbed for the fostering of new small enterprises, has had a mixed reception. Some empirical evidence in favour of it has been found (e.g. in Leicester by Fagg, 1980), but other researchers have found very little evidence to support it (e.g. Nicholson *et al.*, 1981).

(c) *Corporate ownership of plants.* Research by Dicken and Lloyd (1978) examined employment change in Manchester and Merseyside, using the 'components of change' methodology outlined earlier in this chapter. One significant difference between Manchester and Merseyside lay in the average size of plant, and this in turn reflected a difference in ownership. Merseyside has had Development Area status since the last war and, in the 1960s particularly, many large, multiplant firms, both British and multinational, established large branch plants on Merseyside in order to take advantage of the financial incentives offered through regional policy. Manchester has never had Development Area status. Many of the headquarters of firms operating in Merseyside were to be found outside the area, most notably in London and the South-East. Plants in Manchester were far more likely to have local headquarters. Dicken and Lloyd argue that the nature of corporate ownership of plants and the location of the decision makers regarding expansion, closure etc. can be highly influential in the process of industrial change. Merseyside did comparatively well as a 'branch economy' until the mid-1970s, when the world recession led to retrenchment and labour-shedding by many large multinational firms. Dicken and Lloyd suggest that the reduced level of local entrepreneurship in Merseyside is potentially very dangerous for the local economy and that 'in the general climate of manufacturing over-capacity and retrenchment, the real vulnerability of Merseyside's enterprise mix has become apparent' (Lloyd and Dicken, 1983, p.68).

(d) *Structural changes.* Massey and Meegan (1982) have recently suggested three related mechanisms of change within British industry which together help to explain to a considerable degree both why there has been such a drastic overall decline in manufacturing employment in Britian, and also why its spatial impact has been so varied. Massey and Meegan argue that much of the decline in industry is related to *intensification* and *rationalization* of industrial production, and to *investment and technical change*. Intensification involves increasing the productivity of labour, and often therefore achieving the same output with a reduced labour force, leading to job losses. Rationalization essentially involves cutting capacity and is the cause most easily identified with plant closures and unemployment. Investment and technical change has often meant new labour-saving methods of production — part of an increasing drive towards mechanization of many industrial processes, with resultant savings in labour. Massey and Meegan point to evidence of all three of these independent processes at work in a number of industries, all tending to lead to a shedding of labour. Their analysis illustrates the need to examine the nature of industrial production within individual industries and some of the changes occurring in production methods, in order to gain a better insight into why employment decline is occurring and why the spatial effects are so varied.

Fothergill and Gudgin, in their analysis of employment change, suggest that four structural characteristics are crucial in determining the differential growth and decline of manufacturing employment, and that together they exert 'a dominant influence on the changing location of manufacturing jobs' (Fothergill and Gudgin, 1983, p.29). The first characteristic alluded to is that of *industrial structure*, or the 'mix' of industries to be found in a specific city or region. Clearly this will influence employment change significantly if, for example, the 'mix' is of industries known to have undergone severe rationalization in recent years, for example shipbuilding on Clydeside. The second characteristic, *urban structure*, which as has already been discussed, has been crucial in recent years in determining the rate of job loss: essentially the larger the city the more rapid has been its manufacturing decline. The third element identified by Fothergill and Gudgin is the *size structure* of factories. They argue that if the regional or urban manufacturing scene is dominated by large factories (those employing many people), then decline is much more likely, with severe effects when any one plant closes. Where the local economy is dominated by small firms, specific closures have less impact, and there is growing evidence that small firms are both more healthy, and more likely to prosper than large ones.

The final element in the Fothergill-Gudgin analysis is *regional policy*, which must be seen as separate from the other three elements as a generator of manufacturing employment for the Assisted Areas. Regional policy has clearly had some impact on these Areas, though it has proved difficult to quantify. Most authorities are agreed that, given the massive long-term investment involved, the results have been very disappointing, and regional policy has exerted no discernible influence on employment in the Assisted Areas since the mid-1970s. Equally, however, it must be made clear that regional policy has had very little effect as a cause of employment decline in conurbations like London and Birmingham. Dennis (1978) estimated that only 9 per cent of job losses in London between 1966 and 1974 could be attributed to firms moving to Assisted Areas.

In the subsections above an attempt has been made to examine some of the factors that have been put forward to explain the rate and pattern of change in manufacturing employment. It is becoming increasingly clear that a whole series of overlapping factors is at work and that simplistic explanations of the demise of our manufacturing sector are misleading. Further research is required to test hypotheses and confirm or refute some of the arguments which have been outlined here.

The service sector

The discussion so far in this chapter has centred around the changing pattern and often dramatic decline of urban manufacturing. The service sector has not received anything like the attention devoted to manufacturing change and remains a somewhat neglected, under-researched field. This section is based primarily on the work of Marquand (1983). Part of the reason for the neglect of the service sector lies in the problem of adequately defining it. Services cover activities such as transport and the distribution trades, public administration, banking and insurance, the retail trade and the provision of personal services. This is not an exhaustive list and, as Marquand points out, there is a considerable overlap between manufacturing and service job classifications. Service occupations have been a growth area for employment over a long period and, almost unnoticed, have overtaken manufacturing as the numerically most important job sector. In 1971, 61 per cent of those employed were in service occupations, and there was an increase of 28 per cent in service employment between 1960 and 1977 compared to a 16 per cent decline in manufacturing employment over the same period — a decline which has accelerated rapidly in the last decade. *Prima facie* this suggests a shift of jobs from one sector to the other: the de-industrialization of Britain and our emergence as a post-industrial nation providing services for other countries. However, this ignores the nature of growth and decline and the relatively small overlap between the workforces. Female employment is very strongly represented in the service sector as a whole; it rose by 48 per cent from 1960 to 1977 while the growth in male employment over the same period was only 11 per cent. Most of the job losses in manufacturing, with the exception of textiles, have involved male employees. Thus growth in the service sector has not, and will not, replace job losses in manufacturing: redundant miners and foundry workers are not likely to become secretaries or accountants. Also there has been rapid growth of female part-time employment in the service sector, again no substitute for full-time jobs for men with redundant manufacturing skills.

In the 1960s the explosive growth of office employment led to a centralization of this part of the service sector, particularly in central London, but to a lesser extent in all large cities. This trend has reversed itself in the 1970s with increasing dispersion of service-sector activities. As Marquand notes, however, this does not extend to the urban-rural shift which Fothergill and Gudgin have observed for manufacturing employment. Between 1971 and 1977 Marquand found the greatest growth in southern England, within 100 miles of London, from the Bristol area in the West, south to Dorset and east to East Anglia. London itself has experienced a sharp decline in its service sector. But such trends are based on limited studies and scanty information, emphasizing the relative lack of research into the service sector. One final comment is necessary here: there is a widespread assumption that the service sector will continue to expand in employment terms. To some extent this is likely to be true, though the influence of technological innovation (e.g. the increasing use of computers, office word processors etc.) may slow down employment growth significantly. Some authorities suggest that service employment may in fact begin to decline in the fairly near future. All we can say with certainty is that service jobs do not provide a ready alternative for most people who lose their jobs in the manufacturing sector, and that the spatial pattern of service employment reflects the general distribution of population rather more closely than that of manufacturing, with far less dramatic local effects.

Having explored the changing patterns of urban employment, attention should now turn to intervention by local authorities in urban economies.

Local government and urban economic intervention

Until the mid to late 1970s local authority economic intervention remained minimal. Some of the major cities it is true allocated land for industrial development, some manufacturing premises were constructed and the advantages of an area would often be stressed in an attempt to attract footloose companies (Camina, 1974). But compared with the kinds of policies being implemented by the major cities a decade later these earlier interventions have to be perceived as marginal in the extreme. In practice, a sea-change in attitudes towards economic development and employment creation occurred within local government in the late 1970s. Probably policy intervention and innovation in those areas proved more intense than in any other area of urban governance in the late 1970s and early 1980s.

This transformation in attitudes towards economic intervention occurred for a variety of reasons. The enormous increase in unemployment in manufacturing industry endured by the cities (referred to previously) was obviously one factor. Another was the radicalization of some local authorities. Traditional, usually right-wing Labour, or Tory, local administrations were replaced by far more interventionist-minded, left-wing Labour activists eager to embark on policies designed to increase the scope and scale of public-sector influence within the local economy. Authorities such as Sheffield, West Midlands County Council and the Greater London Council were clearly determined by the early 1980s to implement policies designed to moderate the scale of economic retrenchment in the cities, to control more closely the operations of the market and to improve the economic opportunities of those marginalized by prevailing social and economic forces. It was quite obvious that such policies would eventually bring local government into conflict with the centre, but, as many radical authorities remained firmly convinced that Conservative administrations elected in 1979 and 1983 were simply not interested in the economic fortunes of the older industrial regions of the country, this hardly mattered. For many cities independent economic strategies were simply a necessity to counter prevailing market trends that central government appeared determined to accentuate.

It is important, however, to stress that not all authorities in the mid-1980s are wedded to radical policies of intervention in the areas of economic development and employment creation. There has certainly been a considerable change in attitudes, and virtually every urban administration in the country would no doubt perceive the retention or creation of jobs as a most important corporate objective. But it is possible to identify a wide range of strategies adopted by different local administrations. Variations can occur in at least four different ways: the extent to which authorities are prepared to commit resources to economic intervention; the existence or otherwise of specific employment departments or sections; the attitude of the authority towards the market; and the degree to which an authority is prepared to implement more radical proposals in the field of employment creation. However, any classification based on these criteria will prove complex and by no means watertight. In this context a more profitable framework for analysis is one that distinguishes between orthodox and radical approaches towards intervention. In the remaining sections of this chapter an attempt will therefore be made to provide both something of an overview of the kinds of activities these types of authorities might adopt and also an evaluation of the constraints and opportunities intrinsic to economic intervention.

The orthodox authority and economic development

Most cities and many towns implement policies that can be perceived as orthodox rather than radical in direction. As central governments have generally remained convinced that policies towards economic development are a prerogative of the centre, authorities will vary in their approach partly because advice upon, or resources for, innovation in this area are unnecessary. Inevitably, therefore, local authorities undertaking economically orientated policies are operating within something of a vacuum, and hence markedly different strategies have emerged. These have been considered in greater detail elsewhere (Bramley *et al.*, 1978; Robinson, 1979; Collinge, 1983; Young and Mason, 1983; Chandler and Lawless, 1985), but some brief overview should be presented here. There are five major types of activities typical of more orthodox urban authorities intending to intervene in the areas of economic development and employment creation: policies designed to attract industry; industrial development and rehabilitation; support for new enterprises; labour-market policy; and financial innovations. There are, of course, employment or economic implications inherent in many other policies implemented by local government. Environmental improvements can, for instance, help stimulate confidence in an area; improvements to transport infrastructure can ameliorate accessibility and enhance labour mobility; housing investment can create jobs in the construction industry and provide accommodation for key workers recruited by local companies. But space dictates that only policies introduced as part of a specific economic development or employment creation plan should be considered here.

Attraction of industry

Virtually all authorities will provide promotional material, which is usually made available to companies or associations so requesting it, at trade fairs, or on specific trade delegations which an authority may arrange either within the country or abroad. Typically, information will cover the availability of land and industrial premises, assistance from the local authority for incoming firms, educational, housing and recreational facilities, infrastructure and so on. Sometimes an authority will also provide trade directories, or undertake sectoral analyses indicating local market strengths and gaps. Whereas this sort of material can be produced at relatively little cost there are doubts about its effectiveness. It is true that some information, say on the price and availability of land and premises, can be useful for indigenous or incoming companies, but in other ways benefits appear limited. There are few footloose companies within the United Kingdom, and if promotional material simply involves a reshuffling of a few firms at public expense there will be no net gain. Encouraging companies to locate within a British local authority from abroad may be more acceptable. Many regions of the country are, however, familiar with the problems of larger multinational companies establishing branch plants using, say, regional assistance and then closing these during any subsequent corporate retrenchment.

Industrial development and rehabilitation

Powers contained within legislation such as the 1963 Local Authorities (Land) Act allow local government to acquire, control and develop land. These sorts of powers have been used extensively by many authorities in order to service land for industrial use. Increasingly, too, local authorities have become involved in the construction of industrial units, particularly small ones. Frequently an administration might come into agreement with a private developer or an institutional investor to spread risks and returns. The scale of local government intervention in industrial development increased enormously in the 1970s. In 1971 only 5 per cent of authorities were involved in this activity, but by the end of the decade most local administrations had undertaken some development activity (Chalkley and Perry, 1984). This growth, while understandable in the context of massive urban plant closures, is not without its critics. The construction of units may be important, but authorities may have to provide substantial subsidies through rent and rate relief to encourage firms into them. Such companies may not in the event be manufacturing firms, which most authorities would prefer, but rather warehousing establishments, which tend to employ fewer people. Also, interest in industrial development on the part of the private sector and organizations such as the Scottish Development Agency has proved so intense that it is by no means clear that authorities are spending wisely in continuing to allocate scarce resources to this activity.

Industrial rehabilitation has been adopted rather late in the day by many local administrations. Stimulated especially by powers contained within the 1978 Inner Urban Areas Act, many larger cities have declared industrial or commercial improvement areas. Here a variety of grants and loans may be available for, say, the improvement or conversion of industrial or commercial buildings, for the establishment of cooperatives and for environmental improvements. About 60 industrial improvement areas were declared between 1978 and 1980. In some respects the approach appears sensible in that cities may retain their remaining older industrial infrastructure, much of which has been lost due to post-1945 redevelopment. Early indications suggest too that environmental improvements can help build up private-sector confidence in an area and thus encourage substantial market investment (Tym and Partners, 1977). On the other hand, improvement can prove expensive, may not in any case prevent company closures, can represent investment in nonoptimal industrial locations and may, if, say, parking facilities are increased, involve a loss rather than a gain in industrial floorspace.

Local government and new enterprise

From the mid to late 1970s local authorities began to implement a whole range of policies designed to boost local enterprise. Only an indication of these activities can be provided here. However, to give an example, some authorities have been involved through land and planning policies in the designation and evolution of various forms of high-tech estates designed to attract and to foster smaller companies in the new sunrise industries. Other authorities have provided accommodation, finance and managerial assistance for community enterprises, often in association with the local private sector. Small firms are often selected for particular assistance. This may take the form of providing accommodation, providing rent or rate relief on premises, the creation of pooled and subsidized secretarial, marketing and security services for groups of smaller companies, and so on. Finally mention should be made of the enterprise workshop concept. In these, local authorities will allow, often rent free, an individual or a group of workers to explore the market possibilities of a particular product or service for a specified period of time.

Local authorities will continue to implement policies designed to enhance enterprise within their administrations. Although this is undeniably desirable, it should not be allowed to hide some formidable constraints facing many urban authorities in the depressed regions. As Fothergill and Gudgin (1982) have shown, job generation tends to be positively correlated with factors such as high educational attainment within the labour force, the existence of a large number of small companies whose employees tend to be much more inclined themselves to establish new firms, and a settlement hierarchy characterized by smaller, more attractive towns rather than larger, older cities. Quite simply, some parts of the spatial economy are likely to create far more jobs than are others. The cities will not on the whole benefit from these market forces.

Labour market policy

The major urban authorities tend to be much more interested in boosting local demand than in intervening in local labour markets. In times of economic recession this obviously makes sense. If skills improve but demand remains depressed, it is hard to avoid the conclusion that the more skilled will simply bump down the labour market, thus displacing the less skilled, at no net benefit. Nevertheless, assuming that at some time demand does pick up, there are labour market policies that authorities might wish to undertake. These include encouraging the coordination of training within an area or industrial sector, easing the mobility of labour by providing, say, mortgages for those wishing to seek opportunities elsewhere, improving education-industry links, and providing in-house training for apprentices within the local authority itself. However, local authorities will probably have little impact overall in this area, which traditionally depends largely on central government and the market.

Financial innovation

Although many interventionist activities in this area are restricted to a few radical authorities discussed below, many larger administrations have introduced some form of financial support for local producers. Typically, an authority will establish a loan or grant fund which will be used to support local, often small, firms either when such establishments are created or when expansion is being considered. Applications tend to be vetted by some form of committee usually consisting in part of private-sector interests. Such funds rarely amount to a great deal, and it may be the intention of the authority to make a profit from such activities. It is not altogether clear in many cases whether companies so assisted could not have raised equivalent support from the market. Certainly for some authorities this kind of intervention is anyway simply supporting prevailing market forces, which have so devastated extensive regions of the country. For these more radical authorities other policies are required.

The radical authorities

Although not many authorities can genuinely be classified as radical, many of the most interesting developments in the field of economic development have emanated from these administrations. Many of the policies discussed above will of course be undertaken by radical authorities such as Sheffield or the Greater London Council. Equally so, some of the initiatives mentioned below will have been implemented by authorities whose overall position could not be defined as anything other than orthodox. But, even allowing for this inevitable blurring in classification, it is apparent that some administrations are determined to pursue local economic strategies of an altogether more inverventionist nature than any ever undertaken before in the United Kingdom.

Before mentioning some of the key initiatives undertaken by more radical authorities, one or two preliminary observations should be made. It is important to stress the political nature of the activities undertaken by the more radical authorities. The strategies developed by such administrations are designed to counteract market forces, to provide employment opportunities for those who otherwise would seem destined for permanent unemployment, to enhance job prospects for minorities and women and to moderate the impact of Thatcherite economic policies. Whatever the merits of this position it is always important to remember that economic evaluations of radical intervention may be completely misguided: activities are not intended solely — and perhaps not at all — to enhance industrial-sector profits. Frequently instead objectives of a more sociopolitical nature lie at the root of intervention.

A comprehensive list of innovations introduced by more radical authorities is beyond the scope of this book, but some brief indication of key developments should be provided. Local administrations operating within more interventionist perspectives might, for example, attempt to purchase goods and services from local suppliers, provide research facilities for trade union organizations fighting closures or contractions, introduce their own apprenticeship schemes, support initiatives designed to boost employment opportunities for women or ethnic minorities, lobby for, say, import controls to protect local industrial sectors, or encourage the formation of cooperative enterprises. Authorities such as Wandsworth have in the past used the 1970 Local Authorities (Goods and Services) Act to provide goods and services for other public agencies. Many urban authorities have, moreover, established independent economic development or employment creation departments. Sheffield, for example, has formed an Employment Department of more than 50 staff, with an annual budget of around £2m to £3m, and has charged it with a variety of objectives. These include attempting to prevent further job loss, exploring new forms of ownership and widening employment opportunities for the economically, socially and physically disadvantaged. To achieve these ends, various sectors have been created to deal with areas such as research, municipal enterprise, women in the local economy, high-tech developments and so on.

Although the initiatives mentioned above undoubtedly represent a considerable accentuation of local authority intervention in economic development, the most important single development is probably that of the enterprise board. Using Section 137 of the 1972 Local Government Act, which allows authorities to raise 2p in the rates for a wide variety of uses, a number of local administrations have established such boards. In essence they are institutions ultimately controlled by the authorities concerned, which have been granted a considerable degree of autonomy to put together financial packages for industry through the provision of loan funding and, especially, equity finance. Authorities such as the West Midlands County Council and the Greater London Council argued in the early 1980s that British financial markets were proving markedly reluctant to provide longer-term equity finance. Inevitably, therefore, too many companies were forced into loan support and thus became overgeared. If instead, these authorities suggested, publicly controlled enterprise boards were established, more equity finance would be made available, the local authority would have greater control of its productive bases, and the community would eventually see a profit from its industrial investments.

Hence by 1982-83 a number of local authorities had established such boards. The Greater London Enterprise Board (G.L.E.B.) was perhaps the most important, but others had been created in Lancashire, West Yorkshire and elsewhere. Some operated on commercial lines in that financial support depended solely on market criteria.

However, others, such as the G.L.E.B. adopted social as well as commercial consider-ations. For example, support tended to be directed to firms operating in more deprived areas of London, assistance depended on jobs created or sustained, cooperatives and ethnic business were especially favoured, and companies receiving funding had to sign appropriate planning agreements. Typically such agreements would cover issues such as wages, trade union rights, output, employment and health and safety. In essence the G.L.E.B. and other enterprise boards insisted that firms receiving public support should in turn be answerable to the community.

Writing early in 1985, it is unclear whether the enterprise boards created by the G.L.C. and the metropolitan counties will survive the latter's planned demise. Their disappearance would be unfortunate. Perhaps some boards will need to scrutinize their activities more closely, but overall they appear generally to have assisted a wide range of industrial concerns, to have undertaken valuable development and to have created or saved thousands of jobs. For example the G.L.E.B., within eighteen months of its creation, had invested almost £20m in over 140 companies with a direct saving of more than 2000 jobs. There seems no doubt that there is a need for such organizations, which, while remaining generally profitable, have helped boost output and enhance employment creation at relatively little cost — far less, for example, than has regional policy. Moreover, as few firms supported by enterprise boards have folded the community should ultimately reap profits from this investment.

Local authority economic intervention: some broader considerations

Whereas there can be little doubt that local government authorities will continue to intervene in the economic development of their administrations, it has to be accepted that such activities are constrained by a variety of factors of a political, financial and economic nature. These considerations apply to many aspects of urban governance of course, but in the area of economic intervention it appears often to be the case that intervention proves more difficult, complex and uncertain than other activities imple-mented by local government. Some brief indication of these issues should be provided.

(a) Central governments have remained convinced that local authority economic development and employment creation policies should be limited largely to areas such as the allocation of land for industrial use, the improvement of transport infra-structure, and the provision of help and advice for small firms. More interventionist approaches are perceived as illegitimate in that they can undermine centrally deter-mined economic policies. There are of course contrary arguments suggesting, for instance, that local authorities know more about their economic bases and should be able to respond to their deterioration. But whatever the merits in this debate it is important to realize that central government has attempted to reduce local action in this field by, for example, trying to downgrade the 2p in the rate allowance, so crucial to funding of local authority activity in this area, to ½p for most authorities. These proposals were, in the event, defeated in Parliament. It is clear, however, that any controls ultimately imposed on this 2p power would have considerable implications for more interventionist councils. Other sources of funding, such as the urban programme, can be used, and so in some cases can local authority pension funds, but Section 137 of the 1972 Local Government Act is the lynchpin.

(b) There are other political constraints on local authority activities in this area. Intervention will mean higher rates calls. Although there is evidence that public intervention through higher rate demands does create more jobs than would leaving equivalent sums within the market, there are, nevertheless, real political costs. Firms may move elsewhere, electoral defeat can occur, and, it would appear in 1985, rates can be capped. In essence authorities undertaking politically motivated programmes of economic intervention must accept that such activities will be opposed by Conservative central governments.

(c) Authorities must accept too that their activities are likely to have a minimal impact compared with broader trends affecting economic development and employment creation. Central government policies towards interest rates, the scale and direction of public-sector expenditure, regional policy and so on will have a far greater impact on local economic performance than any policies implemented by the local authority concerned. Equally, although authorities may marginally widen public control of production, through support for cooperatives, enterprise boards, direct investment in local firms and so on, the vast bulk of investment and output will remain under the control of the market. Sheffield's Employment Department, for example, in the first two years of its existence saved or created around 1000 jobs at a time when the City was losing 1000 jobs a month.

(d) Local authorities need to be aware of some of the implications of economic intervention. For instance, providing grants and loans for capital equipment may, far from enhancing local employment, actually reduce it as capital replaces labour. Subsidies for one company, moreover, may simply undermine other more efficient local firms. Municipal purchasing may mean the acquisition of inefficiently produced goods and services paid for partly through rate calls on more competent local companies. Where evaluations of the impact of public subsidy have been undertaken in, say, enterprise zones (Catalano, 1983) or industrial improvement areas (Cameron *et al.*, 1982) other disquieting conclusions emerge. Most private-sector investment in enterprise zones and other areas to which public support has been directed seem likely to have occurred in any case irrespective of any subsidy. And there is very little evidence, moreover, to suggest that more deprived, unskilled inner urban residents benefit a great deal from public subsidy. Instead skilled and managerial sectors reap what advantages accrue from intervention. Local authorities will no doubt continue to implement policies designed to boost economic development and enhance job creation. They should nevertheless be aware that their activities are likely to remain marginal to the problems of the cities, are unlikely to benefit many of the unemployed and unskilled and yet, paradoxically, will remain the subject of strong central government disapproval.

Conclusions

Employment, or rather unemployment, in the mid-1980s forms a key issue in the

United Kingdom, an issue whose vitiating effects spill over into other aspects of life — poverty and deprivation, housing etc. Interest in the causes of unemployment, its spatial pattern, and the possible initiatives that central and local government can undertake to combat continuing employment decline has increased dramatically in recent years, producing a growing literature on the subject. It is clear that local authority initiatives can only have a marginal impact on employment and that the decline of our large cities as manufacturing centres will continue. This in turn has implications for the heavily urbanized regions such as the North-West and the West Midlands. Increasing dispersion of new manufacturing industry will also continue, favouring the new 'sunrise' belt from East Anglia to the South-West — the very area which is seeing the greatest growth in service employment. Given the comparative failure of regional policy since the war to reverse the decline of the north and west of Britain and the limited powers of local authorities to offset local job losses, it is difficult to see how even an interventionist government could halt the current trends, which have profound implications for increasing disparities in future regional growth and decline.

References

Bramley, G., Stewart, M. and Underwood, J. (1978) Local economic initiatives, Working Paper No. 1, School for Advanced Urban Studies, University of Bristol

Bull, P.J. (1978) The spatial components of intra-urban manufacturing change: suburbanization in Clydeside, 1958-68, *Transactions of British Geographers, New Series*, Vol.3, No.1, pp 91-100

Bull, P.J. (1983) *Employment and unemployment.* In M. Pacione (1983), Progress in Urban Geography, Croom Helm, Beckenham

Cairncross, A. (1979) *What is de-industrialization?* In F. Blackaby (1979) De-industrialization, Heinemann, London

Cameron, S.J., Dabinett, G.E., Gillard, A.A., Whisker, P.M., Williams, R.H. and Willis, K.G. (1982) Local authority aid to industry: an evaluation of Tyne and Wear, Report No. 7, Inner Cities Research Programme, Department of the Environment, London

Camina, M.M. (1974) Local authorities and the attraction of industry, *Progress in Planning*, Vol.3, Part 2, pp 83-182

Carter, H. (1981) *The Study of Urban Geography* (3rd edn), Edward Arnold, London

Catalano, A. (1983) A review of UK enterprise zones, Paper 17, Centre for Environmental Studies, London

Chalkley, B. and Perry, M. (1984) How many factories do we need? *Town and Country Planning*, Vol.53, No.2, pp 55-57

Chandler, J.A. and Lawless, P. (1985) *Local Authorities and Economic Development*, Gower, Aldershot

Collinge, C. (1983) Investing in the local economy: business finance and the role of local government, Community Projects Foundation, London

Dennis, R. (1978) The decline of manufacturing employment in Greater London: 1966-74, *Urban Studies*, Vol.15, pp 63-73

Dicken, P. and Lloyd, P.E. (1978) Inner metropolitan industrial change, enterprise structures and policy issues: case studies of Manchester and Merseyside, *Regional Studies*, Vol.12, pp 181-198

Fagg, J.J.(1980) A re-examination of the incubator hypothesis: a case study of Greater Leicester, *Urban Studies*, Vol. 17, pp 35-44

Fothergill, S. and Gudgin, G. (1982) *Unequal Growth. Urban and regional change in the United Kingdom*, Heinemann, London

Fothergill, S. and Gudgin, G. (1983) *Trends in regional manufacturing employment: the main influences*. In J.B. Goddard and A.G. Champion (1983) The Urban and Regional Transformation of Britain, Methuen, London

Gripaios, P. (1977) The closure of firms in the inner city: the South East London case 1970-75, *Regional Studies*, Vol. 11, pp 1-6

Hamilton, F.E.I. (1967) *Models of industrial location*. In R.J. Chorley and P. Haggett (1967) Models in Geography, Methuen, London

Hoover, E. and Vernon, R. (1959) *Anatomy of a Metropolis*, Harvard University Press, Cambridge, Massachussetts

J.U.R.U.E. (1979) Industrial renewal in the inner city: an assessment of potential and problems, Joint Unit for Research on the Urban Environment, University of Aston in Birmingham

Keeble, D.E. (1976) *Industrial Location and Planning in the United Kingdom*, Methuen, London

Keeble, D.E. (1978) Industrial decline in the inner city and conurbation, *Transactions of the Institute of British Geographers, New Series*, Vol.3, No.1, pp 101-114

Keeble, D.E. (1980) Industrial decline, regional policy and the urban-rural manufacturing shift in the United Kingdom, *Environment and Planning A*, Vol. 12, pp. 945-962

Lloyd, P.E. and Dicken, P. (1983) *The components of change in metropolitan areas: events in their corporate context*. In J.B. Goddard and A.G. Champion (1983) The Urban and Regional Transformation of Britain, Methuen, London

Lloyd, P.E. and Mason, C.M. (1978) Manufacturing industry in the inner city: a case study of Greater Manchester, *Transactions of the Institute of British Geographers, New Series*, Vol.3, No.1, pp 66-90

Marquand, J. (1983) *The changing distribution of service employment*. In J.B. Goddard and A.G. Champion (1983) The Urban and Regional Transformation of Britain, Methuen, London

Massey, D. and Meegan, R. (1982) *The Anatomy of Job Loss*, Methuen, London

Nicholson, B.M., Brinkley, I. and Evans, A.W. (1981) The role of the inner city in the development of manufacturing industry, *Urban Studies*, Vol.18, pp 57-71

Robinson, F. (1979) Local authority economic initiatives: a review, Occasional Paper 10, Centre for Environmental Studies, London

Tym, R. & Partners (1977) *Time for Industry. Evaluation of the Rochdale Industrial Improvement Area*, HMSO, London

Young, K. and Mason, C. (eds) (1983) *Urban Economic Development, New Roles and Relationships*, Macmillan, London

Further reading

Employment change is poorly covered in general textbooks, though the relevant chapters quoted in the references above from Goddard and Champion (eds) (1983) are excellent sources, and Fothergill and Gudgin (1982), provide a clear though very detailed exposition of spatial change in manufacturing industry.

In the area of local authority economic intervention much material is also relatively inaccessible. The best general reviews are those of Chandler and Lawless (1985) and Young and Mason (eds) (1983).

More than some other aspects of the governance of cities, the transport issue presents a peculiar initial constraint: the exact definition of the problem. Is it, say, about reducing congestion, or improving the efficiency of public transport, or ameliorating the environment, or removing a general dissatisfaction with urban transport facilities? Moreover, as Hills (1974) indicates, there are difficulties for authorities wishing to intervene in the provision of urban transport facilities which impose additional considerations. The physical structure of cities may change only slowly, whereas transport demands and technologies may alter dramatically in relatively short periods of time. In such circumstances urban communication systems become rapidly outdated. As this situation has tended to affect the provision of public rather than private transport, the politically contentious issue of transport subsidy has come ever more to the fore. Indeed, writing in the mid 1980s, it may be argued that the urban transport problem increasingly revolves around the issue of the degree to which society is prepared to support public transport within the older cities. The contemporary state of transport provision within the cities has crystallized out of a number of contextual impulses which can collectively be seen to relate either to national transport policy and its implications for the cities or to socio-economic change and its consequence for urban communications. These two sets of constraints will be examined below. Later, policy considerations will be explored.

National transport policy: implications for the cities

Any analysis of urban transport planning must initially embrace the Buchanan Report (HMSO, 1963). Prior to this there had been little explicit interest in comprehensive approaches to urban transport planning. Buchanan changed this, however.

The Buchanan Committee was established to study the long-term development of roads and traffic in urban areas and their influence on the urban environment. Its conclusions were to prove profoundly important in the emerging urban transport debate. Briefly, it argued that rising car ownership rates were inevitable and desirable and that developing road systems between cities would not be especially difficult. Within cities, however, the Report accepted that rising vehicle ownership rates would create problems. These would tend to arise because, whereas an increasing proportion of commercial, industrial and social trips would be undertaken on the assumption that total accessibility within the urban fabric was possible, this very trend would reduce environmental standards within cities. The Report nevertheless argued that it would often prove possible to accommodate essential business trips within cities, while at the same time protecting residential environments, but that this delicate balance could only be achieved at considerable costs. In essence Buchanan posited the 'law' that environmental standards could be enhanced despite rising road traffic but that this would require extensive and expensive redevelopment proposals. In effect as Bruton (1983) points out, the Report saw that a variety of solutions to traffic problems facing any city was available. Limited increases in vehicle usage might be accommodated through minimal and inexpensive traffic management schemes. An annual growth rate of 4 per cent at the time allowed many to believe, however, that major redevelopment proposals, including underpasses, new and improved urban roads, tunnels, flyovers and the like could be constructed which would substantially increase vehicle usage rates while at the same time preserving environmental standards within residential enclaves.

A number of criticisms can be levelled at the approach adopted by the Report. For example, Hillman (1983) argues that it too readily assumed that a majority of urban residents had access to a car and largely ignored the implications of throwing more traffic onto major highways for those living on or close to them. It perhaps also underestimated the real costs of private transport. These include air pollution, accidents and death due to the private vehicle, distorted travel patterns, compensation for those whose houses are acquired due to road construction and the inordinate costs of urban road improvements or construction. On the other hand, Buchanan (1983) and others (Bruton, 1983) twenty years later were largely to endorse the findings of the Report. It clearly highlighted relationships between environmental standards, rising vehicle usage, and costs. It saw that some essential journeys undertaken by industrial and commercial interests would need to be accommodated while optional private car trips would not. It encouraged the creation of car-free precincts which have dramatically improved the retail and commercial cores of many towns and cities. It perceived the hierarchical nature of urban road provision. Through-traffic needed to be directed onto major highways with lesser volumes being accommodated on narrower, residential feeder routes.

However, although it is true that a range of options for dealing with urban traffic growth was considered in the Report, it is equally obvious that the solutions that attracted both academic and political interest were those that recommended extensive new urban road construction. Academically this interest was reflected in the burgeoning growth of land use and transportation studies in the 1960s and early 1970s. In essence such studies attempted both to predict and to plan for future patterns of travel within city regions. Traffic was seen to be a function of activities taking place within buildings. Hence the siting and organization of such buildings would in turn influence the scale, direction and type of traffic. Once forecasts were made of traffic patterns emanating from different land uses, the pattern of future trips would apparently be established. Unfortunately, in planning for any future growth in trips, the assumption was almost invariably made that an increasing proportion of trips would be made by private car. The concept of any choice between private and public modes of travel was largely ignored. So too were real practical considerations, such as the social and economic costs of highway development and the relatively low car ownership rates which prevailed in many British cities. For reasons that will be considered below, it also seems that even extensive urban road construction will not in any case eradicate congestion and indeed may increase it.

Despite obvious methodological weakness apparent within many land-use/ transportation studies, there was nevertheless a general predisposition towards the construction and improvement of roads, which was recommended by many such studies in the 1960s. Expenditure on new roads increased from about £190m in 1964-65 to over £500m by 1970-71, although much of this was for inter-urban as opposed to intra-urban highways. Nevertheless, following the Buchanan Report on Traffic in Towns, the government in 1964 issued a circular advising local authorities to produce plans consistent with the findings of the Report. In addition, an Urban Unit was established within the Ministry of Transport (McKay and Cox, 1979) which was instrumental in guiding the evolution of the 1966 White Paper, 'Transport Policy' (HMSO, 1966). This accepted the need for a much enhanced urban road programme but also promoted the idea of an integrated and more efficient public transport system. This latter concept was eventually to be formalized in the 1968 Transport Act, which introduced a number of innovations. Passenger Transport Authorities were established to coordinate public transport in four conurbations, and Passenger Transport Executives were created to run services. After the reorganization of local government in the early 1970s additional Executives were created in West and South Yorkshire, and the new metropolitan counties took over the running of the P.T.A.'s. In addition to this rationalization of public transport in the major conurbations, the 1968 Act also introduced grants of 75 per cent for investment in public transport capital projects and smaller subsidies for the purchase of buses. British Rail was also to be paid specific grants for socially necessary but unprofitable routes.

Although the 1968 Act helped to place the planning of public transport within the conurbations on a more efficient footing, this should not in any sense be seen as a major pro-public transport thrust by the 1964-70 Labour government. In money terms for instance, road building increased by more than 100 per cent between 1964 and 1968, and expenditure on public transport declined throughout the decade. Moreover, suggestions that car usage in towns and cities should be subject to a specific tax were never pursued. Although the 1968 Act was undoubtedly an important piece of reforming legislation, it in no way reversed the generally favourable attitudes towards private transport that characterized official thinking throughout much of the 1960s. This was not to change significantly in the following decade.

Public expenditure on transport amounted to between £2 bn and £2.6 bn per annum throughout the 1970s, at 1976 survey prices (HMSO, 1977). In general, however, there was a decline in expenditure on inter- and intra-urban road construction from a peak of over £560m in 1973-74 to less than half this figure by the end of the decade. This decline in part reflected poor economic performance. In addition it is clear that in the early 1970s urban road construction proposals were proving unpopular. Local elections were won and lost on the basis of transport planning. London, for example, changed political complexion in 1973 as a result of massive objections to Conservative proposals for a motorway box. Moreover, these anti-road sentiments were given some degree of authority as a result of a number of official reports, most obviously that undertaken by the House of Commons Expenditure Committee (1972). This argued against increased road spending on a number of grounds: it was an expensive policy; it created additional costs in areas such as housing and health; and there was little evidence that it would substantially moderate congestion since new roads might stimulate as much as satiate demand.

However, although there was some reduction in public investment in road construction this should not be taken to imply a pro-public transport policy. Economic constraints in the post-1976 period dictated declining expenditure in the transport field across the board. The 1976 transport consultation document (HMSO, 1976) promoted a managed market approach which essentially argued for the establishment by central government of a transport framework within which individuals and organizations would be free to make their own transport decisions. This approach largely assumed that users such as lorries would pay heavier taxes to cover their real costs and that, other than in certain selected cases, subsidies would be reduced. As McKay and Cox (1979) suggest, this policy would have effectively reversed postwar Labour policy towards public transport. Any attempt to integrate different sectors of the public transport system would have been abandoned; so too would any pretensions that transport policy should be based on principles of social justice that ensured the universal provision of services. In the event the succeeding 1977 White Paper (HMSO, 1977) presented a somewhat different perspective. It accepted that expenditure in support of public transport should not be reduced. With the election, however, of markedly anti-interventionist Tory administrations in 1979 and 1983, it seems clear that genuinely market-orientated strategies towards public transport appear likely to be implemented within the cities in the later years of the 1980s. This will occur as a result of the planned privatization of public transport, the demise of the metropolitan counties and changes in the system of central support for transport provision.

Although the exact details — indeed the very success — of the 1985 Transport Bill are uncertain, writing in 1985, it appears as if it will allow bus routes to be opened up to competitive tender. Even routes needing subsidy will be open to tender, with some indication of the local authority revenue support that will be available. Local authority bus undertakings may be turned into independent companies, which will be able to bid for suitable contracts on a competitive basis.

Not surprisingly, these proposals have run into a storm of protest. Will all services survive? Fares seem certain to rise, road congestion may increase, safety standards could decline and concessionary fares may be undermined. Jobs may well be lost in the transport industry and elsewhere too as demand for public and private services declines in line with bus usage. Efforts to impose any physical and financial integration of public transport may be undermined. In practice the overall impacts of the proposed change are impossible to estimate in the mid-1980s. The government believes that competition will improve services and reduce costs and subsidies. However, it seems hard to avoid the conclusion that the changes herald a more expensive system of local transport, and this will certainly affect those at the bottom end of the socio-economic spectrum.

Overall assessments of the impact of the proposal are even more obscured in the cities because of the impending demise both of the G.L.C. and the metropolitan counties (discussed in Chapter 8) and because of the planned reductions in central government financial support for public transport services. The 1984 London Regional Transport Act established the L.R.T., which removed control of buses and tubes from the G.L.C. The latter had, however, still to provide a certain degree of financial support. The L.R.T. is particularly required to open up main and ancillary services to competition. In the metropolitan counties, however, it appears as if passenger transport functions will be transferred to joint boards of elected members appointed by the districts. But individual districts may opt out of these arrangements. These byzantine administrative structures will, moreover, be accompanied by a substantial reduction in central government support. This question raises the whole issue of the Transport Supplementary Grant.

From 1975 to 1976 county councils submitted Transport Policy and Programmes to the Department of Transport. The T.P.P.'s specified transport planning objectives for the area, proposals, priorities and success in achieving previously stated goals. In the light of the T.P.P. and subject to the total expenditure available to transport, the counties were provided with a Transport Supplementary Grant which might be used for a variety of capital projects or for subsidizing public transport. Three changes occurred to this system in the mid-1980s. First, the total grant was reduced from about £400m in 1984-85 to about £160m in 1985-86. Secondly, there was a marked swing in support away from the cities to the shire counties. And thirdly, from 1985 only capital projects could be supported through T.S.G. Revenue support would need to come from other expenditure programmes. It is hard to see how this will be possible for many authorities.

The policies implemented by the Tory administration elected in 1983 collectively represent the greatest change in public transport provision since control was imposed on private operators in the 1930s. Far-reaching changes in the operation, control and financing of public transport appear likely to occur. The government has argued that such changes are essential to prevent the continued run down, and enhanced subsidization, of the public transport system. Others would argue that the overall impact of planned changes will be to destroy infrastructures that have taken decades to develop and as a consequence effectively spell the end of conurbation-wide public transport. The later years of the 1980s will certainly prove a rich picking ground for research in transport. However, the changes that will occur then will reflect forces other than those emanating solely from Westminster. Socio-economic trends impose additional constraints on urban transport patterns.

Urban transport and contemporary socio-economic constraints

Urban transport planning must operate within a socio-economic context which can impose substantial changes on the pattern of need and supply within relatively limited periods. Some of these trends will contain implications for urban transport provision across the board. A number of them have created enormous operational problems for public transport in particular and may mean that attempts to run urban public transport at anything approaching an economic profit may be doomed to failure. A number of factors seem important here:

(a) In Chapter 8 the remarkable decentralization of populations from the older conurbations was examined. This has obvious implications for the provision of public transport. Demand will diminish overall. It will, moreover, be increasingly difficult to provide services for expanding lower-density suburban and exurban areas, where demand is much more diffuse than is the case with higher-density urban developments. This problem will be accentuated as public and private services, notably retailing, decentralize too.

(b) Car ownership rates have risen in cities, thus moderating demand for public transport. This should not be exaggerated, however. Some 40 per cent of British households did not have a car in 1981, but 60 per cent of Liverpool's households and fully 70 per cent of Glasgow's fell into this category. Most people in cities still do not have access to a car.

(c) Rising standards of living, which have occurred for most people housed in and around cities, have affected urban traffic patterns. Ownership of freezers, for instance, has increased dramatically. This means that more households make fewer but larger shopping trips, and these are almost invariably undertaken by car. Few people in the 1980s work a six-day week, a marked contrast with the position in earlier decades. This may reduce peak demand for public transport on Saturdays. For that increasing proportion of unemployed urbanites of course peak time travel becomes unnecessary and overall demand for services is likely to decline as a consequence.

(d) After 1974 all transport costs rose relative to the overall price level. But whereas by 1982 motoring and cycling costs were running some 8 per cent above the general inflation rate, public transport fares were fully 20 per cent more (Potter, 1982). There is substantial evidence that even when motoring costs rise dramatically, as was the case with the oil price rise of 1973-74, this has only the most limited of impacts on car usage. This is not as surprising as it might seem. Costs are inevitably incurred by anyone who has acquired a car. The marginal cost of each journey is not particularly great. In essence those who own cars will not willingly switch to public transport, and indeed whatever penalties or subsidies are imposed, aimed at moving motorists to public modes, most will be extremely reluctant so to do.

The combined impact of the factors mentioned above has, not surprisingly, led to a very marked decline in bus usage in Britain (HMSO, 1984). Between 1953 and 1983 the bus and coach share of total travel in the UK fell from 42 per cent, amounting to 82 billion passenger kilometres, to just 8 per cent, 40 billion passenger kilometers. During this same period private motorized transport increased from 30 per cent to 83 per cent of the total, when it amounted to over 400 billion passenger kilometers. Rail travel fell from 20 per cent to 7 per cent. By 1983 there were about 70 000 buses in the United Kingdom. More than half of them were operated by the public sector and it was those that tended to dominate urban and express routes. Two-thirds of all bus journeys in 1978 were made for work, education and shopping trips. As might be expected, per capita bus usage is greater in urban areas than it is in rural ones, and buses are much more likely to be used by groups such as the semiskilled and unskilled, women, children, and the old. An increasing number of the more affluent, especially better-off men, have access to a company car. About three-quarters of the two million new cars registered in 1979 fell into this category. Users of such vehicles may be unable, even if they wish to do so, to switch to public transport.

Urban transport patterns

It is important to stress the varied nature of transport patterns and infrastructure within different British cities. London's system of public transport is more comprehensive than that prevailing in other cities. However, some cities, such as Birmingham, Leeds, Glasgow and Sheffield, are more or less directly linked into the national motorway system. Many, such as Coventry, have some form of inner ring road. Cities vary considerably, moreover, in the extent to which different modes of transport are employed. For example, 16 per cent of residents travelling to work in Britain in 1981 did so by bus, compared with 34 per cent in Manchester and 42 per cent in Sheffield. On the other hand nationally only 6 per cent travel to work by rail or underground, but 22 per cent in London do so. Birmingham has a higher proportion of workers travelling by car than many other cities (O.P.C.S. 1984). Trends through time are revealing too. For instance, whereas commuting into inner London hardly changed between 1951 and 1976, in the same period commuting into Newcastle and into Birmingham doubled and commuting into Glasgow almost quadrupled.

Nevertheless, even when variations are taken into account, certain general trends relating to urban transport patterns can be seen to emerge (Gillespie, 1983; Hall, 1980). Although the information here is dated, much of it being based on the 1971 Census, certain characteristics of urban travel patterns can nevertheless be distinguished. Only a small minority of work journeys are made into the central cores of conurbations — normally less than 20 per cent of the total. Suburb-to-suburb work trips are far more important and amount to fully 60 per cent in South-East Lancashire for instance. More than 50 per cent of work trips in London and 70 per cent elsewhere take less than 30 minutes. As might be anticipated, a large proportion of those travelling into conurbations do so by public transport, and, outside London, most of these journeys are made by bus. Moreover, in virtually all conurbations, in 1981 between 15 per cent and 20 per cent of workers travelled to work on foot.

However, it is increasingly apparent that work trips represent a relatively small proportion of total urban journeys. By 1978-79 only about a quarter of the journeys in the United Kingdom were work trips; almost 60 per cent were for leisure and shopping. Public transport is becoming increasingly unable to cater for journeys of this kind. Rising car ownership rates, however, allow an increasing proportion of households with a car to undertake such journeys. Once a household owns a car, far more, and far longer, journeys are made for a wide variety of purposes. To state an obvious but nevertheless crucial fact, public transport usage will decline. In the remaining sections of this chapter some aspects of urban transport policy, applicable to both private and public sectors, will be examined.

Urban transport planning

Although the distinction between policies towards public transport on the one hand and private transport on the other represents an arbitrary dichotomy, there is some academic, and considerable administrative, justification for dealing with each system separately. In the concluding section we shall attempt an integration of the two systems.

Urban transport policy and the private vehicle

In theory at least, two totally different approaches towards the private car might be attempted: accommodation and restraint. Certainly in the British context it is difficult in practice, to foresee circumstances whereby a firm commitment towards either strategy could successfully be implemented. Nevertheless, cities may move towards one or other of these approaches.

Attempts to accommodate the car will involve the construction of new roads and the improvement of existing ones, the provision of more, and perhaps cheaper, parking, and the introduction of a variety of traffic management devices designed to assist the general flow of traffic. Groups such as the British Road Federation have pushed hard for such policies. As has been outlined above, however, for substantial periods in the post-1970 era central governments proved unwilling to countenance extensive road proposals for political and financial reasons. Nevertheless, it seems evident that a higher proportion of an admittedly smaller transport budget will be spent on roads in the 1980s. Priority is likely to be given to the bypassing of smaller towns on major routes, especially those to expanding east coast ports, and also to the construction of new roads in some inner urban areas, for instance through London's Docklands. Eventually it might be anticipated that most cities will have improved radial and circumferential routes. It is hard to envisage, however, any British city moving towards the pro-car position adopted by some West-Coast American cities. Many observers would regard this as a fortunate state of affairs.

There are in fact formidable problems associated with strategies designed to accommodate dramatically increased numbers of private vehicles (Botham and Herson 1980; Adams, 1982). Acquiring urban land for road construction is expensive, and there are clear opportunity costs involved in such purchases. In effect the land might more effectively be used for other purposes. It is no longer obvious that inner ring roads are justified, moreover, because so many households and so much economic activity has decentralized. Industrial and commercial sites would be displaced and environmental intrusion accentuated. New roads might in addition encourage the decentralization of yet more car-owning households if trips to urban commercial centres were made easier. Many of those living in cities would not benefit since, as indicated above, most people in the conurbations do not have access to a car. As Hillman (1977) has pointed out, the entire approach assumed within pro-car strategies appears contradictory. It would boost, not reduce energy demand. It would increase expenditure on transport, not reduce it, as more households would need to acquire cars. Most crucial of all, road investment is likely just as much to stimulate demand for mobility as it is to satisfy existing needs.

Just as pure pro-car policies raise all kinds of awkward issues, so too do strategies designed radically to restrain the car. A variety of approaches might be adopted here. A simple ban might be effected. To some extent the pedestrianization implemented in many retail cores may be seen as a parallel policy. In this latter case private motorists are often encouraged to drive into cities by the creation of car parks located close to central shopping areas. Authorities genuinely wishing to reduce the penetration of private cars might limit car parking facilities or, where under their control, make it more expensive. In principle other policies such as road pricing or supplementary licensing could be initiated which would force motorists to pay for the use of urban roads. Some attempts have been made, as for example in Nottingham in the mid-1970s, to implement policies of tight physical restraint (Higgins, 1976). Here a 'ring-and-collar' scheme was implemented that made it difficult for motorists either to leave residential areas or to enter into the central core of the city. Elsewhere various forms of park-and-ride schemes have been devised which, because of parking restriction in town centres, strongly encourage motorists to park in peripheral locations and then to use appropriate public provision.

Policies of restraint are not without their critics. Restraint may reduce retail and commercial demand in city centres. Tight policies designed to restrict private mobility effected in one city may simply drive demand elsewhere. Interventionist anti-car strategies are extremely unpopular, and anyway do little to move motorists to the public sector. Perhaps most crucial of all, doubts have to be expressed as to the necessity for restraint in the first place.

Although urban congestion is a problem that affects all cities to some extent, it seems apparent that in general it has not worsened in the later 1970s and 1980s. Centrifugal impulses which have encouraged both demographic and economic decentralization have clearly reduced private vehicle mileage within cities. Urban road capacities have proved greater than had been anticipated. Even when bottlenecks occur these seem limited in time and space (O'Sullivan, 1978). Presumably those affected seek out alternative routes or travel at different times. In many cities relatively modest traffic management proposals have proved effective in maintaining vehicle speeds. Banning right-turns, restricting accesses and introducing clearways, or one-way systems, underpasses, mini-roundabouts, contraflow systems and boxes have all helped to ease urban circulation. In some cities these have allowed speeds to rise throughout the conurbation, and particularly within the central core. Certainly it is hard to envisage the introduction of consistently anti-car policies in any city in the 1980s. Indeed for many urban administrations the real problem will increasingly revolve around the provision of public transport.

Public transport policy within the cities

The question of urban public transport provision has become an ever more politically contentious issue. In part this reflects the socio-economic trends identified above, which make it increasingly difficult for administrations to provide an adequate system. Also there has been a direct clash in the post-1979 era between market-orientated central governments determined to reduce public-sector intervention in transport and the metropolitan counties, a number of which have pursued strongly pro-public transport strategies. They have adopted this stance for a number of reasons. Public transport is usually seen to benefit the less affluent, an equity consideration of great relevance for Labour administrations, which have normally controlled the metropolitan counties. In addition an adequate system is seen as environmentally less intrusive than extensive road construction; it is also cheaper, more energy efficient and more likely to retain commercial, retail and administrative functions in the urban cores where the majority of the populace without the use of a car will be able to utilize them. In passing one might conjecture that transport came to dominate the metropolitan counties' overall strategies simply because this was the policy area over which they were granted widest powers. Nevertheless, whatever the reason, the metropolitan counties have tended to pursue a range of policies designed to improve the efficiency and attractiveness of public transport. Some mention should be made of such policies, which tend to fall into one of the following categories: physical and financial integration; operational innovations; new infrastructure; subsidy; and land-use/ transportation considerations.

Physical and financial integration   The *ad hoc*, pragmatic growth of transport services in cities often led to the development of a loosely knit system consisting of largely unrelated links until well into the post-1945 period. Some improvements were made by the metropolitan counties but, as can been seen from many European cities, much more can be done in the United Kingdom. If possible, rail and bus stations should be located as close to each other as possible. Historic accident and the prohibitive cost of new city centre development may of course prevent this. On the other hand, there is scope for the introduction of both common timetables, covering all aspects of an urban public transport system, and a common fare structure. Too often passengers remain ignorant of fares and may be unable to purchase them anywhere other than on a bus or train. A zonal system of payment seems to ease some of these constraints, especially when allied to the pre-purchase of tickets.

Operational innovations   Just as relatively minor traffic management techniques have improved the flow of private vehicles in cities, so operational innovations can improve the efficiency of the public sector. For example, bus priority turns, bus gates, bus lanes and sensoring devices to alter lights in favour of oncoming buses can all improve the flow of public vehicles. Smaller buses, or dial-a-bus systems can improve the penetration and efficiency of the public sector within large, low-density residential precincts. One-man buses may reduce labour costs, an important consideration when these prove the largest current costs for operators.

New infrastructure   In times of national economic recession, with anti-collectivist national administrations, it is clear that little in the way of new infrastructural investment or innovation will occur. In the 1970s a certain amount was undertaken. Glasgow's antiquated subway system was improved, a railway loop was built in Liverpool and the Tyneside Metro was constructed. This last enterprise cost well over £200m. It involved the upgrading of 41 kilometres of unwanted British Rail line and the construction of 12 kilometres of new line and culminated in an excellent mass transit system running north and south of the river. Such developments are, however, expensive and may shift demand from bus to metro rather than from car to metro. In any event the only parallel development likely to occur in the 1980s is the new light railway into London's Docklands. Equally so, experimentation in public transport provision remains muted. Sheffield at one stage proposed a monorail to link up the ends of its markedly linear shopping centre. But this proposal appears to have passed into oblivion.

Subsidy   Subsidy represents quite the most contentious of policies towards public transport. By 1984-85 revenue support to bus services amounted to over £400m in the metropolitan counties and London — a dramatic increase from just over £100m in 1978-79 (HMSO, 1984). It is apparent, however, as earlier sections of this chapter have made plain, that the long-term continuation of such subsidies appears unlikely because of the demise of the metropolitan counties and the G.L.C. and because any remaining transport grant is likely to be allocated to capital projects. Nevertheless, there are arguments that subsidy for public transport remains essential. Certainly, compared with other European cities, the British conurbations are dramatically undersubsidized. For example, in 1979, whereas only 25 per cent of London Transport's operating costs were met through subsidy, 71 per cent of Milan's were and 72 per cent of New York's (Potter, 1982). Probably in only one area of the United Kingdom can it be argued that a consistently high level of subsidy has been applied: South Yorkshire.

From 1975 to 1976 fares were not changed within the county. By 1981-82 this represented a fall in the real level of fares of about 55 per cent because of inflation (Transport Studies Unit, 1983). During this period there was a 3 per cent increase in the number of passengers when, throughout the country, passenger travel fell fully 23 per cent. This increase in bus usage in the county was achieved in a decade when the population fell by nearly 2 per cent and when there was a decrease of 5 per cent in employment and a rise in car ownership. Between 1972 and 1981 certain clear trends came to characterize the local bus market. The proportion of women using buses rose from 56 per cent to 62 per cent of passengers, there was a marked relative increase in bus usage by both the young and those over 65, and the percentage of nonwork trips rose from 55 per cent to 72 per cent of journeys. Interestingly enough too, whereas there was little evidence to suggest that many had decided against car ownership because of cheap fares, a less attractive bus fares policy would probably have immediately lost about 10 per cent of passengers, and up to 40 per cent might in the medium term have adjusted their travel patterns either by making fewer trips or by acquiring a car.

There seems little doubt that the low fares policy adopted by South Yorkshire has had a considerable impact on usage. It can be argued that as a result of this policy, the region has avoided the cycle of decline so typical of many other areas of the country. Declining patronage has often given rise to fewer buses, more expensive fares, and hence yet fewer passengers. On the other hand, the policy in South Yorkshire has attracted considerable local opposition. It has, for example, been argued that the policy is inordinately expensive and because subsidy is raised through rates this can have a depressing impact on the confidence of local businessmen. In fact by 1983-84 gross expenditure on passenger transport in the County amounted to about £97m, of which £22m was reclaimed through grants and income. Total costs therefore amounted to about £75m, or about 13 per cent of the total rate bill raised by both South Yorkshire and the districts beneath. Of this £75m, £46m went on a general fares subsidy, £26m on concessionary fares for the elderly, children, and the disabled, and £3m to support local rail services. In reality the high rates within the area (high in Sheffield, though not so high in other districts within the county) reflect intervention in a whole host of policies and are not the outcome of cheap fares alone. In any case the high local social wage must have an impact on wages, which are among the lowest in the country.

There are, however, three other reasons why subsidies merit careful assessment. First, bus subsidies may assist those at the lower end of the socio-economic spectrum. This cannot be said for rail subsidies, especially in the case of commuter services in the South-East. These tend to carry more affluent groups in society, who frequently travel to the most profitable of business organizations. Secondly, it has to be remembered that even when subsidies are applied to public transport not all evidence suggests that this will tend to attract many car owners onto public transport. The Fares Fair experiment in London, for instance, involved a 32 per cent reduction in fares but was associated with an estimated 1 per cent decrease in car traffic (Adams, 1983). And thirdly, it seems probable that if subsidies are to be employed they will elicit a much greater response if used to increase mileage rather than reduce fares. Roughly speaking, an additional 10 per cent of expenditure on public transport will generate about 3 per cent more trips if used to reduce fares, but perhaps 7 per cent more journeys if employed to increase service mileage (White, 1976).

Land-use/transportation relationships   The relationships between land use and transport seem frequently to be ignored. Yet they are fundamental to understanding urban traffic patterns. Trips occur between activities such as residential, industrial, retailing, leisure and commercial functions. If such activities are segregated and distanced from other uses, trips will inevitably increase. Trends such as the decentralization of retailing, the amalgamation of health facilities into larger units or the segregation of industry from other urban uses must increase journeys within cities. Mobility of itself is not necessarily a good thing. It can, however, become crucial when accessibility is restricted.

Of course it has to be accepted that most British cities and towns reflect patterns of historical growth which may have occurred over centuries. Dramatic changes to land-use patterns are impossible. On the other hand, the sentiment remains that too often the transport implications of land-use policies are neglected. In particular, if decentralization of all activities continues apace, it is hard to envisage how public transport will even begin to cater for needs within lower-density developments beyond the cities. Virtually all of such households located there will have access to one car, but even in 1982 only 16 per cent of families owned two cars in the United Kingdom. Dispersal of land activities beyond the cities suggests that a lot more households will need two cars. Public transport will be unable to cater for many journeys here.

Urban public and private transport: towards an integrated approach

The distinction between public and private travel is an artificial one, as has been stated before. Some policies designed to ease the flow of the private car might, for instance, reduce the demand for, and the efficiency of, the public sector. Similarly, measures to make public transport more effective may, marginally, reduce congestion for the private car or, as with bus lanes, diminish the availability of road infrastructure for private vehicles. Indeed it can be argued that in practice many transport authorities have, even if by implication, sought out a balanced approach towards urban transport. A determined policy to push the private car seems politically unpopular; also it would prove expensive and might not reduce congestion. Pro-public transport policies face equally severe constraints. Motorists will not switch to the public sector unless absolutely forced to do so. But, even if they do alter modes, will public transport be able to cope? Much of any increased demand would occur at peak hours when authorities might not have adequate infrastructure. Not surprisingly, many local administrations have drifted into a kind of *laissez-faire* strategy of planned congestion. Outside London some problems may well be easing in any case. Traffic management policies and the steady diminution in urban economic activity seem to have ensured that congestion has not seriously worsened and may have eased somewhat. For many older cities the crucial problem in terms of transport will prove to be the ability of the local administration to prevent any dramatic decline in the public sector. Fears, apparent in the early 1970s, that the cities would eventually grind to a halt seem less pertinent in the mid-1980s. The exception remains London. Average speeds within the core of that city have improved if anything. But beyond the core the problem has accentuated. The M25 may attract some circumferential trips, but will itself become a major source of economic activity. Certainly it appears as if the debate about the role of public transport in moderating urban congestion will be pursued more in London than elsewhere. For many other conurbations transport will increasingly figure as one aspect of a broader debate: the extent to which society is prepared to provide material assistance for the disadvantaged in the urban cores.

References

Adams, J. (1982) Motorways in London: from Abercrombie to Archway, *Town and County Planning*, Vol.51. No. 11, pp 312-314

Adams, J. (1983) London's transport: subsidies are not the issue, *Town and Country Planning*, Vol. 52, No. 1, pp 4-6

Botham, R. and Herson, J. (1980) Motorway madness in Liverpool? *The Planner*, Vol. 66, No. 5, pp 118-121

Bruton, M.J. (1983) The 'traffic in towns' philosophy: current relevance, *Built Environment*, Vol. 9, No. 2, pp 99-103

Buchanan, C. (1983) Traffic in towns: an assessment after twenty years, *Built Environment*, Vol. 9, No. 2, pp 93-98

Gillespie, A.E. (1983) *Population and employment decentralisation and the journey to work*. In J.B. Goddard and A.G. Champion (1983) The Urban and Regional Transformation of Britain, Methuen, London

Hall, P. (1980) *Transport in the conurbations*, In G. Cameron (1980) The Future of the British Conurbations, Longman, London

Higgins, F. (1976) Priority for public transport. Nottingham 1972-76, The Royal Town Planning Institute, Summer School, pp 12-15

Hillman, M. (1977) Policy in true perspective, *Built Environment Quarterly*, Vol. 3, No. 4, pp 284-285

Hillman, M. (1983) The wrong turning: twenty years on from Buchanan, *Built Environment*, Vol. 9, No. 2, pp 104-112

Hills, P.J. (1974) *Transport and communications*. In G.E. Cherry (1974) Urban Planning Problems, Leonard Hill, London

HMSO (1963) Traffic in towns: a study of the long term problems of traffic in urban areas (the Buchanan Report) HMSO, London

HMSO(1966) Transport policy, Cmnd 3057, HMSO, London

HMSO (1976) Transport policy: a consultation document, Vols I and II, HMSO, London

HMSO (1977) Transport policy, Cmnd 6836, HMSO, London

HMSO (1984) Buses, Cmnd 9300, HMSO, London

House of Commons Expenditure Committee (1972) Urban transport planning, Second Report, Vol. I, Report and Appendix

McKay, D.H. and Cox, A.W. (1979) *The Politics of Urban Change*, Croom Helm, London

Office of Population Census and Surveys (1984) Census 1981. Key statistics for urban areas, HMSO, London

O'Sullivan, P. (1978) *Issues in transportation*. In R. Davies and P. Hall (1978) Issues in Urban Society, Penguin Books, Harmondsworth

Potter, S. (1982) *The transport policy crisis*, Unit 27, D202, Urban Change and Conflict, Open University Press, Milton Keynes

Transport Studies Unit (1983) Subsidised public transport and the demand for travel. The South Yorkshire example, Transport Studies Unit, Oxford University

White, P.R. (1976) *Planning for Public Transport*, Hutchinson, London

Further reading

McKay and Cox (1979) are excellent on the development of urban transport policy. Potter (1982) is good on political interpretations of policy. A great deal of detailed information on the state of buses is provided in the appendix to HMSO (1984). Hillman's work, some of which is indicated above, provides a critique of the pro-private transport thesis expounded by Buchanan (HMSO, 1963).

16   Inner urban policy

Introduction

For twenty years after the establishment of a formal and comprehensive planning system in the late 1950s planning policies towards the cities, as discussed earlier in Part Two, were very much concerned with urban control and containment at the city-regional scale and with extensive urban redevelopment at the intra-urban level. Policies specifically concerned with inner urban problems really did not surface until the later 1960s. However, it can be argued that since then inner-city intervention has proved one of the most dynamic of urban policies. By comparison with areas such as housing or transport, inner-city resources may not be particularly formidable, but some of the most interesting of urban experiments have been conducted within this area. In this chapter we shall attempt to provide a broad overview of inner-city policy.

However, before embarking on this, one question needs to be raised: Why did an inner-city dimension emerge at all in the mid to late 1960s? In some aspects, such as housing, the inner areas improved relative to the conurbations within which they were located throughout the 1960s (Department of the Environment, 1975). It is not at all clear in fact that in any rational analysis the inner areas merited the additional assistance that came their way. But of course in practice the motives for inner urban policy lie rooted in political considerations. For instance, by the mid-1960s unemployment was rising in the cities, an unfortunate trend for a Labour government whose electoral heartland this was. American experience in urban experimentation had been closely observed by British civil servants eager to embark upon similar innovation. Within the cities there had also been a marked increase in New Commonwealth immigrants. By 1966 many of Britain's 600 000 nonwhite population were living in inner-city areas. Indeed the earliest hints of urban intervention emerged in the 1966 Local Government Act, Section II of which provided additional, though limited, resources for authorities with substantial numbers of immigrants. Not that this was the end of the racial question. Some two years later Enoch Powell's notorious 'rivers of blood' speech was almost certainly influential in forcing a response from Harold Wilson's Labour government. This response was ultimately to culminate in the creation of a formal urban programme (McKay and Cox, 1979) that was to blossom in a manner nobody at the time could surely have ever imagined. In evaluating this policy strand it can be argued that intervention here has consisted of two related but discrete periods: an era of experimentation between about 1967 and 1975 and a subsequent period of more permanent inner urban policy. Each phase merits separate consideration.

Urban experimentation: 1967 to 1975

In this period of eight years or so central governments of both Labour and Conservative persuasion introduced a dozen separate urban experiments. Most were to emerge from the Home Office or the Department of the Environment. Some were to undertake comprehensive reviews of the problems facing quite large areas of cities; others were more limited in scope and scale. Some undoubtedly were to prove important in moulding attitudes towards urban deprivation; others were to become little more than historical footnotes and, having been considered elsewhere (Lawless, 1979), need not detain us here. Some indication of contrasting strategies ought, however, to be undertaken. One approach that can be adopted here is to perceive the experiments as falling into three major classifications: first, the more important resource-allocating projects, such as the urban programme; secondly, those experiments charged with creating a more coordinated approach towards the delivery of urban services; and thirdly, the major investigative projects.

The urban programme was to prove quite the most important of the urban projects in financial terms. A few million pounds were usually made available annually by the Home Office for capital and current investment in social and community facilities. Both local authorities and community groups could bid for relevant resources. Demand always tended to outstrip supply, although during the decade when the traditional programme ran, from 1968 to 1978, over 200 local authorities benefited in some way or other. Although there was little to indicate any formal research programme underpinning the initiative as a whole, it is evident that certain models of deprivation — of which more below — guided the evolution of the programme (Edwards and Batley, 1978). It did not concern itself either to any large degree with educational issues, which in the urban context were channelled instead into the concept of the educational priority area. These emerged from the 1967 Plowden Report, 'Children and Their Primary Schools', which recommended that additional resources should be directed to educational establishments in more deprived urban localities. This was to happen in association with a research programme under the general direction of A.H. Halsey (1972). The conclusions of this research can be seen as extremely penetrative: deprived children were not to be found, for example, in easily defined areas of cities; positive discrimination towards educational provision could only ever be seen as one aspect of an attack on disadvantage; the scale of educational support administered through educational priority areas had to be perceived as minute.

By the early 1970s many working in the inner areas were arguing that one potentially significant strategy that might reduce deprivation was for the coordination of services to be improved. A 'total approach' might theoretically be devised wherein all public agencies which in some way or other featured in the governance of cities might be pulled together through the creation of integrative urban strategies. A number of the urban experiments had this aim of improving service coordination as one aspect of their brief. But one or two, notably the Comprehensive Community Programmes, were entirely based on this approach. The convoluted evolution of the C.C.P.'s has been dealt with elsewhere (Higgins *et al*, 1983). Ultimately, however, two programmes — at Gateshead and Bradford — were developed in some detail, and, although considerable doubt has been expressed about the validity of coordination as a strategy through which disadvantage might genuinely be reduced, it has remained a persistent theme in the inner-city debate.

The third type of project, the major investigative experiments, proved extremely important in changing attitudes towards deprivation. Two experiments should be mentioned. When the Home Office established the urban programme in the late 1960s it was decided to balance the approach adopted there, the scattering of relatively small sums to many authorities, by the introduction of concentrated projects exploring the causes of, and possible responses to, deprivation in a number of disadvantaged areas in the United Kingdom. This latter approach culminated in the creation of 12 Community Development Projects. Not all were urban based. Some were to be supported by relevant local authorities for only relatively short periods. But the analysis of urban problems and policies undertaken by Projects such as that at Coventry (Coventry Community Development Project, 1975) were, when read in conjunction with the findings of the Inner Area Studies, to prove profoundly important in changing official attitudes towards urban deprivation.

The three Inner Areas Studies were commissioned in 1972 by Peter Walker, then Secretary of State for the Environment in the 1970-74 Conservative administration. They were undertaken in the urban cores of Birmingham, Liverpool and Lambeth in South London. As with the C.D.P.'s, there were variations in approach adopted by the three teams. That based in London, for example, was to pursue the concept of balanced dispersal, arguing that the extent of disadvantage might be moderated through moving some of the more deprived from inner London to suburban and new town locations. But this somewhat maverick approach was not typical of the conclusions that many of the Inner Area Studies and indeed the C.D.P.'s were to present. Rather their lasting impact was to explore, and in some cases reject, prevailing models of urban deprivation.

Models of urban deprivation

Throughout the late 1960s and early 1970s there was substantial political and academic (Holman, 1978) interest in the question of deprivation, and particularly urban deprivation. In a relatively short period, that is in the seven or eight years before 1975, a number of models were to be expounded and in some cases undermined. In the inner urban context mention ought to be made of four such approaches.

(a) The culture of poverty

Culture of poverty arguments were to be proposed by a number of central government politicians, notably Sir Keith Joseph. Briefly the argument is that families, of a certain kind often concentrated in specific localities, imbued those born into such areas with a kind of antisocial culture. There was in effect an intergenerational weakness, often termed pathology, which encouraged life-styles based on early school leaving, vandalism, early marriage and child-rearing, crime and so on. Such arguments were convenient for central government to promote since clearly they implied that deprivation was concentrated in certain areas, was essentially generated by the deprived themselves and might be moderated at relatively little cost. This approach certainly did not call into question the equity of prevailing social and economic structures.

In many respects the debate about urban poverty revolved around the reality of cultural arguments. Academics had for many years doubted the effectiveness of this explanation in accounting for the perpetuation of urban poverty (Townsend, 1974). In the event these doubts were to be strongly reinforced through the findings of the C.D.P.'s and the Inner Area Studies. For example, deprivation did not appear to be concentrated in certain easily definable localities. On the contrary it appeared to have a widespread distribution throughout the country, a conclusion that the 1971 Census was generally to confirm (Holtermann, 1975). Equally so, the deprived in the urban cores did not appear in any discernible way to be different from the more affluent. Moreover, research undertaken at the specific request of Sir Keith Joseph, commissioned when he was Secretary of State at the Department of Health and Social Security, confirmed what those working in the area strongly supposed (Rutter and Madge, 1976). Many born into circumstances that might be described as deprived escaped. Similarly, many disadvantaged were often born into relatively well-off families. In effect there was a great deal of intergenerational change. Other more substantial models needed to be invoked if the totality of deprivation was ever to be understood.

(b) Life-cycle of poverty

Although cultural arguments were largely to be rejected by the urban experiments, it is worth pointing out — and different nomenclature can apply here — that a life-cycle of poverty can often be identified. It does appear nationally, for example, that large groups in society may well be deprived because income tends radically to decline at certain times in the life-cycle of many households, old age and child rearing periods in particular. The cities with heavy concentrations of such groups, increasingly in fact the elderly, will inevitably find an intensification in demand for certain social services. Moreover, it should be pointed out that inner urban policy, as will be explored later, has concentrated largely on aspects of economic development and employment creation. However successful such approaches might be it must be accepted that for many of the urban deprived beneficial consequences will be minimal. For those dependent upon social welfare their position will vary according to nationally derived policies. Inner urban policy as such has normally not been concerned with their interests.

(c) The search for coordination

As has been mentioned previously, one central objective assumed in many of the urban experiments was the attempt to better the coordination of services within the cities. In fact this approach towards moderating urban problems has persisted. Late in 1984, for example, the Conservative administration appeared likely to announce the creation of a number of task forces drawn from the private sector, one of whose aims would be to formulate coordinated urban strategies for selected cities.

There seems little doubt that the administration of cities is frequently undertaken by a myriad of agencies, which may operate according to different objectives and within different time-spans and contrasting boundaries. It may make sense to try to bring relevant organizations together in some sort of formal arrangement. The effectiveness of such strategies should not be overestimated, however. The search for better management can deflect attention from the total resources available to the cities for instance. It may prove impossible to create an agreed agenda that will embrace all organizations. In practice this search for consensus may disguise the reality of conflict between and within urban agencies. Perhaps in any case some variety in response to urban disadvantage is to be welcomed. It would be hard to point to organizations or strategies that had proved so incontravertibly successful in moderating urban decline that their approach and no other should be embraced.

(d) The impact of structural forces on the cities

By the early 1970s the Community Development Projects and the Inner Area Studies were clearly beginning to direct their attentions to alternative explanations of deprivation. No doubt certain inadequate families could be identified in the cities. Some groups, such as the old, were deprived because of the welfare system. There might also be some limited mileage in improving the coordination of services, but these explanations of themselves were not sufficient for an understanding of the totality of urban deprivation. Other forces needed to be invoked.

In essence the argument that developed from the Inner Area Studies and Community Development Projects was that the primary generator of urban disadvantage was quite simply lack of income and wealth. This had historically always characterized many in the cities. Twenty years of the welfare state had, however, clearly not eradicated poverty. It might be the case that the degree of disadvantage in the 1970s was neither as extensive nor as acute as had been the case in earlier eras but it nevertheless remained a reality for many in the cities.

The causes of inadequate and declining income were varied. As has been mentioned above, some were disadvantaged because of the welfare benefits system. But many others were unemployed, underemployed or employed in less skilled and less well paid jobs than had previously been the case. The causes for this contraction in urban employment are dealt with in Chapter 14 and need not detain us here. But, in brief, manufacturing jobs had been lost largely because of extensive corporate restructuring, rationalization and reorganization.

A large proportion of Britain's manufacturing output comes from a relatively small number of multinational or international firms. Their pursuit of profit has ultimately culminated in a dramatic transformation in patterns of industrial investment away from traditional industrial products manufactured in the older industrial regions and cities towards newer goods and services produced in more environmentally attractive areas of the south of England and indeed increasingly abroad. These processes, which were identified in the urban experiments and which were in turn to be refined by later analyses (Fothergill and Gudgin, 1982; Massey and Meegan, 1982; Scott, 1982), differed in their operation from region to region. In some areas, such as Coventry (Coventry Community Development Project, 1975), the fluctuations in the car industry were crucial in explaining the extent of unemployment; on Tyneside it was heavy engineering and shipbuilding (North Tyneside C.D.P. 1978); in London's Docklands it was the demise of port-related activities (Canning Town C.D.P. 1977). But whatever the immediate cause, this massive contraction in manufacturing and the associated decline in community income created impacts across the board. It affected investment in housing, retailing, transport provision, and other services. When, as was usually the case, local and central government proved unable to counterbalance declines in personal income through greater public-sector investment, whole swathes of cities became characterized by depressing physical environments, outdated infrastructure, poor educational and health facilities and limited, ineffective political activity.

Although the Inner Area Studies and the Community Development Projects tended to produce similar analyses of the urban problem, somewhat different prescriptions tended to be promoted. The Lambeth Inner Area Study (1977), for instance, argued for a socially balanced dispersal of urbanities from inner London. The Southwark C.D.P. promoted the idea of area management. A substantial number indicated the need for a reformist programme of intervention based on enhanced local and central investment in both production and consumption. Some of the C.D.P.'s also adopted radical prescriptions arguing for an intensification of trade union and resident group activity in conjunction with sympathetic national and local political institutions in order to implement dramatic changes in, say, the ownership of production (National Community Development Project, 1977).

Despite this plethora of prescription, the fundamental message emanating from the experiments was that urban malaise was economically based and was affecting many older cities and regions. The implications of this analysis were profound. The experiments were arguing in effect that the urban problem related to broader national and international economic trends over which local or even central government might have little control. Moderating such processes would prove expensive and would require additional and substantial public-sector investment. The problem was not, moreover, one limited to certain pockets of cities, but one that affected entire regions of the country. Older dispensations based on culture of poverty arguments would simply have to be abandoned, and in effect this is what central government did. From 1975 onwards there is evidence (Castle, 1980) that the then Secretary of State for the Environment, Peter Shore, saw inner-city support as a primary objective which should be retained to the detriment of other policy goals. Some two years later, moreover, after the deliberations of a Cabinet committee on the problem, a White Paper was produced which, in a telling phrase, argued that 'the decline in the economic fortunes of the inner areas often lies at the heart of the problem' (HMSO, 1977, p.2). This position was a long way divorced from the cultural arguments that had dominated official thinking only a few years earlier. More crucially, too, it was to herald the emergence of a permanent inner urban policy.

Inner urban policy post-1977

With the publication of the White Paper on policy for the inner cities in 1977, it became evident that the period of urban experimentation was in effect terminated. Some projects were to continue for a few more years, but the entire inner-city emphasis undeniably shifted towards the implementation of substantive policy. In the following years a number of initiatives were to be introduced by central governments of both political persuasions. Before its electoral defeat in 1979 the Labour government was to instigate the concept of 'partnerships'. In the post-1979 era Conservative administrations were in turn to implement additional urban innovations, in particular enterprise zones and urban development corporations. Each of these initiatives merits separate consideration.

The partnerships

The main proposal contained in the 1977 White Paper was for the establishment of Partnerships in England. As a general review of existing inner-city funding it was announced that the urban programme would be transferred from the Home Office to the Department of the Environment and would be increased from £30m to £125m by 1979-80. By 1983-84 total resources had risen to about £350m. Although a traditional programme would be retained in that any urban local authority with special social needs would be able to apply for grant, it became clear that a substantial proportion of enhanced inner-city investment would be allocated to Programme and Partnership authorities. By 1983 there were 23 Programmes or second-tier authorities, and seven Partnerships.

Central government argued in the 1977 White Paper that in a strictly limited number of areas it would be prepared to enter into a formal agreement with other public and voluntary organizations to produce programmes to assist the regeneration of the urban cores concerned. This action, it was argued, was necessary in order to bring national experience to bear on the problem, to create coordinated urban strategies and to underline the government's commitment to the inner cities. Formal Partnerships Committees were to be chaired by a Department of the Environment Minister. A whole range of organizations were invited to participate. These included central government departments, such as the Department of Industry and Employment, the Manpower Services Commission, the police, local health authorities, voluntary organizations and representatives from relevant departments within two tiers of local government — the counties and the metropolitan districts. Ultimately Partnerships were offered to London's Dockland authorities, Lambeth, Islington and Hackney, Birmingham, Liverpool, Manchester and Salford, and Newcastle and Gateshead. When elected in 1979, the incoming Conservative government reviewed the concept but decided to retain it, although a greater emphasis was to be placed on cooperation with, and assistance from, the private sector. However, to some extent this had already occurred, particularly in industrial improvement areas, which had been given formal recognition in the 1978 Inner Urban Areas Act. This legislation allowed the Partnership and Programme authorities to declare industrial improvement areas within which a variety of grants and loans could be made available to employers for improvements or for the conversion or improvement of industrial and commercial buildings.

By the early 1980s it was becoming clear, however, that Partnerships were encountering problems. It was proving difficult for example to tease out a comprehensive, coordinated strategy from the myriad of agencies that in some way or other might have a role to play in urban regeneration. Not all relevant organizations considered an inner-city dimension at all appropriate. The Department of Industry has often been seen as having at best a lukewarm attitude towards an inner urban dimension — an important consideration, bearing in mind the substantial regional and national resources under its control. Some organizations, such as health authorities, did not wish to assist certain inner urban areas and not others. The operational aims of participating organizations conflicted at times. For example, the views of the police did not always equate with those held by some voluntary organizations. As Hambleton (1981) points out, it is quite clear that many Partnerships abandoned any idea of defining a coherent and logical strategy towards the inner areas and opted instead for the *ad hoc,* pragmatic spending of urban programme assistance on capital projects. Many local government departments certainly used urban funds to implement long-cherished projects that could not be funded from other sources. Because of this approach, urban programme expenditure was often allocated not to the priority area of economic development but to other social and community projects (Nabarro, 1980). In the early programmes produced by the Partnerships it was almost invariably found that economic demise was the most important single problem. From then onwards most money was spent elsewhere, partly because local authority departments such as Social Services normally retained considerable influence with Partnership Committees.

The concept of 'partnership' was, moreover, undermined by persistent conflicts between participating organizations. The metropolitan counties often disagreed with the districts (House of Commons Environment Committee, 1983). Central government was frequently criticized on the grounds that it was in reality subjecting the cities to severe financial constraints through cuts in main programmes of expenditure such as housing. Far from receiving more the Partnerships in real terms lost about 10 per cent of central government support in the first three years of the Conservative administration elected in 1979. Local conflict was apparent too. Some authorities in the combined Partnerships, notably Hackney and Islington, differed sharply in approach. Within the individual authorities too there was little to indicate that a coherent approach towards more deprived areas could be developed from the often opposing positions of different departments (Spooner, 1980). In retrospect it was not surprising to see the emergence in the early 1980s of alternative inner urban innovations.

Enterprise zones

When in opposition in the 1970s the Tories had promulgated the idea of zones free from financial and physical constraints. Radical right-wing opinion within the party believed that economic development and employment growth could be achieved by removing controls that apparently hindered the flourishing of enterprise. At one stage it appeared as if many concessions were to be applied to the zones that were announced in the 1980 Budget and given legal status in the 1980 Local Government, Planning and Land Act. In the event, however, due in part to opposition from a wide range of national and local organizations, the exemptions ultimately to apply were relatively modest (Taylor, 1981). In particular, a relaxed planning regime was to be introduced, Development Land Tax and local rates would not be levied and 100 per cent capital allowances for industrial and commercial buildings were to be allowed. These benefits were to last 10 years, and by 1983 there were more than 20 zones throughout the United Kingdom, about half of which were located in older urban areas.

Only a few years into the experiment it is impossible to evaluate with any great confidence the likely impact of enterprise zones. It can be argued that the experiment is worth trying. The government indicated that over 3000 jobs had been created by May 1982, at which time only 11 zones were in operation.

Many of the areas to receive zones had been subject to extensive economic decline and perhaps any intervention is an improvement of sorts. It has become clear too that a widespread return to the physical despoilation typical of Victorian *laissez-faire* development is not going to occur in enterprise zones. Although more relaxed planning schemes have been implemented, dangerous or polluting industries remain the subject of planning control. Interestingly enough, the concern that some authorities expressed about a widespread proliferation of retailing, of which only a certain proportion can be sustained in any urban economy, has tended to be unfounded. Larger shopping projects normally need permission in enterprise zones. Authorities wishing to retain the primacy of city centre shopping have thus been able to refuse applications that might lead to an imbalance in retailing provision.

It is clear, however, that some local authorities and some independent observers (Catalano, 1983: Tym and Partners, 1984) retain a considerable degree of scepticism about the entire concept. For instance the vast proportion of jobs created in zones have come from neighbouring areas, and their relocation involves little net job creation. Much of the private-sector investment that has occurred would anyway have been undertaken. In fact the entire concept that public intervention somehow reduces enterprise and that the private sector should be allowed to operate in an unrestrained fashion is completely undermined by experience within the zones: those that have received the most public-sector infrastructural assistance have attracted the most private-sector investment. Zones such as those at Swansea or Corby, where site preparation has been rapidly implemented by single agencies, often owning much of the land, have been the most successful. Even then it is not of course certain that all companies renting property will remain after the ten-year exemption period ends. Many may simply move on to take advantage of other publicly funded benefits. It is, moreover, far from clear that those who were supposed to benefit from the approach will in the event do so. Landlords may benefit more than industrial tenants if they can raise rents. Commercial developments have found the exemptions more favourable than have manufacturing firms — probably an unfortunate tendency because of the former's relatively limited ability to take on additional labour. It is also uncertain whether many of the unskilled will be helped at all by these exemptions, which clearly relate to economic development rather than employment growth. Ultimately, as more caustic commentators might well point out, the basic premises of the concept are simply untenable: the United Kingdom is neither especially highly taxed nor tightly planned. Genuine economic development will require the combined talents of private and public sectors, not the absurdly simplistic assumption that the private sector alone can create and sustain wealth.

Urban development corporations

Part XVI of the 1980 Local Government, Planning and Land Act allowed for the creation of urban development corporations. In the event, by 1984 two had been declared, in the docklands of London and Merseyside. They are appointed development organizations with wide powers to acquire, reclaim, sell, or develop land. By 1983-84 central government funding amounted to about £70m, although it has always been assumed that considerably greater sums would eventually be forthcoming from the private sector, the involvement of which has been perceived as central to the operations of the U.D.C.'s.

The Merseyside U.D.C. now controls about 860 acres of what had been virtually redundant docks. Much of its activity has concentrated on the reclamation of land, part of which was used for the 1984 Garden Festival. In addition the Corporation has acted as a catalyst in the extensive redevelopment of the Albert Docks which are to be converted for residential, industrial and commercial purposes. Because of the relatively uncontentious nature of this Corporation's activities and because so few people live in land vested in it, its operations have proved less controversial than those of the London Dockland Development Corporation (L.D.D.C.).

The L.D.D.C. operates within 5000 acres downstream of Tower Bridge. More than 40 000 people live in the areas whose traditional port-based activities have moved downstream. The Corporation has consistently argued that it should act as a catalyst in the transformation of the area through encouraging private-sector investment, which will eventually transform the social and economic base of the area (London Docklands Development Corporation, 1984). In essence the Corporation has tried to encourage investment in new employment sectors, such as financial services, high-tech, printing and communications, which have never traditionally located within the area. Paralleling this policy of economic readjustment the Corporation has also actively pursued a policy of encouraging owner-occupation, some of it of a prestigious nature, in an area where public-sector accommodation has dominated tenurial patterns.

It is not surprising that the creation of the corporations, especially the one in London, has proved unpopular (Leaders of the London Boroughs of Greenwich, Lewisham, Newham, Southwark and Tower Hamlets, 1979; Joint Docklands Action Group, 1980; Newman and Mayo, 1981; Hebbert, 1982). In brief, it has been argued that they create administrative chaos because they assimilate some but not all local functions. They have, moreover, proved secretive in that they are largely unwilling to consider local community representations. They have determined instead undemocratically to pursue policies that may not assist the economic, housing and social needs of local residents at all. Ultimately their very necessity has been questioned. In London the 1976 Docklands Strategic Plan had been agreed by the five London Boroughs concerned and by the Greater London Council. In many respects this Plan had been relatively successful, although, for reasons beyond the control of the authorities concerned, job creation had not matched job loss in the area in the late 1970s. Why many observers believe the U.D.C. was established here was not therefore so much that local planning had failed in its objectives but rather that the policies outlined in the 1976 Plan were at variance with those preferred by the Conservative government elected in 1979. In particular the emphasis in the 1976 Plan on public and cooperative housing within an economy based largely on manufacturing industry was not acceptable to central government.

There are, however, contrary arguments that suggest that the U.D.C's are an appropriate vehicle within which urban regeneration can be guided. They can operate more quickly and with less bureaucracy than can local authorities. They bring attitudes and skills from the private sector — a vital consideration when so much investment for these areas will ultimately emanate from the market. Also, they follow demand-led policies that attract and guide the private sector, rather than pursuing strategies based on what are likely to be declining, public resources. They encourage development in growth sectors and propose balanced socio-economic communities. Moreover, they are ultimately democratic in that they are responsible to the Secretary of State for the Environment and hence in turn to Parliament. In the final analysis it could be argued for the U.D.C.'s that it should be national rather than local government that decides policies appropriate for an area such as London's Docklands, which represents an enormous, perhaps unique, opportunity for both the nation and the capital. The area's ability in particular to sustain the commercial and financial functions of London is not one that should be lost because of the parochial attitudes of the few local authorities concerned. Perhaps there is some truth in this last argument, but the doubt remains nevertheless whether the huge scale of public-sector investment in land reclamation, road construction, the creation of a new light railway and so on will do anything to boost the social and economic fortunes of many resident within the area.

Other inner urban innovations

Brief mention ought to be made of a number of other inner-city initiatives that had been introduced by 1984. Local authorities have, for example, to produce land registers indicating vacant public land. Once such sites are listed the assumption is that authorities will ensure development is carried out either by the public or the private sector. In the case of the latter it should be pointed out that urban land will frequently be sold by local government at much lower prices in real terms than was paid for its acquisition. Often such acquisition was imperative if authorities were to undertake housing, education, health or traffic policies that they, or central government, thought essential in the 1960s and 1970s.

One clear feature of inner urban policy in the 1980s has been the determination on the part of Conservative central administrations to involve the private sector in urban regeneration. Thus companies contributing to local enterprise agencies, which try to boost local economic development through, for example, assistance to small firms, receive benefit through tax relief. The Financial Institutions Group, consisting of private-sector managers, was established in 1981. It made a number of recommendations intended to boost private-sector investment in the older urban cores. One proposal that was implemented in 1982 was the urban development grant. This is payable where local authorities can guarantee the involvement of the private-sector in the implementation of projects. In essence public funds are used to 'lever out' at least comensurate private-sector investment. Frequently a ratio of one public-sector unit of investment to four of private-sector investment can be attained, a figure high enough to suggest that some schemes might have been implemented anyway irrespective of urban programme assistance.

Inner urban policy: some interpretations

Any analysis of inner-city intervention over the last twenty years or so would have to conclude with certain incontrovertible findings. The sums involved have been tiny and indeed in real terms the cities have lost resources for many years. No one could realistically argue that the scale of public-sector investment will moderate, let alone reverse, market contraction. The cities are simply no longer appealing locations for a wide range of industrial, retail, commercial and residential investors. At the same time it would be unwise universally to overstress urban malaise. In some respects, such as housing, standards have not consistently declined. There have often been impressive improvements in terms of environmental standards and the provision of leisure and recreational facilities. But if the primacy of economic regeneration is accepted, there can be no doubt that unemployment has continued to rise in the major conurbations and that the inner urban programme has done little to enhance job opportunities, especially for the more disadvantaged. It would surely be impossible to argue that the limited scale of inner-city innovation is a rational response to the perceived problems of the cities. Other motives must be invoked.

It can be argued that the programme has been an ill coordinated, irrational, misguided and pragmatic response on the part of a relatively small number of central government ministers and officials. Secretaries of State such as Walker, Shore and Heseltine realized that considerable political advantages could accrue from pursuing an urban programme. Resources could remain limited while innovation proceeded and political reputations were made. Indeed Higgins (1978) has argued that, especially in the 1960s and through to the middle of the following decade, central government essentially used the urban experiments as demonstration projects. Experiments could be established at limited financial cost and considerable political gain whose recommendations, which the projects themselves believed would be implemented, could in practice be ignored or delayed while other limited experiments were developed.

Other observers (Bridges, 1981-82) have, however, perceived not so much an incremental and random evolution of inner-city intervention as a conspiratorial one. Here inner-city intervention is explained as the state's response to the problems endured by the cities as a result of dramatic market withdrawal and contraction. Inner-city innovation is essential both to boost declining profit accumulation — hence grants and loans to employers — and to legitimize a system that seems patently to have failed many in the urban cores — hence the emphasis within the Partnerships on aspects of social consumption such as leisure and social services. Although there can be no doubt that the scale of urban economic retrenchment has proved so severe that central administrations have intervened both to boost accumulation and to legitimize prevailing economic and social structures, the minimal scale of intervention and its patent inability independently to achieve either objective make this analysis partial at best.

Perhaps the most useful device within which to locate inner-city intervention is through the central-local debate. There can be little argument that central government has tightened its control over local authorities in recent years. Inner urban intervention can be seen to reflect this in that, for example, the urban development corporations allow the centre to direct both local production and local consumption. As Rhodes (1980) points out, central-local relations are, however, in practice rather more complex than central domination models would suggest. For instance, national policies may in effect be compromises worked out between central and local government wherein the latter retains considerable discretion. This analysis appears valid in terms of the inner-city policy. Enterprise zone proposals were altered as a result of local authority comment. Finally, also in terms of the central-local debate, the dualism thesis developed by Saunders (1981) contains valuable perspectives from the point of view of the urban dimension. In brief, Saunders argues that decisions relating to aspects of production have typically been taken at the centre through a corporatist form of policy making embracing major business and trade union interests in conjunction with central government. On the other hand, decisions with regard to aspects of consumption, such as housing, education and social services, have tended to be made locally through pluralist decision-making mechanisms. This analysis can be seen as useful in any dynamic interpretation of urban intervention. In effect central government appears no longer to be satisfied with control over aspects of production but rather is using inner urban innovation, such as urban development corporations, to intervene locally in consumption too. Simultaneously, more radical local authorities are realizing that if economic decline is the root cause of urban malaise then influence over local production should be a primary objective. As pointed out in Chapter 14, this is the direction in which such administrations are moving.

References

Bridges, L. (1981-82) Keeping the lid on: British urban social policy 1975-81, *Race and Class*, Vol. XXIII, No. 2/3, pp 161-185

Canning Town Community Development Project (1977) Canning Town's declining community income: a case study, Tate and Lyle, London

Castle, B. (1980) *The Castle Diaries*, Weidenfeld and Nicolson, London

Catalano, A. (1983) A review of UK enterprise zones, Paper 17, Centre for Environmental Studies

Coventry Community Development Project (1975) Final Report Part I, Coventry and Hillfields: prosperity and the persistence of inequality, Coventry C.D.P., Coventry

Department of the Environment (1975) Study of the inner areas of conurbations, D.O.E., London

Edwards, J. and Batley, R. (1978) *The Politics of Positive Discrimination*, Tavistock Publications, London

Fothergill, S. and Gudgin, G. (1982) *Unequal Growth, Urban and Regional Employment Change in the United Kingdom*, Heinemann Educational Books, London

Halsey, A. (1972) *Educational priority*, Report of Research Project Sponsored by DES/SSRC, Vol. 1, Educational Priority EPA, Problems and Policies, HMSO, London

Hambleton, R. (1981) Implementing inner city policy: reflections from experience, *Policy and Politics*, Vol. 9. No. 1, pp 51-71

Hebbert, M. (1982) A style of its own, *Town and Country Planning*, Vol. 51, No. 2, pp 35-36

Higgins, J. (1978) *The Poverty Business, Britain and America*, Blackwell, Oxford

Higgins, J., Deakin, N., Edwards, J. and Wicks, M. (1983) *Government and Urban Poverty*, Blackwell, Oxford

HMSO (1977) Policy for the inner cities, Cmnd 6845, HMSO, London

Holman, R. (1978) *Poverty: explanations of social deprivation*, Martin and Robertson, London

Holtermann, S. (1975) Areas of urban deprivation in Great Britain, an analysis of the 1971 Census data, *Social Trends*, No. 6, pp 33-47

House of Commons Environment Committee (1983), The problems of management of urban renewal, appraisal of the recent initiatives in Merseyside, Third Report of the Environment Committee 1982/83, HMSO, London

Lambeth Inner Area Study (1977) *Inner London. Policies of Dispersal and Balance*, HMSO, London

Lawless, P. (1979) *Urban Deprivation and Government Initiative*, Faber and Faber, London

Leaders of the London Boroughs of Greenwich, Lewisham, Newham, Southwark and Tower Hamlets (1979) Local democracy works, London

London Docklands Development Corporation (1984) Corporate strategy, L.D.D.C., London

Massey, D.B. and Meegan, R.A. (1982) *The Anatomy of Job Loss*, Methuen, London

McKay, D.H. and Cox, A.W. (1979) *The Politics of Urban Change*, Croom Helm, London

Nabarro, R. (1980) Inner city partnerships. An assessment of the first programmes, *Town Planning Review*, Vol. 51, No. 1, pp 25-38

National Community Development Project (N.C.D.P.) (1977) The costs of industrial change, C.D.P. Inter-Project Editorial Team

Newman, I. and Mayo, M.I. (1981) Docklands, *International Journal of Urban and*

Regional Research, Vol. 5, No. 4, pp 529-545

North Tyneside Community Development Project (1978) North Shields, living with industrial change, Final Report, Vol. 2, North Tyneside C.D.P.

Rhodes, R.A.W. (1980) Some myths in central-local relations, *Town Planning Review*, Vol. 51, No. 3, pp 270-285

Rutter, M. and Madge, N. (1976) *Cycles of Disadvantage. A review of research*, Heinemann, London

Saunders, P. (1981) *Social Theory and the Urban Question*, Hutchinson, London

Scott, A.J. (1982) Locational patterns and dynamics of industrial activity in the modern metropolis, *Urban Studies*, Vol. 19, No. 2, pp 111-142

Spooner, S. (1980) The politics of partnership, Planning Studies No. 6, Polytechnic of Central London, School of Environment, Planning Unit

Taylor, S. (1981) The politics of enterprise zones, *Public Administration*, Vol. 59, Winter, pp 421-439

Townsend, P. (1974) The Cycle of Deprivation. The History of a Confused Thesis, British Association of Social Workers, Birmingham

Tym, R. and Partners (1984) Monitoring enterprise zones, Year Three Report

Further reading

On the deprivation debate generally Holman (1978) is very comprehensive. The urban experiments are dealt with in Edwards and Batley (1978), Higgins (1978), Higgins *et al.* (1983) and Lawless (1979). Lawless, P. (1981) *Britain's Inner Cities, Problems and Policies*, Harper and Row, London, considers some aspects of post-1977 inner-city policy.

The British city in the 1980s:
                     a concluding comment

In this book three major tasks have been attempted: to explore the scale of urban growth and societal responses to this process in the 1760-1939 period; to analyze the British conurbations in the post-1945 period within prevailing institutional constraints; and finally to examine some of the dynamics of the contemporary city. A central emphasis has thus been placed throughout on the mutually interdependent relationships between urban growth, societal responses towards urban development, and the prevailing institutional and political parameters which have proved so important in delineating the evolution of the city. Whatever the defects in this approach it has the undeniable advantage of placing sociopolitical impulses at the very centre of the urban debate. Too frequently they have been undervalued or indeed ignored. But the city moulds society and in turn mirrors its evolution. Contrasting sociopolitical tensions would have culminated in a markedly different urban Britain from the one that faces us in the mid-1980s. From this somewhat depressing vantage point we will briefly raise three concluding issues: the likely fate of the British city in the coming years; theoretical developments in urban studies; and some directions for future research.

Into the 1990s: the city within British society

Writing in 1985 it would be hard to present anything other than a depressing picture of the contemporary city. Much of what has been written in Parts Two and Three of this book must inevitably lead to a pessimistic assessment. Demographic and economic decline, combined with diminishing political power, would have placed the cities in a difficult position, irrespective of central government's prevailing ideology. In the event, in the post-1979 era the cities ran into the most market-orientated, anti-interventionist administration elected in Britain for many decades. Many of the policies implemented by Tory administrations returned to power in 1979 and 1983 will appear bizarrely anachronistic to future generations faced with the consequences of inadequate educational, physical, industrial and technical investment. This may offer the cities longer-term consolation. Political and hence economic change appears less than imminent in 1985, however.

In the mid 1980s indeed it appears probable that the cities will continue to suffer from the implementation of policies whose adverse effects have been explored earlier in the book. Financial restraint will be tightly imposed on current and capital expenditure with obvious implications for employment, local services and physical investment. Necessary improvements to, say, transport infrastructure, health provision or educational investment will simply not occur. New housing will be increasingly concentrated in the owner-occupied sector and will be constructed beyond the cities. Many of the less affluent will remain trapped in deteriorating public housing within the major conurbations. Here public services of all kinds are likely to become more expensive and less effective. Transport services, for example, seem certain to become less extensive and much more costly in the years to come. In addition, proposed amendments to the social security system may well substantially reduce the status of groups such as the unemployed, young families and the old, many of which are particularly concentrated in the urban cores.

Anti-interventionists will of course argue that reduced public intervention and expenditure are essential to achieve national economic growth, and that declining support for the cities is therefore inevitable and even desirable. Such arguments need to be treated with disdain. There is no evidence that private enterprise will flourish in line with reduced public investment. The opposite is more probably correct: public investment helps to lever out private expenditure. In any case, if deprived groups are to be granted some public support and sympathy, it is clear that an increasing proportion of welfare expenditure will be directed towards the cities. Quite simply, more and more of the disadvantaged are living there. This will no doubt raise Tory hackles. It should, however, be pointed out that a society which imposes minimal constraints on the market must accept some of the consequences of such insouciance. If companies can leave established urban premises and pay nothing towards the social and economic costs of such relocations then inevitably social expenditure will rise. And trite comments that those displaced from employment should follow the market must be dismissed as simplistic nonsense. How many of those made redundant from the contraction in manufacturing in the older cities and regions of the country are likely to find accommodation in, say, the Cambridges and Newburys of the world, to say nothing of the booming industrial zones of Singapore?

Reality concerning the scale of the urban problem should not give way to despair. However bleak the urban picture may appear in the 1980s it would be wrong to imagine any universal acceptance of continuous decline on the part of many living and working in the cities. Indeed the cities reflect a variety and richness of experience that holds out hope for the future. It may well be true that the best prospect for the major conurbations would be the return of a non-Thatcherite government prepared to implement policies over, say, capital investment that would help to re-employ more of the semi-skilled and unskilled and would improve the disastrous state of the physical infrastructure apparent within many of the urban cores. But even if anti-interventionist administrations are re-elected in the later 1980s and early 1990s, as seems possible writing in 1985, there is still much that can be achieved locally.

Donnison (1983), for example, has outlined the sorts of policies that urban local authorities may still be able to initiate, despite tightening central control. Local economic strategies (discussed in Chapter 14) can be fostered. Community and cooperative enterprise can be stimulated. There is evidence, for instance, that some jobs can be created locally in areas such as waste disposal, furniture renovation, odd jobbing, environmental improvement programmes and so on. The scale of market contraction should not in any case be overstressed. Most of those living in cities are still employed. Many companies may reduce output but not close altogether. Local authorities can better their prospects through land-use planning, improving access for example, or purchasing policies; councils can themselves buy local land. Although there will be severe constraints on the scale of local resources, funds will still be available from central government departments, the E.E.C., local business, charitable organizations and so on. Authorities will, however, need to be made more aware of resources that might be tapped and prove more effective in applying for them. In this context it will also have to be accepted that publicly inspired and implemented projects will prove the exception rather than the rule. Local authorities will need to mould alliances with local chambers of commerce, with trade and industry and with local financial institutions such as banks, insurance companies and pension funds. The resources available to the latter will prove of an altogether different nature from those within the direct control of many urban councils. It may prove galling for many administrations to embark upon local economic strategies in cooperation with regional business interests, but the political climate may well dictate this. Certainly there seems an increasing willingness on the part of financial institutions to fund local projects, partly no doubt because regional capital has no wish to preside over perpetual economic decline. All local administrations should be able to concur with that general objective.

Although resources, especially those available for local economic development, must be seen as a primary issue in the evolving urban debate, there also seems some scope for the improved administration of cities. As has been discussed in the previous chapter, attempts within the inner-city programme to create unified, coordinated urban strategies have tended to prove less than totally successful. Despite this there is still scope for the development of coherent, integrated action plans embracing as many agencies involved in urban activities as possible. Certainly traditional land-use planning, undertaken by traditionally trained planners, appears increasingly irrelevant to the needs of the cities. More flexible policy documents are required to enable rapid responses to be made to changing demands and opportunities.. Planners implementing such documents also need to be much more responsive towards the market, local residents, the business community, other agencies of urban governance and regional offices of central government departments. Planning without implementation is a complete waste of time. Finally, in terms of improving the administration of cities, there is a strong case for the decentralization of many services to mini town halls. Housing, local planning, environmental protection and personal social services might all then be regrouped locally. This would not make a great deal of difference to the scale of urban disadvantage. But at least it would enable local residents to be made more aware of the available services and therefore they would be able to make greater use of them.

Theoretical developments in urban studies

The authors intended that this book should present an empirical account of urban change and growth in Britain in the last 200 years. Because of the sheer scale of this exercise it became rapidly apparent that a determinedly atheoretical stance would have to be adopted. Space dictated this. It is crucial, however, that those embarking on disciplines addressing urban questions should be aware of the dramatic theoretical developments that have occurred since the mid to late 1960s. Anyone familiar with, for example, the work of Dunleavy (1980) or Saunders (1979, 1981) will be aware of the immense intellectual strides that have been made in urban studies. The incorporation of sociological and political conceptualizations in particular within the general ambit of the subject area have given it a depth, structure and synthesizing framework that has undeniably elevated its academic status.

Although any comprehensive analysis of theoretical developments in urban studies is obviously beyond the scope of this text, some brief mention of key issues should be presented as a signpost for those intending to pursue the subject. This task has been made immeasurably easier by the work of Dunleavy (1982), to which those proposing to explore this area should turn. In essence, however, it is apparent that the subject of urban studies has been developed through four major paradigms: spatial definitions, sociocultural approaches, institutional definitions and political economy perspectives. A brief comment should be made on each.

Spatial definitions of urban studies have emanated largely from geography and urban economics. The approach has been much concerned with questions such as the spatial distribution of cities and towns or how urban land uses can be explained. Major advances have included central place theory (discussed briefly in Chapter 13). Despite its historical importance, however, it seems apparent that the perspective suffers from a number of grave weaknesses. For instance, can 'urban' areas, which presumably form the focus of attention here, readily be distinguished from 'rural' areas? Increasing economic interdependence between different areas of the United Kingdom suggests not. Even more critically, it might well be argued that the very questions addressed are unimportant. Should urban studies be concerned with issues such as the pattern of land uses within cities, for example? There seem far more important problems facing the cities in the mid 1980s.

A second strand of thought within urban studies, sociocultural analyses, also seems to be of historical rather than contemporary relevance. Important figures here include Burgess, Park and Wirth whose collective work in Chicago in the interwar period was to lay down the alignments of the subject area for many decades. In essence the Chicago School argued that a specifically urban way of life, with its own intrinsic processes, could be identified, which was in some way different, and inferior, to an apparently rural arcadia. To some extent these sentiments influenced postwar planning in Britain. New towns and neighbourhoods developed in the late 1940s and the 1950s (and discussed in Chapter 11) were constructed on the assumption that localized communities could be developed that would be superior to their counterparts within the larger cities. As with spatial definitions, however, the approach has waned. One clear defect is that it is far from certain that an urban way of life can be identified as having been articulated by processes different from those operating elsewhere. Increasingly indeed practitioners in urban studies have moved towards alternative perspectives: institutional and political economy definitions.

As the name suggests, institutional definitions concentrate on urban social structures, such as local communities, or on urban political creations, such as local authorities. A variety of major academic developments can be identified within this broad definition. Some analyses have, for example, explored the issue of the distribution of power within cities. Dahl's (1961) classic work on New Haven tried to penetrate formal power arrangements to answer questions such as who benefits from urban policies and who decides local policies? In the United Kingdom on the other hand a major neo-Weberian line of thinking can be identified within the overall ambit of institutional definitions. Weber has proved important in the urban debate because of his concern with bureaucracy and because he argued that social change and social stratification can occur for reasons other than those pertaining to the economic mode of production. This effectively distanced him from Marx, for instance, whose work was to prove so crucial in the evolution of the political economy perspectives mentioned below. Certainly for observers such as Rex and Moore (1967) or Pahl (1970) neo-Weberian thinking was to prove a dominant impulse in their explorations into British local government and, in particular, the extent to which local institutions such as housing departments could impose constraints upon, or even articulate classes within, the housing market. In the 1970s many neo-Weberians were themselves to react against institutional analyses, tending instead to adopt political economy approaches. By the mid-1980s their reaction appears somewhat premature. Of course we cannot explain the totality of urban experience by focusing solely on local authorities or local institutions. But to ignore them is equally misguided. Despite increasing control from the centre, different local authorities will employ different policies, will react differently to local circumstances and will develop contrasting relationships with the centre.

Despite the undeniable value of institutional explanations, it is evident that the major development in urban studies since the late 1960s has come through political economy approaches. These have emanated largely from neo-Marxist writings and have proved absolutely crucial to the evolution of the subject area. A whole range of insights emerging out of neo-Marxist analyses have been assimilated by those examining the state of the contemporary city. For instance, vicissitudes ordained by the economic mode of production have been used to explain the collapse of manufacturing industry in many cities. The role of the state has been perceived by radical observers too as a vital determinant in understanding urban policy. On the one hand, the state may wish to legitimize prevailing politico-economic circumstances and hence is prepared to invest in aspects of social consumption, especially in the cities. But on the other hand the state must ensure the continued accumulation of profit and hence devise, say, inner urban policies that attempt to enhance the viability of urban firms.

These and other conceptualizations have been used by radical observers in an attempt to locate cities and urban policy towards them within a holistic, all-embracing framework. There are undeniable weaknesses in the perspective, however. Whether for example one can argue that the capitalist system is doomed, or that a subjugated proletariat can be identified, or that class relates solely to an individual's relationship to the prevailing economic system seems doubtful. The authors indeed would prefer to operate within something of a dualistic interpretation. It seems undeniable that at a higher level of analysis the primacy of economic forces in explaining the state of the British city is of fundamental importance. The state of the economy, the implications for the cities of changing investment patterns, or the decline of manufacturing output in the United Kingdom are the kinds of basic considerations that any analysis of the city in the 1980s must of necessity embrace. But within these structuring parameters there is variety. Contemporary cities reflect historical diversity, political innovation and policy initiative. In accepting the guiding principle of economic vicissitude the variety and dynamism of urban growth and change must not be ignored. Urban analyses needs therefore to proceed within a two-tiered explanatory framework rooted in political economy perspectives but moderated by institutional approaches emerging out of neo-Weberian explanations. The authors believe that this dualistic interpretation can provide a stimulating and synthesizing framework within which substantial advances in urban studies can be made.

Future directions for research

Within the investigative framework outlined above one area of work that still provides scope for important developments is the whole question of the evolution and structure of urban economies. Too often little is known for instance about the dynamism of local capital. Historical investigations allow us, however, to appreciate the role and impact of local entrepreneurs in organizing, expanding and rationalizing urban output. Contemporary explorations of individual economies can, moreover, provide us with a wealth of information on issues such as the scale of economic contraction, the extent of job loss and creation, and sectoral growth and decline. Such analyses nevertheless increasingly seem of importance, not so much because of their intrinsic merits but rather because they can assist in the evaluation of policy initiative, which seems a particularly fertile avenue for urban studies.

One of the initial problems facing those evaluating urban policy is that many commentators come from disciplines wherein the methodology of policy analysis has hardly been explored. The work therefore of, say, Stewart and Underwood (1981) or Dunleavy (1984) is particularly useful in that it can help identify parameters pertinent to the evaluation of policy initiative. There is certainly plenty of scope for such assessments. Urban economic intervention, inner-city policy, and the transport and housing innovations discussed earlier in the book merit evaluation in terms of criteria such as equity, cost-effectiveness and efficiency. In a book concentrating on the British city in general, inevitably many of the crucial differences between the conurbations are lost. Yet detailed comparative analysis can prove of crucial interest. Cities clearly differ in political complexion, the intensity and direction of intervention, their relationship with the centre, and internal managerial structures. Are some cities more effective in the evolution and implementation of policies than others? There is every reason to imagine that this is so. It is certainly one function of urban studies to explore this issue in greater detail.

Although a great deal of the work undertaken in urban studies will concentrate on local government, it will be crucial to embrace the impact on the cities of other forces, notably the market and central government agencies. In terms of the former, inadequate attention has been paid to questions like market perceptions of the cities and their administrations, the real attraction to the market of suburban and ex-urban locations, and the degree and direction of subsidy likely to lead to some market rein-vestment in the urban cores. In turn such considerations raise specific research topics such as the costs of urban development, land prices, and the impact of rates on financial institutions and developers.

Just as market-orientated topics have raised insufficient interest within urban studies, so also too little effort has been directed towards research issues relating to aspects of central government policy. Central control over local authorities has clearly been accentuated in recent years. But the degree of constraint has varied from city to city and policy to policy. Some cities appear to have retained better relationships with the centre than others. Why is this so? How have some cities apparently managed to carve out a more independent position *vis-à-vis* the centre than have other urban administrations? Generally tightening central control has, moreover, resulted in the implementation of policies, such as rate-capping and the demise of the metropolitan counties and the G.L.C., that appear to offer rich research agenda for those working in the subject area. Central government has argued that such administrative innovations can be carried out at limited cost and with minimal consequences for the governance of the cities. Independent observers need to question these assertions.

Central government's impact on the cities extends beyond questions such as rate-capping. The entire tenor of economic policy since 1979 seems likely severely to have reduced the ability of urban authorities to intervene at all effectively within their administrations. More work needs to be directed towards issues such as the implic-ations for the cities of reduced expenditure in areas such as housing, transport, social services and regional policy. Governments elected in 1979 and 1983 have of course attempted to guide the urban debate away from these areas of orthodox funding towards innovations such as enterprise zones. As an earlier chapter has made clear, however, considerable doubt has been expressed about the ability of such initiatives to moderate social and economic disadvantage dramatically. Such evaluations need constantly to be grounded in continuing empirical research.

As previous pages have made clear, it is apparent that trends that have proved disastrous for the cities open up enormous possibilities for urban studies. These oppor-tunities, however, impose responsibilities too. The cities have become the focus for racial and class strife in the Britain of the 1980s. There is little to suggest that the situation will do anything other than deteriorate in the medium term. Policies imple-mented by the central governments elected in 1979 and 1983 have unquestionably worsened the status of the conurbations and many living within them. These admin-istrations were returned to power while arguing that diminishing public-sector inter-vention, borrowing and expenditure would open up opportunities for the market. The impression was, moreover, given that such a transformation could be achieved without any extensive deterioration in public services. Those involved in urban studies are in an ideal position to expose such statements for the fallacies and half-truths they undeniably are. Despite some reductions in public-sector spending the market appears consistently reluctant to invest in extensive parts of the UK, notably in the older industrialized regions and cities. And the concomitant assumption that market-orientated strategies could be implemented with minimal disruption to essential services must be seen as a poor joke for many in the older urban cores. The nation may again decide to elect an anti-interventionist administration. It is one function of urban studies to help ensure that the implications of such an event are better understood than ever before.

References

Dahl, R. (1961) *Who Governs? Democracy and Power in an American City,* Yale University Press, New Haven, Connecticut

Donnison, D. (1983) Urban policies: a new approach, Fabian Tract 487, Fabian Society, London

Dunleavy, P. (1980) *Urban Political Analysis,* Macmillan, London

Dunleavy, P. (1982) *The scope of urban studies in social science,* Units 3/4, D 202, Urban Change and Conflict, Open University Press, Milton Keynes

Dunleavy, P. (1984) *The limits to local government.* In M. Boddy and C. Fudge (1984) Local Socialism, Macmillan, London

Pahl, R. (1970) *Whose City?* Longman, London

Rex, J. and Moore, B. (1967) *Race, Community and Conflict,* Oxford University Press, London

Saunders, P. (1979) *Urban Politics: a sociological interpretation,* Penguin Books, Harmondsworth

Saunders, P. (1981) *Social Theory and the Urban Question,* Hutchinson, London

Stewart, M. and Underwood, J. (1981) *Inner cities; a multi-agency planning and implementation process.* In M. Healey, G. McDougall and M.J. Thomas (1981) Planning Theory. Prospects for the 1980s, Pergamon, Oxford.

Index